Philosophy
Goes to School

Philosophy
Goes to School

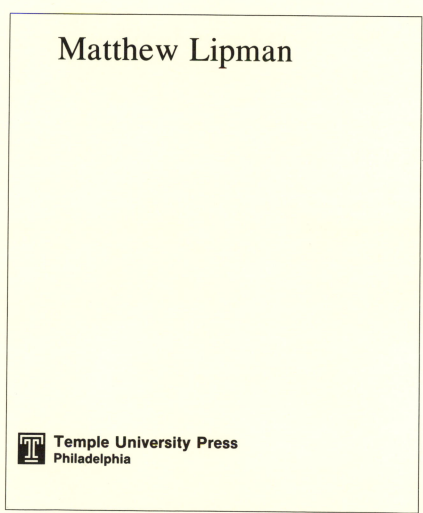

Matthew Lipman

Temple University Press
Philadelphia

Temple University Press, Philadelphia 19122
Copyright © 1988 by Temple University. All rights reserved
Published 1988
Printed in the United States of America

Library of Congress Cataloging-in-Publication Data

Lipman, Matthew.
  Philosophy goes to school.

  Bibliography: p.
  Includes index.
  1. Philosophy—Study and teaching (Elementary)—
United States.   I. Title.
B52.L559   1988   372.8   87-18071
ISBN 0-87722-537-0 (alk. paper)

Contents

Preface

The trickle of philosophy into the schools is still tiny, but it is perceptible and growing steadily. Many educators concerned with improving the quality of children's thinking have become aware that philosophy is a living and reliable educational option. The same is true of educators seeking elementary school humanities programs with which to enrich the skill-oriented curriculum typical of today's schools: philosophy offers children a chance to discuss those concepts, such as truth, that cut across all other disciplines but are openly examined by none. It provides a forum in which children can discover for themselves the relevance to their lives of the ideals that have shaped the lives of everyone. With every day that passes, the presence of philosophy in the schools is more accepted, more taken for granted, and the fact that it has hitherto been absent is what is found more and more to be astonishing.

Accompanying the emergence of philosophy as an elementary school discipline has been a small parade of studies documenting the feasibility of engaging in philosophical inquiry with children—works such as Gareth B. Matthews's *Philosophy and the Young Child* and *Dialogues with Children*, Ronald F. Reed's *Talking with Children*, Michael S. Pritchard's *Philosophical Adventures with Children*, and Lipman and Sharp's *Growing Up with Philosophy*.

When the focus shifts from the possibilities of children's philosophical conversation to the broader question of the practice of philosophy as a school subject, the central work has been *Philosophy in the Classroom*, by Lipman, Sharp, and Oscanyan. On the one hand, this book has provided a theoretical rationale for the Philosophy for Children curriculum developed by the Institute for the Advancement of Philosophy for Children at Montclair State College. On the other hand, it has become a handbook for teachers seeking practical cues for guiding philosophical discussions, engaging in ethical inquiry with children, and helping children find more meaning in their reading, listening, speaking, and writing. These are only a few of the many difficult and complex issues with which *Philosophy in the Classroom* attempts to deal but perforce must touch on rather lightly in its effort to be comprehensive. Some of these issues are of sufficient weight such that an amplified discussion of them cannot be too long postponed. Examples are the relationship of the teaching of philosophy to the improvement of thinking, the nature of a community of inquiry, and the educational significance of grade school philosophy.

This book seeks to address the educational significance of grade school philosophy, although it occasionally may throw a sidelong glance at some of the other issues just mentioned. In doing so, it has sought a balance of generality and specificity.

Part II of the book discusses the general question of the contribution of philosophy to elementary and secondary school education. Several flashbacks to Plato attempt to provide a historical perspective, and some references to the contemporary educational scene indicate where philosophy is to be found in the spectrum of curricular offerings available to the present-day school administrator.

Part III and Chapter 14 explore the contributions to education that may be expected from two particular branches of philosophy—ethics and aesthetics. The questions of creativity treated in Chapter 14 were among those most noticeably absent from *Philosophy in the Classroom*. The discussion here is hardly definitive but may be seen as an introduction to further exploration. The same is true of the remarks dealing with ethical and civic education.

In Part IV, an effort is made to deal with particular subject areas at particular educational levels to illustrate how philosophy can be relevant in these respects. The subject areas are language arts, science, and social studies.

Part V returns to the themes of educational practice and educational reform that had appeared in Chapter 1. It offers some reflections on the significance that elementary school philosophy holds in store for curriculum development, teacher preparation, and teaching for thinking in the classroom.

Several chapters appeared originally in other publications. The Introduction was originally published in *Federation Reports: The Journal of the State Humanities Councils* 5, no. 5 (Sept.-Oct., 1982): 1-4. "Philosophical Practice and Educational Reform" appeared in *Journal of Thought* 20, no. 4 (Winter, 1985): 20-36 (with a response by Kurt Baier, pp. 37-44). "The Role of Philosophy in Education for Thinking" was part of the proceedings of *Conference 85 on Critical Thinking* (April), published by Christopher Newport College, pp. 41-52. Though previously unpublished, "Education for Civic Values" was a position paper commissioned in 1981 by the New York State Department of Education. "Ethical Inquiry and the Craft of Moral Practice" appeared in the *Journal of Moral Education,* 16, no. 2 (May, 1987): 139–47, by permission of NFER-NELSON, Windsor, England. Chapters 7 through 10 have served as introductions to instructional manuals in the Philosophy for Children curriculum. Chapter 11 originally appeared in *CT News* 5, no. 3/4 (Jan.-Feb., 1987): 1, 5–7. Chapter 12 was published originally in *Philosophy Today* 31, no. 1/4 (Spring, 1987): 90–96, and a portion of Chapter 13 was published in *Analytic Teaching* 3, no. 1 (Nov.-Dec., 1982): 19–25. Chapter Fifteen (the Epilogue) is taken from *Thinking: The Journal of Philosophy for Children* 2, nos. 3–4, pp. 4–7. A portion of the Appendix appeared originally in *National Forum* 65, no. 1 (Winter, 1985): 22–23. Reprinted with permission from *National Forum,* "Critical Thinking," Winter 1985.

I

Introduction

1 Remaking the Foundations

Against the Conventional Wisdom

A sneering Callicles in the *Gorgias* insinuates that philosophy is for children only: grown-ups had better get on with the serious business of life. Subsequent commentaries on Plato have agreed that Callicles must be wrong: philosophy is for adults only, and the older, presumably, the better. (An odd inference to draw, especially when one notes the relish with which Socrates welcomes conversation with young and old alike.)

It must therefore come as a rude shock to many that thousands of children, perhaps even tens of thousands—from kindergarten to mid-high school—are currently taking one-year courses in philosophy, reputedly that most abstruse, bewildering, and impenetrable of disciplines. What has happened? Has the subject been unspeakably vulgarized? Must one now memorize the *Enchiridion* of Epictetus in early childhood and be able to parrot David Hume and John Stuart Mill by the time one completes grade six? Have hitherto sober and responsible superintendents and principals lost their minds?

On the contrary. It had long been suspected that philosophy, its crusty, forbidding exterior notwithstanding, carried within it pedagogical treasures of great munificence, and these treasures might someday follow the "Socratic method" in making their own rich contribution to education. If philosophy is now finding a respected place in elementary and secondary schools, it is because hard-headed educators have discovered that children are delighted with it and that it contributes significantly to the improvement of their education, even in the area of "basic skills" such as reading and mathematics.

Perhaps nowhere is philosophy more welcome than in early childhood education, which has hitherto been a wasteland of missed opportunities. But the reasoning skills philosophy provides find themselves quite at home in the middle school and in the high school. Every subject seems easier to learn when its teaching is infused with the open, critical spirit and logical rigor characteristic of philosophy, but at every grade level philosophy is being taught as an autonomous and independent discipline as well, so that students and teachers never lose sight of it as a model of creative, yet disciplined, intellectual inquiry.

All of this, of course, flies in the face of conventional wisdom. A fashionable "taxonomy of educational objectives" had established a Gibralter-like pyramid of cognitive functions, of which the recall of grubby facts formed the ignominious base and of which analytical and evaluational skills formed the exalted apex. From this it was all too easy for teachers, professors of education, and curriculum developers alike to infer that education must necessarily proceed from lower-level to higher-level functions. That inference has been singularly unhelpful, and it is evident that educational progress will henceforth depend on our ability to invert such mischievous pyramids so as to inject analytical skills into every level of the curriculum.

In no way does this mean that reflective education, in which philosophy rubs shoulders as an equal with other disciplines, springs out of nowhere and can cite no ancestry or tradition. One has only to reread Montaigne and Locke, Richard and Maria Edgeworth, Coleridge and I. A. Richards, or Dewey and Bruner to discern that a crude but powerful notion was here struggling to be born.

John Dewey's contribution, it must be acknowledged, dwarfs those of all the others, much as does his standing in the philosophy of education. For surely it was Dewey who, in modern times, foresaw that education had to be redefined as the fostering of thinking rather than as the transmission of knowledge; that there could be no difference in the method by which teachers were taught and the method by which they would be expected to teach; that the logic of a discipline must not be confused with the sequence of discoveries that would constitute its understanding; that student reflection is best stimulated by living experience, rather than by a formally organized, desiccated text; that reasoning is sharpened and perfected by disciplined discussion as by nothing else and that reasoning skills are essential for successful reading and writing; and that the alternative to indoctrinating students with values is to help them reflect effectively on the values that are constantly being urged on them. Rejecting both romanticism and its opponents, Dewey saw the child neither as "trailing clouds of glory" nor as a "barbarian at the gates" but as a being of such creative promise as to require on our part a grasp of the whole of civilization for any understanding of the meaning and portent of the child's developing conduct.

From Dewey, it is only a short step to Jerome Bruner's contention that the cultural heritage of mankind can be taught with undiminished integrity at every grade level, to Michael Oakeshott's insistence that all disciplines, the sciences as well as the humanities, are languages to be learned, languages whose interanimation constitutes "the conversation of mankind," to Wittgenstein and Ryle on thinking, and to Buber on dialogue. Another short step and we see the text replaced by the philosophical novel and the instructional manual (how it would have delighted Wittgenstein!) composed almost completely of philosophical questions.

Implications for the Disciplines

The beleaguered humanities may well take a second look at what is happening with philosophy: there may be much to learn from the way a discipline that had previously been limited to the cloisters of the university has begun to penetrate levels of elementary education to which other humanities have had as yet only limited access. This is not to deny that philosophy may in some respects be unique and that it has pedagogical potentials that other disciplines cannot match. Even if this were so, however, there would be much to be learned, for the self-transformation philosophy that has had to perform to make itself eligible for consideration at the elementary school level is now beginning to work its way back to the university and to modify the way philosophy is presented even in that heady atmosphere. After all, if the position of the humanities is not conspicuously secure even at the university level, this may well be due less to the philistinism of the society in which we live than to the failure of these disciplines to engage in the searching self-appraisal with regard to curriculum and pedagogy that philosophy, albeit reluctantly at times, has seen fit to perform.

Thus to make itself acceptable to children, philosophy has had to sacrifice the hermetic terminology by means of which, since Aristotle, it has contrived to make itself unintelligible to the layperson and only barely intelligible to the undergraduate philosophy major. The case of the subdiscipline of logic is particularly instructive. Logic, of course, is an indispensable accompaniment to the cultivation of reasoning, since logical criteria are the only criteria we have by means of which better reasoning can be distinguished from worse. But logic turns out to be a fairly disorderly family of many logics that has grown wild over the centuries, and few textbook authors in the field agree on what is logically prior to what or on what is pedagogically prior to what. Consequently, the translation of traditional philosophy into philosophy for children required a sequencing of the materials of logic so that students could intuitively grasp each new step and how it followed from the last.

As has already been indicated, the traditional text gave way to the philosophical novel, a fictional work consisting as much as possible of dialogue so as to eliminate the objectionable, behind-the-scenes voice of the adult narrator. Philosophical ideas are strewn about lavishly on every page, so that it is a rare child who can read a page without being struck by something puzzling, something controversial, or something wonder-making. As the children who people the novel come to engage in intellectual cooperation, and so to form a community of inquiry, the story becomes a paradigm for the live children in the classroom. Indeed, every such novel aims at being exemplary by portraying fictional children in the act of discovering the nature of the discipline in which and about which the children in the classroom are expected to think.

In like manner, the traditional "teacher's manual," a compendium of wearisome drills and exercises with answers, has given way to concordances—questioning strategies and discussion plans keyed to specific lines and pages of the text and designed to elicit dialogue through which the concepts broached by the text are to be operationalized and understood. If in the course of such classroom dialogue unsuspected ranges of alternatives are discovered, the objective is not to bewilder students into taking refuge in relativism but to encourage them to employ the tools and methods of inquiry so that they can competently assess evidence, detect inconsistencies and incompatibilities, draw valid conclusions, construct hypotheses, and employ criteria until they realize the possibilities of objectivity with regard to value as well as to fact.

The Tasks Ahead

There is no point to teaching children logic if one does not at the same time teach them to think logically. Likewise, the objective of teaching history is to get children to think historically and, in the case of mathematics, to get them to think mathematically. For to learn any language (including foreign languages) is to learn to think in that language. If education has the production of reasonable children as its goal, they must be children who can both think in and reflect on the disciplines of instruction.

To upgrade elementary and secondary school education in the direction of this objective is a monumental task, one that the schools are not in a position to accomplish by themselves. (The idea that present-day school teachers can, with no more effort than a weekend of "brainstorming," come up with strategies by means of which public education can be lifted to a new level of excellence is as unrealistic as the idea that a person can "lift himself off the ground by his own bootstraps.") The schools have no choice but to turn to the college and the university—that is, to more advanced practitioners of the disciplines. The initial step would likely entail a sweeping overhaul of curricula. The arid, didactic text would have to be replaced with materials (not necessarily novels) that exhibit as well as communicate what it is to think in a discipline. And that discipline would have to be presented to students as something welcoming, something to be discovered and appropriated for one's own, not something alien and intimidating. The reasoning skills indigenous to every subject would have to be made explicit and cultivated in every subject. And the classroom would have to be devoted to reasoning, to inquiry, to self-appraisal, until it turns into an exploratory, yet self-correcting, community where teachers are skilled both in fostering reflection and in engaging in it.

The pages that follow explore the prospect before us: what education can be with the infusion of philosophy into the curriculum. Many pages are devoted to a defense of that infusion, and at this stage, such justifications are indispensable. And yet, in the long run, it will not be theoretical justifications that make philosophy an essential component of the elementary school curriculum but the fact that children like it and teachers and administrators respect it. Philosophy will take its rightful place at the core of the curriculum only when it has shown educators that it belongs there. That is something this book alone cannot do, for it is here that theory must wait upon practice.

II

Philosophy in Education

2 Philosophical Practice and Educational Reform

Did Plato Condemn Philosophy for the Young?

We all know that philosophy emerged in Greece about a hundred generations ago, and for this achievement we honor such figures as Thales, Anaximander, Anaxagoras, and Anaximines. Apparently philosophy was first embodied in aphorisms, poetry, dialogue, and drama. But this variety of philosophical vehicles was short-lived, and philosophy became that which, by and large, it has remained—an academic discipline, access to which was limited to college and university students.

For the most part, these students in the upper echelons of education have been expected to *learn* philosophy rather than to *do* it. Often they study the history of systems of philosophy (perhaps from the pre-Socratics to Hegel, or from Aristotle to St. Thomas, or from Russell to Quine) in preparation for final examinations, or they prepare extended philosophical arguments on obscure but respected topics to qualify for academic degrees.

Yet philosophy is a survivor. In an era in which most of the humanities have been driven to the wall, philosophy has somehow managed to stay afloat—if only barely—largely by converting itself into a knowledge industry: *pace* Socrates! But the price of survival has been high: philosophy has had to abdicate virtually all claims to exercising a socially significant role. Even the most celebrated professors of philosophy nowadays would be likely to admit that, on the vast stage of world affairs, they appear only as bit players or members of the crowd.

Oddly enough, despite the continued social impotence of philosophy, it has remained internally a discipline of incredible richness and diversity. Only in the past few centuries has a new note sounded, suggesting that philosophy has practical applications undreamt of by academicians, and here and there are those who marvel (like Descartes amazed that mathematics offered such powerful foundations but was unused) at the great, sweeping panorama of its applicability.

11

Nevertheless, *applying* philosophy and *doing* it are not identical. The paradigm of doing philosophy is the towering, solitary figure of Socrates, for whom philosophy was neither an acquisition nor a profession but a way of life. What Socrates models for us is not philosophy known or philosophy applied but philosophy *practiced.* He challenges us to acknowledge that philosophy as deed, as form of life, is something that any of us can emulate.

Any of us? Or just the males? Or just the adults? To many philosophers, reasonableness is found only in grown-ups. Children (like women) may be charming, beautiful, delightful, but they are seldom considered capable of being reasoned with, logical, or rational. Descartes, for example, and the young Piaget seem to have thought of childhood as a period of epistemological error that is fortunately sloughed off as one matures. The adult/child dichotomy has an obvious parallel in the dichotomy between ideal industrial management ("rational") and ideal workers ("cheerful"). Nevertheless, it is likely that the dichotomy between adults and children, insofar as the capacity to pursue the philosophical form of life was concerned, would have seemed absurd to Socrates.

Generally, when a discipline is available only on the college level or above, it is because it is considered a discipline inappropriate for children or inessential to their education. However, this has not consistently been the case with philosophy, and Jacques Derrida has shrewdly noted that, until the Reformation, philosophy had been part and parcel of the education of adolescent princes and princesses.[1] But the Reformation put an end to all that: philosophy appeared utterly superfluous when it came to the preparation of future businessmen and scientists. With the ascendency of the business ideology, philosophy was banished from the scene as far as the education of children was concerned. Not even Dewey, easily the most insightful of all philosophers of education, could bring himself to advocate philosophy as an elementary school subject, but that was because he had already committed himself to rebuilding education along the lines of scientific inquiry. For others, philosophy appeared too difficult for children or too frivolous or too arid; some even thought it too dangerous. What was it about philosophy that gave rise to these misgivings?

Let us turn back to Plato and re-examine his attitude toward teaching philosophy to the young. In the earlier dialogues, it will be recalled, Socrates talks to young and old alike, although just how young they are is not clear. (Robert Brumbaugh, for example, places the ages of the two children in the *Lysis* at eleven.) There is no indication that Socrates has any misgivings about these conversations with children (although on other occasions he is certainly capable of expressing the unease he feels about what he is doing: we have only to recall here his bizarre conduct in the *Phaedrus*). But then comes a seemingly dramatic reversal: in Book 7 of the *Republic,* after genially admonishing us to keep children to their studies by play and not by compulsion and after having perhaps overgenerously praised dialectic ("he who can view things in their connection is a dialectician; he who cannot, is not"), he urges that children not be exposed to dialectic, for "its practitioners are infected with lawlessness" [537]. Young people, he says,

> when they get their first taste of it, treat argument as a form of sport solely for purposes of contradiction. When someone has proved them wrong, they copy his methods to confute others, delighting like puppies in tugging and tearing at anyone who comes near them. And so, after a long course of proving others wrong and being proved wrong themselves, they rush to the conclusion that all they once believed is false; and the result is that in the eyes of the world they discredit, not themselves only, but the whole business of philosophy. [539][2]

Certainly this latter remark is not to be taken too lightly. The situation of philosophy in those turbulent times was precarious enough, without incurring additional risks by encouraging logic-chopping and speculation by Athenian urchins. Nor can we forget that even Aristotle had to make a hurried exit from Athens so as not to afford Athenians an opportunity to do to him what they had done to Socrates and thus "sin twice against philosophy."

This, then, is one reason for sequestering children and philosophy from one another: doing so is for the protection of philosophy, for if children are allowed to do it, philosophy will appear unworthy of adults. The other reason is for the protection of children: dialectic will subvert them, corrupt them, infect them with lawlessness. These reasons, it must be presumed, have been taken as conclusive ever since Plato wrote, and his authority has been invoked to deter educational initiatives that might have given children access to philosophy earlier on. What are we to say about this? Was Plato wrong to have opposed dialectical training for children so vigorously in Book 7? Here it may be helpful to consider the picture of intellectual Athens painted by Gilbert Ryle. Ryle offers us a highly speculative portrayal of the manner in which the procedures and techniques of eristic or dialectic were taught to students. Intellectual contest was paramount: debaters were assigned theses to defend or attack, regardless of their personal beliefs, and it was through these "moot court" procedures, Ryle contends, that cogency in argumentation was fostered and achieved. These moot conditions "proved to be the beginning of methodical philosophical reasoning." Nothing in Ryle's account indicates that he found these forensic or sophistic techniques of instruction objectionable in any way.

Elsewhere, indeed, Ryle seems to feel that Socrates likewise was not inclined to distinguish between philosophical reasoning and philosophy. Thus he argues that in the *Apology* Socrates provides "only a perfunctory answer to the charge of impiety but a protracted defense of the practice of elenctic questioning." Ryle identifies such questioning as "the Socratic method" and tells us that it was the right to engage in such questioning that Socrates was most concerned to justify.[3]

Here we must tread with great care. It is one thing to say that debate and argument can be useful disciplinary devices in the preparation of those who are to engage in philosophical reasoning; it is quite something else to assume that philosophy is reducible to argument. The eristic method of teaching, probably introduced into Athens by the sophist Protagoras, may have been suitable for preparing future lawyers and politicians, but was it really serviceable for the preparation of everyone else (including would-be philosophers) who sought a more reasonable view of life? It would be strange indeed if Socrates, for whom the shared examination of the concepts essential to the conduct of life was of the greatest urgency, would have been content to equate that all-important pursuit with the dry, technical procedures of dialectical argumentation. What Socrates stresses is the continued prosecution of philosophical inquiry by following the reasoning wherever it leads (confident that, wherever it leads, wisdom lies in that direction), not the heavy breathing and clanging of armor in dialectical battles, where the premium is not on insight but on victory.

What made classical rhetoric and dialectic dangerous, for young people at any rate, was their separation of technique from conviction. Children should be given practice in discussing the concepts they take seriously. To give them practice in discussing matters they are indifferent to deprives them of the intrinsic pleasures of becoming educated and provides society with future citizens who neither discuss what they care about nor care about what they discuss.

Forensic education, the preparation of lawyers who can argue for any side regardless of their own convictions (if they have any), should be considered a very special case, in no way a model for the rest of education. The breeding ground of amoralism is the training of technicians who assume that ends are given (or do not matter), so that their concern is merely with means, with tactics, with technique. If children are not given the opportunity to weigh and discuss both ends and means, and their interrelationship, they are likely to become cynical about everything except their own well-being, and adults will not be slow to condemn them as "mindless little relativists."

One may readily conjecture, therefore, that what Plato was condemning in the seventh book of the *Republic* was not the practice of philosophy by children as such but the reduction of philosophy to sophistical exercises in dialectic or rhetoric, the effects of which on children would be particularly devastating and demoralizing. How better to guarantee the amoralism of the adult than by teaching the child that any belief is as defensible as any other and that what right there is must be the product of argumentative might? If this is how philosophy is to be made available to children, Plato may be supposed to have been saying, then it is far better that they have none at all.

Plato's condemnation of eristic argumentation by children is consistent with his general suspicions regarding whatever it was that the sophists were up to in Greece. Evidently he saw them as his rivals in subversiveness: they seemed to him to be undermining the foundations of Greek morality, while he was trying to undermine the foundations of Greek *immorality*. When they glibly equated dialectic with philosophy—equated, in short, the part with the whole—he and Socrates were not taken in. Nowhere does Socrates ever draw the line when it comes to doing philosophy with people of different ages, for doing philosophy is not a matter of age but of ability to reflect scrupulously and courageously on what one finds important. Indeed, when Callicles suggests to Socrates that philosophy is unworthy of grown men, we may imagine Plato's amusement at being able to implant so seditious an idea into the conversation.[4]

It can hardly be doubted that the traditional prohibition of philosophy for children is much indebted to citations from Plato's *Republic*. Nevertheless, it must be concluded that, insofar as that prohibition has rested on an appeal to Plato, it has rested on a mistake.

Philosophical Inquiry as the Model of Education

The contemporary educational system is frequently depicted as monolithic, inflexible, and impenetrable. However, it is considerably more pluralistic than these accounts suggest—more loose woven, open-textured, and diversified. Within its many crevices and interstices are school administrators to whom philosophy for children, for whatever reason, seems irresistible. Some prize it for its promise of improving reasoning skills; others admire it because students seem to enjoy it for its own sake rather than for the sake of grades or because it is relevant to their vocational aspirations. Some see it as the central stem of the elementary and secondary school, out of which the specialized disciplines can emerge; others see it as a wholesome preventive to drug and alcohol abuse. These educators may be familiar with the traditional rejection of philosophy for children, but they are pragmatic enough to reject it in turn. They like what philosophy does when children do it. They may be quite unaware that philosophy for children happens to fulfill Plato's pedagogical admonition that education be conducted "not by compulsion but by play." Although it may not be easy to put philosophy in place, it is enough for them that it works when it is put in place correctly.

Under these circumstances, philosophy for children will continue to find its way into the elementary schools. After all, word of a good thing gets around; already, children who take philosophy are boasting of it to those who do not, and far from being viewed with odium and contempt, philosophy has become a status symbol of elementary school. But all of these changes may be merely symptoms of a shift in fashion. How can philosophy as a required elementary school discipline—perhaps even as the core or armature of the curriculum—be justified?

This will not be easy, because it relentlessly demands of us the kind of self-knowledge that we, as educators, know to be highly elusive but that Socrates was wont to insist is indispensable to the worthwhile life. We must put aside any illusions we may have about the benign influence we exercise as educators and speak frankly to one another as Santayana speaks of the "magnificent example" Spinoza offers us

> of philosophic liberty, the courage, firmness, and sincerity with which he reconciled his heart to the truth. . . . Many a man before Spinoza and since has found the secret of peace: but the singularity of Spinoza, at least in the modern world, was that he facilitated this moral victory by no dubious postulates. He did not ask God to meet him half way: he did not whitewash the facts, as the facts appear to clear reason, or as they appeared to the science of his day. He solved the problem of the spiritual life after stating it in the hardest, sharpest, most cruel terms. Let us nerve ourselves today to imitate his example, not by simply accepting his solution, which for some of us would be easy, but by exercising his courage in the face of a somewhat different world.[5]

If we examine the present educational system with such candor, it is fairly predictable that we will be bound to conclude not simply that our educational system is imperfect but that its imperfections are more responsible than we have cared to admit for the grave circumstances in which the world currently finds itself. If we deplore our leaders and electorates as being self-centered and unenlightened, we must remember that they are the products of our educational system. If we protest, as an extenuating factor, that they are also the products of homes and families, we must remember that the unreasonable parents and grandparents in these families are likewise products of the selfsame process of education.

As educators, we have a heavy responsibility for the unreasonableness of the world's population.

Socrates must have known that the tincture of self-knowledge provided by philosophy would in itself hardly suffice to deter an Athenian state hell-bent on its own destruction. Nevertheless he persisted, even to the point of demonstrating that what he was doing was worth more to him than life itself. (Always the teacher, even his final act was intentionally instructive!) Surely Socrates realized that the discussion of philosophical concepts was, by itself, just a fragile reed. What he must have been attempting to show was that the doing of philosophy was emblematic of shared inquiry as a way of life. One does not have to be a philosopher to foster the self-corrective spirit of the community of inquiry; rather, it can and should be fostered in each and every one of our institutions.

There is, then, a narrower and a broader case for philosophy for children. The narrower case is simply that it makes a wholesome contribution to the present curriculum and the classroom. But the broader justification would have to rest on the way in which it paradigmatically represents the education of the future as a form of life that has not yet been realized and as a kind of praxis. The reform of education must take shared philosophical inquiry in the classroom as a heuristic model. Without the guidance of some such paradigm, we will continue to drift and the curriculum will continue to be a hodgepodge.

What Is It to Be Fully Educated?

Some educators today see philosophy for children as prefiguring a thoroughgoing reappraisal of education, and they are eager to recite the characteristics of elementary school philosophy that they think the educational process as a whole should exhibit. This is without a doubt an appealing approach, but it should be accompanied by a comprehensive rationale. One does not usually attempt to redesign something unless one first knows what to expect of it or what to try to accomplish by means of it. The Greeks were probably the first people to insist that institutions (and not only people) needed to be perfected and that only by means of ideals such as justice and freedom could the reform of existing institutions be measured and judged. The notion of perfection is unlikely to stir us in quite the way it did the Greeks. Nevertheless, we may still agree with Dewey that nothing in human society commands our admiration as much as the way human institutions such as science and art, medicine and law seek in their practice to approximate their respective ideals of truth and beauty, health and justice.

What, then, is the ideal that educational practice seeks to approximate? This would seem to be the primary question that the redesign of education must confront. Thus put, the question may be too formidable to answer. Perhaps we should try putting a different question first: in what respect has education most greatly disappointed us? Here our response need not be in the least equivocal, and in answering the second question, we automatically answer the first: the greatest disappointment of traditional education has been its failure to produce people approximating the ideal of reasonableness. (This is not to say that all who are reasonable must have been educated, but rather that whoever is educated ought to be reasonable.) It may well be that in previous centuries unreasonableness was a luxury that human beings could afford, even though the costs were high. It should be evident, however, that the costs of our tolerant attitude toward unreasonableness are now far beyond our reach. We may still smile indulgently as we read of the legendary figures of history who were splendidly capricious and magnificently illogical: they savaged their victims, but they did not endanger everything. This is no longer the case; we will have to reason together or die together.

Traditionally, education has been conceived of as initiation into the culture, and the educated person has been thought to be the "cultivated" person or even the "cultured" person. But a closer look at traditional education might reveal students studying the disciplines, and in fact learning them, while yet failing to think in terms of them or to appropriate them fully. Seldom has traditional education been able to meet Vico's challenge—that the only way really to understand something is to re-enact it in some fashion. (One can understand what it is to be a story-teller only by becoming a story-teller, a painter only by becoming a painter, a dancer or a worker or a slave only by becoming a dancer or a worker or a slave.)

To be fully educated, one must be able to treat every discipline as a language and to think fluently in that language; be cultivated in one's reasoning as well as in everything else, remembering that reasoning is most effectively cultivated in the context of philosophy; and demonstrate educational accomplishments not merely as acquisitions of intellectual properties or as the amassing of spiritual capital but as a genuine appropriation that results in the enlargement of the self. Because philosophy is the discipline that best prepares us to think in terms of the other disciplines, it must be assigned a central role in the early (as well as in the late) stages of the educational process.

Converting Classrooms into Communities of Inquiry

It would be unrealistic to expect a child brought up among unjust institutions to behave justly. Abusers of the rights of others often turn out
themselves to have been abused. Likewise, it is unrealistic to expect a
child brought up among irrational institutions to behave rationally. The
irrationality of institutions must be considered preventable. There is no
excusing them, for to do so permits them in turn to become the excuse
offered by children who have been reared in such institutions and who
adopt the irrationality of the institutions that fostered them.

The institution with which we as educators have primary concern is
education. The irrationalities or "socially patterned defects" that permeate
education have to be rooted out because they do not die out on their own:
they have a marvelous capacity for self-perpetuation. This involves our
bringing a greater degree of rational order than currently exists into the
curriculum, into the methodology of teaching, into the process of teacher
education, and into the procedures of testing. The adjustments made
within each of these must in turn be determined by the interrelationships
they have among themselves, as components of education, just as the
structure of education depends on what kind of world we want to live in,
since it will have much to do with the character of that world.

All too often the components of education have that kind of bizarre
interrelationship of which the best analogy is the tail wagging the dog.
Testing, which should have only ancillary status at best, tends to be
the driving force of the system. The content of the tests structures the
curriculum, which in turn controls the nature of teacher education. (This
is not to deny that current practice in schools of education is consistent
with the ethos of higher education generally, just as that ethos is in general
consistent with that of the larger society of which it is a part. Schools
of education tend to reflect the values of their societies, rather than the
other way around.)

As long as the major goal of education is thought to be learning, as is
the case in all tribal societies, the recall model will dominate testing, and
teachers will find it difficult not to teach for the tests. Equally sad is that
the information-acquisition model that dominates education, rather than
encouraging children to think for themselves, is a failure even on its own
terms, for we are constantly appalled at how little our children seem to
know about the history of the world or about its political and economic
organization. The effect of the tribal model is to stifle rather than to
initiate thinking in the student. This does not mean we need to begin by

producing better tests; we need to ask ourselves what kind of world we want to live in, what kind of education is most likely to contribute to the emergence of such a world, and what kind of curriculum is most likely to produce such an education. We must then set about producing that better curriculum.

There is good reason to think that the model of each and every classroom—that which it seeks to approximate and at times becomes—is the community of inquiry. By inquiry, of course, I mean perseverance in self-corrective exploration of issues that are felt to be both important and problematic. In no way do I mean to imply that inquiry sets a greater premium on discovery than on invention or a greater premium on rule-governed as opposed to improvisational activities. Those who produce works of art are practitioners of inquiry no less than those who produce new epistemological treatises or new discoveries in biology.

If we begin with the practice in the classroom, the practice of converting it into a reflective community that thinks in the disciplines about the world and about its thinking about the world, we soon come to recognize that communities can be nested within larger communities and these within larger communities still, if all hold the same allegiance to the same procedures of inquiry. There is the familiar ripple effect outward, like the stone thrown in the pond: wider and wider, more and more encompassing communities are formed, each community consisting of individuals committed to self-corrective exploration and creativity. It is a picture that owes as much to Charles Peirce as to John Dewey, but I doubt they would quibble over the credits if they thought there was a hope of its realization.

As so often happens when people describe the cloud castles of their dreams, the nitty-gritty realities are all too easily overlooked—realities such as the ladders by means of which the cloud castles are to be reached and the fearsome dragons and lurking trolls that are to be avoided along the way. Here are some considerations that we should not fail to take into account.

Appropriating the Culture

The tribal model of education, in which the child is initiated into the culture, in effect provides for the assimilation of the child by the culture. In contrast, the reflective model of education provides for the appropriation of the culture by the child. A good case in point would be the textbook. As it currently stands, the textbook is a didactic device that stands over against the child as an alien and rigid *other*. It has this obdurate nature because it represents the final end-product of the received or adult view of the discipline. As Dewey would put it, the textbook (a century after *The Child and the Curriculum*) is still organized logically, like a table of contents or a sequence of lectures, rather than psychologically, in terms of the developing interests and motivation of the child. It is not something the child wants to enjoy and possess in the way one enjoys and assimilates a story or a picture; it is instead a formal, dreary, oppressive, and in many ways unintelligible summary of the contents that the child is expected to learn.

All of this is unnecessary, since we know from the work of Bruner and others that the child views material that is contextualized (i.e., presented in the form of a story) as something to be appropriated rather than rejected. If children are to learn to think in the disciplines so as to appropriate their humanistic heritage, they must begin with the raw subject matter of the disciplines and refine it for themselves. Masticating it for them in advance, the way mother birds masticate worms for their fledglings, is hardly the way to provide an education. Children presented with logic as a finished discipline find it repugnant, but they can find it delightful to discover it bit by bit and to see how it all interlocks and applies to language if not the world. This is how logic was probably discovered, and we can surmise that the early Greeks felt the same excitement and sense of power and mastery in discovering the same logic. Indeed, to learn something well is to learn it afresh in the same spirit of discovery as that which prevailed when it was discovered or in the same spirit of invention as that which prevailed when it was invented. When this spirit, which is truly the spirit of inquiry, prevails in the classroom, children will eagerly work through the materials of the arts and sciences and humanities for themselves and will appropriate them to themselves.

Acquiring the Conceptual Tools

Introducing a budding artist to the great works of the past can be inspiring if it happens at the right time but intimidating if it happens too soon. It is of primary importance, therefore, that young artists learn the tools of their trade at the same time that they learn to explore their own experience and discover their own intentions. All of this is equally applicable to the budding student. Children may be inspired by the stories they read of the lives of heroes and heroines, but if they are to think for themselves about ethics, they must engage in ethical inquiry. This entails learning the tools of the trade; getting practice in weighing the relationships of means to ends and parts to wholes; getting used to inquiring about rules and consequences; and getting experience in exemplifying, illustrating, universalizing, ferreting out underlying ethical assumptions, and deducing or inducing implicit conclusions. In time the use of these tools will become second nature to such students (and will be productive of presumptively justifiable moral intuitions), but until it does, the study of ethics entails the construction and appropriation of an ethical tool kit, and much the same can be said with regard to the study of any other discipline.

An example of the way in which education essentially provides students with tools has to do with the use of criteria. Now it is commonly accepted that a democratic society consists of citizens equipped to assess how well the institutions of that society are working. Such evaluation necessarily requires citizens who have facility in employing criteria. If, however, our educational pundits are to be understood as saying that evaluation is a higher-order skill that one can employ only when one reaches the rarified atmosphere of secondary or higher education, we might as well forget about equipping students with such ability. The truth is that almost from the time they start speaking children cite reasons, among which are the purposes and criteria that they employ for evaluational purposes. It is therefore possible to give children systematic practice in the employment of criteria throughout their stay in school so that, by the time they are ready for active citizenship, they will have become quite well prepared to engage in the kinds of evaluation of institutions that democratic citizens must be able to perform.

The Rationalization of the Curriculum

The advent of philosophy for children requires that the massive corpus of philosophy, the accumulation of thousands of years of philosophical scholarship, be reviewed in outline to determine how it can be sequenced into the successive grade levels of elementary and secondary schools. This must be done without prejudice to the intense curiosity and readiness for discussion of very young children with regard to cosmological, ethical, epistemological, and other philosophical issues. It must be done so as to strengthen rather than weaken intergenerational and familial ties and understandings. And it has to be done in such a way as to demand the utmost professionalism from the teacher rather than in a way that would not be in keeping with the teacher's educational role (such as asking the teacher to play therapist).

For teachers of other disciplines to follow this example, they must likewise review the entire corpus of their materials, rethink the serial order in which such materials as they selected for children could best be presented, and coordinate their sequences with the sequential offerings of the other disciplines. This might mean that much of the present offerings (in, say, mathematics) might be dropped or reassigned to earlier or later grade levels, depending on what a rational reassessment would deem necessary. On the other hand, the rational sequencing of curriculum would disclose many gaps and hiatuses that would have to be filled to produce smooth transitions from one point in the curriculum to the next. A rational curriculum is so arranged that each step prepares the way for the steps that follow it and presupposes for its mastery the steps that precede it. It is quite unlike the present curriculum, which resembles a ladder with numerous missing rungs so that the students who attempt to move upward are too often likely to fall through and drop out.

The Transition to the Text

The secondary text, so much relied on in education, is a barrier between children and their humanistic heritage, just as "methods" courses are a barrier between teachers and the academic disciplines. To replace the secondary text with primary texts would be like rolling the stone away from the mouth of the cave and allowing the sunlight in. Unfortunately, the mass-education process required by young democracies like ours must operate without the high degree of cognitive preparation provided children born into the elite families of previous societies. As a result, a transitional literature must be created to prepare the way for the encounter with primary texts in later schooling. This transitional literature (an example of which would be the Philosophy for Children curriculum) would have consummatory as well as instrumental values in that it would be enjoyable for its own sake just as it would pave the way for the primary texts to be encountered in the future. Many students who will never read primary works in philosophy can nevertheless enjoy reading, discussing, and writing about *Pixie* and *Harry Stottlemeier's Discovery,* but many others who have read these philosophical children's novels will be lured by them into investigating Plato and Aristotle for themselves. If they are to encounter the Platos and the Aristotles of other disciplines, they will have to be led to them by cognate versions of *Harry* and *Pixie* or by other kinds of transitional curricula that will provide children with provocative experiences that will cause them to be thoughtful and discursive. For precisely as the children's stories based on the works of Homer, which we read long ago, prepared us for the almost déjà vu thrill of actually encountering the *Iliad* and the *Odyssey,* so a vast literature of original but preparatory texts will have to be produced as a stepping stone to the less accessible landmarks in our humanistic heritage with which high school and college students should become acquainted.

The Primacy of Discussion

Just as a cat can be more readily encouraged to find its way out of a box if the latching mechanism is operated by a string rather than by a key, so a child is more readily encouraged to participate in education if it emphasizes discussion rather than paper-and-pencil exercises. Discussion in turn sharpens the child's reasoning and inquiry skills as nothing else can. Yet in many classrooms talking has a bad name, and students' efforts to engage in it covertly are treated as evidence of disobedience rather than as evidence of healthy impulses needing only to be effectively organized so as to be harnessed in the service of education. Indeed, although we should be ready to acknowledge that virtually every elementary school educational experience should involve or point in the direction of all five factors—reading, writing, listening, speaking, and reasoning—we have to be prepared to see that these exist on different levels, that reasoning is common to all of them, and that speaking and listening form the foundations on which reading and writing can be superimposed.

Eliminating Curriculum Fragmentation

We keep demanding that the individual academic disciplines do some-thing to reduce their isolation from one another because we see the be-wilderment that such a fragmented curriculum can produce in students. Unfortunately, the disciplines are virtually helpless to resolve this prob-lem, so long as they continue to define themselves as subject areas to be learned rather as languages in which students must learn to think. The disciplines also appear to be remote from one another because they have shrunken away from their former contours by aping the technical disciplines in repressing the philosophical aspects that had once been vi-tal to their integrity. When a discipline attempts to divest itself of its ethical, logical, aesthetic, and epistemological presuppositions and ram-ifications because these are "contestable" or "controversial," it removes the very features that enabled students to see it as a piece with all other academic disciplines. This is why the introduction of philosophy into the school curriculum tends to reduce rather than to intensify the students' sense of fragmentation. Philosophy is, so to speak, at right angles to the other disciplines, so that together, like warp and woof, they interpenetrate and interweave until they produce a seamless texture. Education cannot recover itself without eliminating the suppression of the philosophical concerns indigenous to each and every one of the disciplines.

Transcending the Concepts versus Skills Dichotomy

Some educators, critical of the way in which some schools seem to take for granted that they are preparing their students for higher education while others assume they are preparing their students for lower-level vocations, have charged that the former schools emphasize conceptual development whereas the latter schools are dominated by a "skill and drill" mentality, stressing the correction of error rather than originality. Although much is meritorious in this view, conceptual development is not irreconcilable with skill development, nor is the acquisition of skills dependent on the performance of drills. Moreover, there is nothing incompatible in encouraging original thinking and at the same time encouraging students to find the errors in their thinking. There are teachers who embrace elementary school philosophy joyously because they think they have at last escaped the "tyranny of right and wrong answers" and are somewhat crestfallen when they learn that this is not altogether so. The injection of philosophy into the other academic disciplines does not so much eliminate reliance on "right and wrong answers" as it introduces a critical awareness as to when such answers are or are not appropriate, as well as a greater judiciousness when it comes to deciding what counts for wrong and what counts for right. If the Philosophy for Children curriculum should be permitted to serve as an educational paradigm, surely one way in which it can be most useful is precisely in demonstrating that skill acquisition and concept development (in this case the skills being reasoning and inquiry skills and the concepts being the ideas prevalent in the history of philosophy) can accompany and reinforce each other.

Recognizing the Importance of the Metacognitive

Educational psychology has suddenly discovered the importance of thinking about thinking: of studying, monitoring, and reviewing one's own thinking processes. This in turn has focused attention on the educational role of mental acts (e.g., assuming, supposing, assenting, guessing, surmising, recalling), of metacognitive acts (e.g., knowing that one remembers, assuming that one knows), of meta-affective acts (e.g., desiring to desire or hoping to love), and of corresponding mental acts (e.g., my inferring that you infer). If these acts are treated as performances to be improved on by classroom drills, the results will almost certainly be counterproductive. Nevertheless, through some procedures students can be induced to become more attentive to their own employment of such behaviors.

For example, one novel in the elementary school philosophy curriculum has a blind girl telling about an accident at which she was present. The third and fourth grade readers of *Kio and Gus* have their work cut out for them: distinguishing what she perceives from what she infers, what she accepts as true based on the testimony of others, and what she infers from that testimony. What is especially significant, however, is that the readers must infer what the girl infers, surmise what she surmises, guess what she guesses. They do not learn about these mental acts so much as they are compelled to perform them—and to perform them proficiently.

In general, this is how thinking skills should be improved, by voluntary performance rather than by compulsory drill, whether or not one can recite the taxonomic definition of the skills involved. The metacognitive act is what makes self-correction possible. It is one thing for mental acts and thinking and inquiry skills to be directed at the world, but it is something else again for them to be directed at themselves. When we begin to draw inferences about the way we draw inferences, develop conceptions of the ways in which we form concepts, and define the ways in which we construct definitions, our thinking becomes cybernetic. But each mental act or reasoning skill may be turned on any or all of the others, as in two columns where each component matches with every other (see Figure 1).

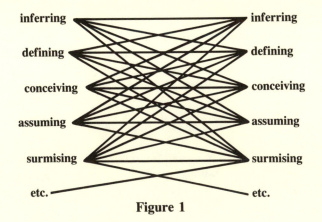

Figure 1

The ferment of mental activity we see here is the self-monitoring aspect of the mind at work. Obviously, we must learn how to foster it, for children are unlikely to reason better if they cannot reason about how they reason.

Educating the Educators

Schools of education seem to be continually in the throes of identity crises. Like adolescents, they seem to be constantly trying on new personae, depending on whatever seems to be momentarily fashionable. At one moment it is group dynamics, at another moment it is classroom management, or right brain/left brain, or some other harebrained, short-lived panacea. If the education of the future is to have substance, the education of teachers will require more integrity than it currently does. It will have to discover its own identity, its own sense of direction, and this should give it a sense of proportion in terms of how it is to distribute its energies with respect to the hierarchy of its concerns.

It cannot be assumed (as the academic disciplines used to assume) that mere knowledge of a given domain ensures competence in the teaching of that domain. There have simply been too many teachers and professors who have known their fields but were incompetent teachers for us to believe that. On the other hand, it cannot be assumed (as schools of education have more recently assumed) that teachers can dispense with knowing the fields they teach if only they study courses in the methods of teaching those fields. This is a bit like trying to develop future novelists by giving them courses in how to write a book. It is not that these approaches are altogether wrong; it is just that they are hopelessly one sided.

The teachers of the future should be conversant with the major aspects of the disciplines they teach, at whatever grade level they teach, as well as with the elements of instructional methodology that are appropriate to their disciplines. By and large, teachers should be taught by the very same procedures as those that they are expected to employ in the classroom. If discussions are desirable and lectures abhorrent in the classroom, there should be as little lecturing and as much discussion as possible in the schools of education. If the teachers of children are to encourage thinking for oneself, then professors of education must encourage thinking for oneself among teachers in training. Nevertheless, just as teachers cannot be effective if they dislike or are indifferent to children, they cannot be indifferent to the disciplines they teach. They must love them, for only if they love them will they love to rediscover them with each teaching. And only with that delight in rediscovery will there be that infectious enthusiasm that thrills children the moment they suspect it and that motivates them as little else can, for they recognize it as an invitation to share in an experience of understanding or in an encounter with meaning. Children will find education an irresistible adventure only when teachers find it so, and if schools of education are unable to provide teachers with this love of the disciplines they teach, we have to find other ways of preparing teachers.

Distinguishing the Philosophical from the Pseudo-philosophical

In the light of this plea for educational reform Plato's misgivings about the educational approach of the sophists should be reassessed. No doubt Plato, especially in his early years, was attracted by much of what the sophists had to say about education, but he drew the line when he suspected that the stress on grammar, rhetoric, and dialectic was not to be balanced by the student's immersion in and appropriation of the humanistic wealth of the culture. Having had a teacher like Socrates and a pupil like Aristotle, Plato would indeed have been peculiar if he had not felt distressed by the peddlers of educational nostrums who descended on Athens in droves. The situation has not been without its parallels in later periods. Even now, the word "thinking" is on everyone's lips, and educationists have taken to dressing up even the most unlovely of their offspring as some manner of cognitive processing or problem-solving. In the past, this gambit was fairly often successful, and many of today's educational administrators continue to accept it. But today there are alternatives to it that were lacking in previous years, and the difference these alternatives can make can be enormously significant. We must now be prepared to hear it parroted from every quarter of the educational community that the goal of education is to produce reflective and reasonable students and that this can occur through the teaching of "thinking skills." We must also be prepared to expect that pseudo-philosophical approaches of every manner and description are going to vie for entry into the schools. It is up to us to devote ourselves as energetically to distinguishing the philosophical from the pseudo-philosophical as to distinguishing the philosophical from the non-philosophical.

3 The Role of Philosophy in Education for Thinking

Since thinking skills are alleged to be the missing ingredient in education, it is not surprising that many school administrators are becoming increasingly impatient with teachers who teach their subjects but not the thinking skills that students require to master those subjects. Teachers, on the other hand, feel themselves under increasingly intensive pressure: the schools of education they attended did not prepare them to teach thinking skills, and most teachers feel that, although they are competent, they can teach only what they have been taught to teach. So they feel responsible and guilty and resentful, and yet it is not at all clear how they could have been trained to teach thinking skills, what they would do with such training if they had in fact received it, and whether it would make the least difference, since it is quite possible that all the talk about the deficiency in thinking skills merely addresses the symptoms of the problem and not the problem itself.

The teachers of any discipline are understandably concerned when their students merely memorize the contents on which they expect to be tested rather than learn to think in the discipline. Now this notion of thinking in a discipline is a very tricky one indeed. Does it presuppose that only thinking in a discipline is really thinking? Or perhaps that education occurs only in disciplines, so that only thinking in a discipline is truly educational? Is it to be taken for granted that thinking skills are discipline-specific and that, in consequence, there can be no such thing as generic thinking skills? Perhaps this last question is the best one to take up first.

The Generic Use of Thinking Skills

Whenever we inquire, we employ a variety of cognitive skills. These may be extremely elementary, such as making distinctions and connections, or extremely complex, as in description and explanation, which are intricate composites of simpler skills used in a coordinated fashion. For educational purposes, we may consider the generic skills as consisting of reasoning, inquiry, concept-formation, and translation skills.

It may be profitable to recognize the different roles played by these skills. Thus reasoning is thought in movement, progressively pressing forward. Concept formation takes place in moments of concentration and organization. And those reasonings known as inferences may be contrasted with translations in the sense that valid inferences preserve truth, irrespective of meaning, while accurate translations preserve meaning, irrespective of truth. Translation and inference are both critical for reading comprehension, since we need to infer what a given passage implies and to translate what the passage both states and implies if we are to be able to paraphrase it. (Although the ability to paraphrase is one way of testing to determine if reading comprehension is taking place, it is still possible for people to think well in the language of a discipline even when they are inexpert in paraphrasing what they read in that language.)

The references just made to meaning and truth bring to mind another contrast, which is that the rules that govern reasoning and translation within a given language, or from one language to another, stand in marked contrast with the conventions that otherwise govern a particular language and the ways in which it may be used. Thus the conventions regarding, say, spelling and punctuation, traditionally emphasized by teachers of English, are of minimal significance with respect to meaning and truth, whereas the rules of reasoning and translation, traditionally *not* emphasized by such teachers, are of maximum significance when questions of meaning and truth are involved.

Who Should Teach What Skills?

It is customary for the teachers of beginning algebra to feel put upon when they discover each year that their students lack the skills needed to solve elementary algebraic problems, to say nothing of their inability to "think algebraically." But, they wonder, what is the solution? Do such students need a specific set of skills so that their lethargic and inept minds will suddenly, magically catch fire and be animated with the spirit of mathematics? And even if this were so, does it follow that the algebra teacher should be teaching these skills, or should students have acquired them earlier so that they were prepared to use them from the very first day of the algebra course? The teachers in other disciplines might well echo these questions and argue that the skills specifically needed to master a given discipline should always be acquired earlier: to wait until the subject must actually be studied is inevitably to wait too long.

In thus pointing out that students being introduced to a new discipline should have been antecedently provided with the skills needed to master that discipline, teachers are not shirking their duty but displaying their pedagogical sagacity: it is just too much to ask of students that they acquire at one and the same time the skills that a subject presupposes, which students must bring with them, and the skills needing to be learned in order to think *in* the subject. In support of their opinion, the teachers may well cite the findings of psychologists that the onset of adolescence generally retards the rate at which students can acquire new cognitive skills. And yet, if everyone were to disclaim responsibility, how would the necessary skills ever be taught? Surely it would be absurd to maintain that no teacher teaches the skills needed to master the subject that that teacher teaches—or would it?

At this point it is difficult to resist bringing to mind a rather similar discussion portrayed by Plato in the *Republic*. In the interchange with Thrasymachus, Socrates maintains that no discipline or form of inquiry ever seeks its own improvement. Either it is already perfect (in which case it needs no improvement) or it is imperfect (in which case it is the responsibility of some *other* discipline to improve it). Thus when medicine, the art of healing, finds itself inadequate, it turns to medical research for help, and if medical research finds itself inadequate, it may turn to medical technology or biochemistry and so on. Putting the matter in terms of the individual practitioner, a dentist qua dentist never looks out for himself or herself. Either the dentist treats other people's dental problems or, when he or she has such problems, turns to some other dentist for assistance.

Now the analogy between the argument advanced by Socrates and the problem with regard to the teaching of thinking skills might be phrased in this fashion: the teachers at any grade level teach their students the skills that will be needed in subsequent grades, not the skills needed at their own grade level, for those skills will have been implanted in the students earlier on. When expressed in this way, the analogy has considerable plausibility. But a fourth-grade teacher might nevertheless wonder aloud, "All right, my job is to prepare my students to cope with the fifth- and sixth-grade curricula and to provide the skills presupposed by those curricula. But how in the world do I do it? I'm no more prepared to teach the cognitive skills needed for later grades than I am for my own grade!"

Those who have gone through this process of self-doubting and who have become really desperate might find themselves forced back into a re-examination of the conclusion of the argument according to Socrates: *no discipline ever seeks its own improvement.* Sufficiently discouraged and ready to grasp at any straw, they might find themselves studying that negative quantifier, that formidable, monolithic "no." No discipline?

Not even one? What if Socrates were right about all but one? What if there were a discipline that sought both its own improvement and the improvement of all other disciplines as well? What if there were a discipline that concerned itself with the problematic and contestable aspects of every discipline, fastening upon just those perplexing aspects of the disciplines in which they had become a problem to themselves?

Is There a Discipline that Prepares Us To Think in the Other Disciplines?

It would not be amiss here to fall back on Aristotle, who defines or identifies something by seeing how it is subsumed under the principles of inclusion and exclusion. Thus all humans are animals (principle of inclusion), but only humans are rational animals (principle of exclusion). All particular goods have the highest good in common (principle of inclusion), but only the highest good is always an end and never a means (principle of exclusion). Analogously, one might say something like, "All disciplines, to be properly practiced, require thinking in the language of the discipline" (principle of inclusion). We could then add that only _____ prepares one to think in the other disciplines (principle of exclusion). Alternatively, another principle of exclusion might be suggested: only _____ concentrates on the logical conditions that apply generically to thinking in the languages of the disciplines. Still other formulations might refer to some discipline that seeks to provoke thinking per se or to promote better thinking.

One does not have to be gifted with special insight to recognize that the discipline under discussion is philosophy. True, some will demur. Collingwood, for example, holds that philosophy's role is not to make us think but to make us think better. Presumably he means that philosophy does not motivate us to think, but it makes us think better by strengthening our reasoning, inquiry, and concept-formation skills, once we have them. Given the alacrity with which normally unreflective persons can be prodded into wonder and reflection by philosophy, this comment by Collingwood is somewhat puzzling. But let us glance at another part of the same book (*Essay on Philosophical Method*) by Collingwood, in which he discusses the differences between philosophy and other disciplines—in particular, the differences in their respective approaches to classification.[1] Collingwood argues that philosophy's approach to classification is radically different from that of other disciplines. In other disciplines, the object of classificatory inquiry is the establishment of a taxonomy made up of non-overlapping classes, which together comprise completely the domain under investigation. Simply put, the classes are mutually exclusive and jointly exhaustive of the domain. The philosophical approach, however, is to keep open the possibility that classes are overlapping. Thus the rationalistic disposition of the non-philosophic disciplines leads to their insistence that there is a clear-cut distinction between, say, differences of degree and differences of kind. Philosophers, on the other hand, may find this distinction acceptable in some situations and unacceptable in others. They will argue that there are fuzzy zones where classificatory systems overlap or break down, as when we cannot decide whether or not it is raining when a single drop of rain has fallen.

Now the contrast between the approach of philosophy and the approach of other disciplines with regard to classification is merely an illustration of a more fundamental difference: philosophy's concern with "essentially contestable concepts." Philosophy is attracted by the problematic and the controversial, by the conceptual difficulties that lurk in the cracks and interstices of our conceptual schemes. It is not that philosophers are inclined to celebrate such difficulties and make no effort to remove them by proposing clarifications and elucidations. It is simply that philosophers recognize such efforts as inherently Sisyphean: the problematic is inexhaustible and reasserts itself remorselessly, whatever our efforts.

Philosophy goes for the problematic as a moth is drawn to a flame or as a combatant is drawn to his opponent's jugular; indeed, it is not unusual to observe philosophers seeking their own jugulars at times. The significance of this quest for the problematic is that it *generates* thinking. And so when we encounter those prefixes, "*philosophy* of science," "*philosophy* of history," and so on, we are grappling with the problematic aspects of those disciplines. For insofar as academic disciplines take themselves to be non-problematic, the instructional approach they favor is that their students must learn what they are taught, whereas the more problematic the image these disciplines have of themselves, the more they will favor an instructional approach of joint, shared inquiry by teachers and students alike. For a discipline to stay alive, it must re-animate the thinking that went into it at its inception and subsequent formation.

The present crisis among the disciplines no doubt stems from their belonging to an exploding universe whose members are moving farther and farther apart, in a kind of redshift. Yet the problem lies not with their expansion, which is constructive and commendable, but with their divesting themselves of the philosophical integument that would normally bind them together. It is when a discipline conceives its integrity to lie in ridding itself or its epistemological, metaphysical, aesthetic, ethical, and logical considerations that it succeeds in becoming merely a body of alienated knowledge and procedures. Nevertheless, it cannot be forgotten that the subdisciplines of philosophy just alluded to—epistemology, metaphysics, aesthetics, ethics, logic, and the like—are equally vulnerable to becoming alienated if they are taught independently of the parent discipline of philosophy, for it is only within the humanistic context of philosophy that students can experience the cultural relevance and methodological rigor that can be lacking when, for example, "critical thinking" courses are offered by non-philosophers or when "thinking skills" are taught in isolation.

What has now emerged is that thinking is becoming the very foundation of the educational process and that education built on any other foundation (such as the kind of education we have now) will be shallow and sterile. Since the skills needed to think in the other disciplines must be perfected before the other disciplines themselves are encountered, we see why philosophy had to cease being exclusively a college or university subject and become as well an elementary school subject—the discipline whose task it is to prepare students to think in the other disciplines.

A century and a half ago, Eduard Hanslick formulated his famous thesis that music is unique among the arts because in music, form and content are one and the same.[2] Be that as it may, one might effectively argue that philosophy is the discipline whose form and pedagogy are one and the same. To the extent that this is so—that the dialectical form of philosophy is identical with its pedagogy—philosophy provides a formidable model for the educational process as a whole.

4 Philosophy, Critical Thinking, and the Core of Common Culture

Philosophers have been understandably reluctant to accede to the proposal for an auto-da-fe with which Hume concludes in *An Inquiry Concerning Human Understanding:*

> If we take in our hand any volume—of divinity or school metaphysics, for instance—let us ask, *Does it contain any abstract reasoning concerning quantity or number?* No. *Does it contain any experimental reasoning concerning matter of fact and existence?* No. Commit it then to the flames, for it can contain nothing but sophistry and illusion.[1]

Indeed, the followers of Hume might have cause to wonder if the *Inquiry* itself might someday be classifiable as school metaphysics and burned along with the rest. The cautious philosophical response to Hume's inflammatory proposal has been to confine one's philosophical activities to analytical or positivistic pursuits. The many philosophers who have followed this path have seemed to their colleagues to be making unnecessary concessions to Humean intimidation.

And yet, in the past few years, the atmosphere has begun to change. Philosophy's vigor is undiminished, but it is now active in a variety of ways rather than in just a few. With this show of strength, philosophers are developing renewed respect for their own discipline, and non-philosophers are beginning to admit that philosophy may be a legitimate and meritorious academic discipline after all. Moreover, recognition is growing that the enormous achievements of analytical and positivistic philosophers were made possible not by writing off other forms of philosophy but by reworking what had been done in ways that other forms of philosophy had insufficiently explored. The change in atmosphere has provided an opportunity to inquire into the ways in which philosophy might do things better than other disciplines and into the ways in which philosophy might do things—very worthwhile things—that no other discipline could do.

Both of these considerations come into play with the surfacing of the problem of teaching rationality. But even before that, they came into

play with the surfacing of the problem of education itself. Confronting
the disciplines to be taught, specialists in education have taken this tack:
"Show us what you want to teach, and we will show you how to teach
it more successfully than any way you could devise yourselves." This is
somewhat like the technical writer who tells a client, "Tell me what you
want to say, and I will invent a way of saying it better than any way you
can invent." It is not that either of these comments is objectionable but
that they do not go to the heart of the problem.

The better physicists, historians, and teachers of English are not merely
concerned with injecting their knowledge into their students. The better
historian is not simply concerned with producing students educated in
history but with producing educated students who think historically as
a part of that education, and neither the historian qua historian nor
the educationist qua educationist is equipped to transcend his or her
specialties and spell out the aims of education. On the other hand, it
is the very nature of philosophy to transcend the points of view of the
individual disciplines, to be, as it were, transparochial, and yet to have
an overall sense of proportion that would put it in a better position to
formulate those aims than either the representatives of the disciplines or
the specialists in education. It is not that philosophers, in claiming this
prerogative, are arrogating unto themselves a privilege to which they can
have no legitimate claim; it is rather that when specialists in education
and representatives of the disciplines attempt to formulate the aims of
education, they can do so only by becoming philosophers.

According to conventional wisdom, the aim of education is to take
ignorant children and make them knowledgeable by transmitting to them
the knowledge currently possessed by adults. It involves the acquisition
of a considerable amount of information—of "knowledge that"—as well
as initiation into the tribal rites of the society—of "knowledge how."
Although this is a splendid model for a tribe that is relatively fixated—that
is, well adapted to an unchanging environment—it is virtually suicidal for
a society in which cultural change occurs at such a velocity that the
knowledge enabling us to function successfully today will be obsolete a
decade from now.

Confronted with the probability that the rate of cultural change is
unlikely to recede, some commentators have advocated that we identify
at least a core of common heritage and impress this core on the young,
whatever else we do.[2] The perennial wisdom contained in this priceless
core of humanistic values will shore us up among the ruins and provide us
with a minimal continuity from generation to generation. The alternative
is endless social fragmentation under the guise of autonomy and pluralism,
which is anathema to these commentators.

At the other end of the spectrum are those who accept the inevitability of rapid and even accelerating social change and, having seen the handwriting on the wall, are aghast at the prospect of voters, consumers, students, workers, and other social groups helplessly exposed to and totally vulnerable to those who would engineer their consent by manipulating their thoughts and emotions. Here, too, are to be found those who fear that democratic institutions, already precariously balanced in many parts of the world, will totter and collapse if education does not prepare children to become autonomous, reflective, and critical citizens. Here, likewise, are those who perceive burgeoning bureaucratization and rationalization everywhere they turn, whether in capitalistic or collectivistic societies, and who consequently fear that children unprepared for the demands of such rationality will be doomed. To many individuals with anxieties such as these, the goal of education must be switched from knowledge acquisition to thinking, and such thinking must be critical, or logical, or both.

Under the banner of "critical thinking," a groundswell of well-intentioned effort has begun to make itself felt in educational circles. In the proliferation of books and articles on this topic, one only infrequently encounters those longer-range studies that would evaluate critical thinking in terms of how well it might serve as a means to desirable but more general educational goals. Much more fashionable is the discussion of whether a separate version of critical thinking should be developed within each discipline or whether critical thinking involves the learning of generic rather than discipline-specific skills, so that critical thinking is a kind of autonomous discipline, sui generis. Few discussants seem to have much affection for the possibility that partisans of both sides may be right, and one is led to wonder if perhaps the battle is so heated because it is a vestige of the still older controversy over whether education courses should be given within each discipline or as part of a separate and autonomous school of education.

Thus the advocates of a core of common culture hope to ride out the storm by pinning their hopes on the character building that they claim occurs with the acquisition of that core. The advocates of thinking-skill education, on the other hand, hope to develop students with such a high degree of intellectual flexibility and resourcefulness that they will survive the storm no matter how bad it gets. It is hardly an accident that those who take seriously the question of what is to be done—that is, those with strong moral concerns—split up, as they have always done, into advocates of character development and advocates of intelligence strengthening. We must keep in mind that these concerns may be wholly authentic and legitimate, even if we feel we must reject as inadequate the solutions advocated by one of these groups.

With these considerations in mind, let us return to the question of the primary goal of education. Immediately we are besieged by words like "civilized," "cultured," "learned," "knowledgeable," "rational," and "reasonable" as characterizations of the fully educated person, and each term vies with the others for nomination as the end toward which all our educational efforts must be directed. Now the selection of "the most desirable end" from an array of ends is as pointless, in exclusion of consideration of potential means, as would be selection of "the most desirable means" in exclusion of consideration of possible ends. The array of both ends and means must be taken into consideration together, so that learning what is available can illuminate the understanding of what is ideal, and vice versa. Thus, instead of matching up ends and means, we will find ourselves matching up "ends in view" and "means in view." The phrase "matching up" can also be problematic. It recalls the matching exercises that children are often asked to perform, but is this really the route we want to take? Is the relationship between ends in view and means in view quite so arbitrary? Is it not possible that every procedure projects an outcome? There is a sense in which Kant's dictum is convertible: not only is it the case that to will the end is to will the means, but it is also the case that to will the means is to will the end. The objection, that this confuses end as goal with end as consequence, misses the point: what good is the ideal if it cannot be realized in the consequence?

Another way to put this, borrowing from a recognizable classical text, is to say that every educational enterprise, program, or project aims at some educational end. What, then, is the end at which all these endeavors aim? And which approach promises to be both the most comprehensive in terms of aims and the most successful in terms of outcomes?

We are proceeding here in a very sketchy fashion, scanning the field in a most cursory way in an effort to ascertain its general outlines. Earlier we noted the core of common culture proposal, which was aimed at solidifying and strengthening intergenerational continuity while inculcating humanistic standards and values. We also looked at the thinking-skill movement, the aim of which is to strengthen intellectual virtuosity so as to enable students to deal effectively with the unforeseeably novel situations they would encounter in their study, their work, and their lives. To explicate the ideals projected by each of these approaches is no more capricious or arbitrary than to discover the angle that subtends a given arc. Those advocating the core of common culture approach conceive of education as producing cultured, civilized human beings; those advocating the strengthening of thinking skills look forward to developing human beings who are rational.

Now, none of these means in view and ends in view is in any way reprehensible. In fact, they may all be highly desirable. But we earlier resolved to seek the most comprehensive solution, and it is questionable that either of these approaches, or the ideals that they can appeal to, offers a satisfactory degree of comprehensiveness. Indeed, as we investigate still other approaches and come to realize that they entail still different and perhaps preferable ideals, we realize that this stage of our inquiry is not one at which we can comfortably rest.

The educational approach we are looking for is one that does all the desirable things that the other approaches do, plus other desirable things that the other approaches fail to do. With this in mind, let us consider philosophy, giving particular attention to elementary and secondary school philosophy.

To begin with, how does Philosophy for Children compare with the "core of common culture" approach? The latter, of course, represents the adaptation to the elementary school of the Hutchins-Adler view that the educated individual is familiar with the essential findings in the major disciplines—the essentials of history, physics, art, mathematics, and so on.[3] Simply to know these essentials qualifies one as a civilized, cultivated human being. Those possessing such knowledge form a small, select elite, and they bear the burden of human understanding from generation to generation, so that the community they form is broadened by the membership of those with like attainments in past and future generations. It is intimated that, by immersing our students in all that is noblest and best, by having them learn summary versions of each major discipline, we can preserve our common cultural heritage and establish a standard of educational excellence that the remainder of the society can be encouraged to emulate.

The proponents of elementary school philosophy are not content with the notion that erudition of this kind can serve as an educational ideal in an era in which great masses of people are aspiring to or attempting to preserve democracy. The student who learns only the products of inquiry in the various disciplines does not thereby become an inquirer but merely a learned student. This allusion reveals one of the educational aims of philosophy: that every student should become (or continue to be) an inquirer. Toward the achievement of this goal, there can be no better preparation than philosophy. Philosophy is conceptual inquiry, which is inquiry in its purest and most essential form. Education in the other disciplines does not involve knowledge of their products so much as learning to think in the disciplines—to think historically, physically, anthropologically, mathematically, and so on. What philosophy involves is learning to think about the thinking in the disciplines, while at the same time learning to think self-correctively about one's own thinking. (Thus the graduate student in philosophy is expected to take a variety of courses that are discipline-specific, such as the philosophy of science, the philosophy of literature, and the philosophy of religion, and at the same time to take courses that are philosophically generic, such as logic, epistemology, and ethics.)

Moreover, when we talk about philosophical thinking, we are not speaking in the taxonomic sense that would classify any thinking as thinking. We are speaking rather of reasoning guided by the ideal of rationality, and this, to the philosopher, is not merely thinking, but better thinking. The educational significance of this point is that importing philosophy into elementary school experience is a way of bringing about better thinking—more logical, more coherent, more productive, more successful—than the kinds of thinking now prevalent at that level or likely to be prevalent if other educational approaches are employed.

How, then, does philosophy compare with the common core of culture approach as educational alternatives at the elementary school level? First, philosophers would note that their discipline, as much as any in existence, is representative of the heritage of human thought. Philosophy does not cannibalize its past but holds the thought of any philosopher ever available for re-inspection and re-interpretation. It is thus in philosophy that the values and ideals of the past may be reconsidered for their relevance to the present and the future. Second, then, philosophy infuses education with a spirit of critical reasonableness and judiciousness that no other discipline can hope to provide. Third, as has already been pointed out, philosophy is the discipline that prepares us to think in the disciplines. We may conclude, therefore, that the admixture of philosophy into the elementary school curriculum would accomplish all that the core of common culture approach would accomplish, while achieving other desirable objectives not attainable by that other approach.

If we turn now to the thinking skill approach, we can see very quickly that it presents a number of difficulties. The concentration on the sharpening of isolated skills provides no procedure leading to the convergence and orchestration of these skills. Little may be done to motivate the students to improve their cognitive skills or to engage in inquiry, either because they are presented with nothing that grips their attention and curiosity or because the problems presented are not ones they have discovered for themselves but rather problems posed by the teacher. Such problems, moreover, are generally not the kind that students find challenging because it is understood that there are answers, and these answers are already known to the teacher.

A second objection to the thinking skill approach is that its advocates (such as Benjamin Bloom) so seldom include reasoning skills in their purview.[4] The skills they have in mind tend to encompass only those that are familiar from the teaching of social science practice, whereas philosophy-based programs are concerned with reasoning skills along with inquiry skills. The absence of logical skills in the usual thinking skill approach ensures that little will be done to overcome student incoherence in the formulation of explanations and arguments, in the ferreting out of underlying assumptions and implications, or in the unification of meanings.

A third objection is to the frequent emphasis on non-linguistic skills, such as identifying and discussing dot patterns. Improved ability to cope with non-linguistic symbol systems simply presents the student with new problems of transfer into the linguistic systems that are the standard language of the schools. A language-based approach such as philosophy directly improves reading, writing, listening, and discussion skills; alternative approaches must be indirect and consequently less efficient.

This brings us to still a fourth objection, which is that psychologically based approaches to thinking are essentially descriptive, whereas philosophical approaches are normative. That is, psychologists seeking to produce better thinkers must necessarily borrow their standards of logicality and rationality from philosophy, since philosophy has always studied these criteria assiduously and has devoted itself to spelling out the steps required to improve thinking so as to conform to these ideals. Philosophy need not look far afield in order to provide itself with standards of good thinking. Moreover, the relationship of psychology to thinking is external and contingent, whereas the relationship of philosophy to thinking is internal and recursive. Philosophy is self-corrective thinking. It is thinking inquiring into itself for the purpose of transforming itself into better thinking. (This is not to say that philosophy is concerned with no discipline but itself, but rather, when it considers other disciplines, it is concerned primarily with the thinking going on in those disciplines.)

There is a fifth point that may seem to be an advantage rather than a disadvantage of the thinking skills approach. That is, teaching students cognitive skills directly can be accomplished in the conventional classroom by means of conventional methods of instruction. Neither students nor teachers need be involved in inquiry. The teacher can retain the guise of omniscient authority. The students can sit in silent rows, giving answers when called on and doing paper-and-pencil exercises. Philosophy, on the other hand, cannot be done in that fashion. The doing of philosophy requires conversation, dialogue, and community, which are not compatible with the requirements of the traditional classroom. Philosophy entails converting the classroom into a community of inquiry, where students and teachers can talk together as persons and as members of the same community, where they can read together, appropriate ideas together, build on one another's ideas as well as think independently, seek reasons for their views, explore their presuppositions, so as to bring into their lives a fresh new sense of what it is to discover, to invent, to interpret, and to criticize.

The integral link between philosophy and the classroom community of inquiry is more than the connection between a subject matter and an instructional methodology. In the past few decades, there has been a growing sense in some quarters, such as political science, sociology, social psychology, and philosophy, that some significant shifts in cultural emphasis are beginning to take place. Instead of the freezing of social groups into antagonistic positions so that little can be done but bombard each other with arguments, there is a developing sense of the merits of conversation and dialogue before the fixed positions can congeal. Instead of democratic practice being limited to the annual pull of a lever in a ballot box, there is an increasing emphasis on participation and community at a variety of grass-roots levels, thereby avoiding the noxious extremes of rampant individualism and collectivism. If this direction of social change is to prosper, it must have an educational component. The community of inquiry will perhaps be seen more and more as not simply that component, but as a paradigm of the process and a specimen of its benefits.

Finally, it must be pointed out that philosophy as a discipline is eminently suitable for the elementary and secondary schools. It has a vast traditional literature that can be translated into ordinary language and sequenced according to grade levels. Its concepts are intrinsically interesting to children, and their discussions of these concepts prepares them to deal more effectively with the concepts in other subject areas, such as science. And it offers children a model of the reasonable life as a member of a participatory, collaborative community. The internalization of this model can reinforce the positive aspects of the family model already internalized by the child, so that together these introjected dynamics can serve as a kind of internal gyroscope, helping to keep the individual on an even keel through life's vicissitudes.

Rationality is probably an indispensable notion, but it will always remain problematic as an aim of education. It seems more appropriate to armies, factories, and computers. Reasonableness, on the other hand, would seem more akin to the well-tempered life, in closer touch with the whole person rather than with just the intellect, and more representative of the spirit and outcome of shared inquiry. If the doing of philosophy—

philosophical praxis, as it were—is the embodiment of reasonableness, every phase of childhood should have access to that experience, both for its immediate enjoyment and for the preparation it provides for personal and social experiences in the future. If both philosophy and education are seen to share reasonableness as the same goal, it might not seem at all outrageous to contend that fundamentally all true philosophy is educational and all true education is philosophical.

**Ethical Inquiry
in the Schools**

5   Education for Civic Values

It is generally agreed that, in a democratic society, parents would like their children to be able to identify, want, and have what is best. The same hopes are characteristic of democratic societies with respect to their future citizens. But what values does the adult world agree are *best?* Here there is a broad range of disagreement.

Controversy over value education is unavoidable in a democratic society. The most common form of controversy is found when the question is formulated as, Whose values are to be taught—theirs or ours? In state after state throughout the country, the typical confrontation is between antagonists who believe themselves to be engaged in a struggle of change versus stability. Consider how these opponents view themselves and each other.

In the eyes of its proponents, the first position (education as preparation for change) is an expression of the liberal values of urban diversity and cultural innovation. City life requires considerable tolerance for a variety of life-styles and promotes skepticism with regard to the possibility of any broad consensus of views. Interest and pressure groups abound; factions are matched against factions. Since no one faction can be victorious, the goal is a balance of power, the achievement of which requires ceaseless efforts at persuasion and negotiation. Thus skills in argument and rhetoric become invaluable for the fabrication and unmasking of ideologies and for efforts to resolve disputes through mediation. The first position stresses skills over educational content.

The second position, in contrast, conceives itself as representing the permanent repository of traditional, civilized values. The same moral codes are to be passed from generation to generation, thereby guaranteeing the integrity and continuity of the social group. There is reverence for the past, for the sources of the nation's being, and there is respect for the ideals that are a heritage of that past as well as a faithful guide to the future. Proponents of this conservative position tend to feel that values are better shown than explained, just as they tend to find indoctrination unobjectionable. The second position stresses content rather than skills.

From the point of view of the first position, the second is provincial, if not reactionary. From the point of view of the second position, members of the first group are relativists and skeptics, if not nihilists.

There are accuracies as well as distortions in the way each set of proponents sees the other. But neither can have any hope of convincing the other. Those who uphold the second position see all too well the precariousness of argument as a basis for value education; those who uphold the first position see all too well the precariousness of an overreliance on character training. What neither sees is that, in a democratic society, committed to pluralism and diversity, no one set of values can be taught at the expense of other sets of values, without infringement on someone's constitutional rights. On the other hand, the diversity of ends characteristic of a pluralistic society may rest on a uniformity of means, and it is precisely this consensus with regard to procedures that can form the accepted context of value education. For example, whatever our political or religious commitments, we all accept due process and the sovereignty of the Constitution, for we realize that without these things there would be little left to our society as we know it.

From whatever background they come, most children enter the educational system alert and eager to learn, bright-eyed, and trusting. But all too many of them find the process meaningless as they move through the system, and as this happens, they become progressively more apathetic and despairing. As a result, every year the educational system dumps into the pool of adult citizens a vast number of individuals who are ignorant of the mechanisms of the society in which they are to participate, skeptical of its traditions, and cynical with regard to its ideals. We cannot resign ourselves to this sort of thing, but what can be done—if only as a start—to turn matters around?

To begin with, the educational system must be one that gives pupils reason to hope; indeed, this is the first step with any population that feels its situation to be hopeless. Children must therefore be allowed to experience what it is like to exist in a context of mutual respect, of disciplined dialogue, of cooperative inquiry, free of arbitrariness and manipulation. The casual observer may dismiss what seems to be happening in such a classroom as "just talk." But this ignores the fact that nothing sharpens reasoning skills like disciplined conversation. It ignores the fact that children love to talk, and wise educators have always tried to build on what children are already motivated to do rather than what they have to be made to want to do. And finally it ignores the fact that conversation (as every diplomat or labor-management negotiator knows) is the minimal condition for civility. It is when conversation stops that we must prepare for the worst; it is when conversation resumes that we can breathe easier and begin to hope again.

Value education must be conducted in such a cooperative and communal context, far from the contentiousness and invidiousness of the undergraduate seminar in ethics and equally far from the sophistry of forensic debate. The objective is not to present children with elaborate ethical theories from which one to live by is to be selected, but rather to equip children with the tools of reflection, within a context of inquiry—that is, a context whose methodology is one of continual self-criticism and self-correction. (Needless to say, the capacity for self-criticism and the capacity for self-control are intimately connected.)

There is no single thinking skill whose cultivation will suffice for competence in value inquiry, for sensitivity to the incredible subtlety of social issues demands every thinking skill that philosophy can cultivate. Developing concepts, forging definitions, drawing inferences, making connections and distinctions, and reasoning analogically are only a few of the major reasoning skills. Nevertheless, indispensable as these skills may be for citizenship in a society where it is considered important to reason together about the issues, reason alone is insufficient. There is also a question of character.

A person who has the character of "good citizen" is one who has internalized—that is, adopted as his or her own—the social mechanisms of rationality in institutional practice. Thus members of a search committee whose personal beliefs and attitudes are poles apart will nevertheless agree on the need for openness of evidence, clear and precise job specifications, goals and objectives, and criteria of evaluation if the candidates are to be considered fairly. The members of the committee may view any given candidate differently, but they do not differ with regard to the procedures of valuation, for these are what all the members have internalized and taken for granted. Likewise, civilized individuals generally have internalized due process and the rule of law, the parliamentary procedures, the codes of fair play, the prudential guidelines of diplomatic practice, and even to some extent the methodology of scientific inquiry. These are not mere matters of opinion or of conflicting ideologies: they represent the rational basis of civilization, and legitimate socialization involves their internalization by each and every individual. So internalized, they represent the dispositional readiness of the citizen to treat like cases similarly and different cases differently—a readiness without which one cannot be just.

To link value education to any particular ideology—whether liberal, conservative, radical, or reactionary—is to doom its chances of being found acceptable in a public school setting. Moreover, intergenerational communication being what it is, for an older generation to attempt to compel a younger generation to accept a particular set of values is virtually to guarantee their rejection. Nor can educators who recognize that each and every criterion is a means of distinguishing the better from the worse confirm the bland prejudice of so many young people that "everything's relative." This is mindless relativism, and to indoctrinate it as the way to resolve all value conflicts is particularly reprehensible.

When consideration is given to the various ways in which value education has been successfully incorporated into existing subject areas and to promising new approaches in the field, it becomes evident that the means do exist for the fashioning of an objective and workable program in value education—one about which there can be a community consensus, one that fosters the development of moral character, and one that promotes the education of reasonable and reflective individuals. The aim of this chapter is to suggest promising directions for further work that would in turn be conducive to a unified approach to awakening in students an awareness of the advantages and responsibilities of citizenship.

In mentioning instances in which values have been successfully taught in direct, explicit, and overt ways, we should not overlook the vast array of approaches that are tacit and indirect. If, for example, we were to ask what goes on in school that helps make students more fair-minded, and if by "fair-minded" we mean a readiness to treat like cases similarly and different cases differently, then no subject area would be found that failed to contribute significantly to the development of such fair-minded individuals. Surely science contributes heavily, with its stress on the value of objectivity, the need to search scrupulously for causes and effects, and the value of careful description and explanation. Surely the humanities contribute enormously: how else can we become sensitive to the subtleties of the present moment and the possibilities of the future unless we have suitably surveyed the history of the past and immersed ourselves in literature and art? Where do we learn the nuances of social roles and relationships, apart from direct personal experience, except as we see them modeled in Antigone and David and Cordelia, in the oration of Pericles, in *Tosca* and *Fidelio,* in Piero della Francesca's *Queen of Sheba* and Rembrandt's *Prodigal Son,* in the *Phaedo* and *The Brothers Karamazov,* in *The Canterbury Tales* and *In Memory of W. B. Yeats?* We perceive and understand human beings through the windows of science and history and the arts and languages; indeed, every sentence is a prism through which perception takes place, so that the values that shape our linguistic expressions also shape our experience of the world around us as well as of our selves. Wittingly or unwittingly, whoever teaches teaches values. Thus education for values is already being done, and being done pervasively, so that the problem is not to do it but to do it better.

It must be done better, if students are to be better armed against the cruelty and violence of the world into which many of them will graduate and in which many of them already exist. In this sense, education for citizenship is more than just preparing young people to be good decision-makers, for they must learn how to live so that social crises will be less likely to arise and can be better circumvented if they do. Such education is preventive with regard to crime and addiction, and it makes for a new generation of parents who may be more effective in transmitting reasonable and wholesome values to their own children.

Although moral values represent only one value category among many, it would be difficult to deny that ethics is the most critical area for value education. One of the major branches of philosophy, ethics is generally thought of as the theory of moral conduct. That is, human conduct is subject to a kind of appraisal that we call moral and that results in particular instances of conduct being termed better, worse, right, wrong, good, bad, and so on. Ethics represents the philosophical endeavor to examine the rational grounds of such appraisals and to devise theories that would, among other things, suggest ways in which ethical principles could be brought to bear on the moral predicaments of human life.

Philosophers such as Aristotle, Kant, and Mill developed ethical theories of great elegance and complexity, and it is normally these theories, along with many others, that are studied and discussed in college and university courses in ethics. Unfortunately, it is the very sophistication and subtlety of such theories, couched as they usually are in highly specialized terminologies, that have caused the teaching of ethics to be limited to college and university students or to high school seniors. Elementary school students would find Aristotle, Kant, and Mill unreadable, although this does not mean they could not, starting with examples, eventually comprehend the general principles espoused by these philosophers. Nor does this mean we should ignore the recommendations of traditional writers on ethics as we seek ways of improving value education in the schools. We cannot ignore Aristotle's stress on the connection between thinking and morality: something is good when it performs its function well. The function that humans possess exclusively is to live in accordance with reason; therefore, human beings who are most reasonable in the way they live are most deserving to be called good.[1]

Likewise, we must not fail to take into account Kant's contention that moral law is universal: morality is not a matter of doing whatever it is that everyone else is doing, nor is it a matter of merely carrying out our natural impulses and appetites. Rather, each of us must act as all of us ought to act: we therefore recognize our duty when we ask ourselves if the way we are now considering acting is the way everyone should act. In other words, what sort of world would it be if everyone were to act this way? In forging the policies by which we choose to live, either as individuals or as nations, we would find it costly to overlook Kant's maxim.[2]

The same may be said of the utilitarian approach favored by Mill. Like Aristotle, Mill sees human beings as motivated by the desire for happiness and as able to maximize that happiness through reason. This refers to not just our own happiness but the happiness of all concerned—a goal toward which we aim when we pursue courses of action that might reasonably be expected to increase the happiness or decrease the unhappiness of all who might be affected by such courses of action. Mill's approach reminds us that reason and morality can no more be severed in the case of individuals than in the case of nations: both are concerned with the relationship between the good of each and the good of all.[3]

This is not the place to cite a spate of corroborating or critical theories; it will have to suffice to take the preceding views as typical and to proceed by asking what has happened in more recent intellectual history, which, while building on classical theories of ethics, has prepared the ground for more effective programs of value education. In this regard, mention would have to be made of the following developments, which suggest that a fresh start in value education can be a highly promising one:

1. the insights of Durkheim, Weber, and Piaget into the ways in which individuals internalize social controls;
2. G. H. Mead's recognition that the child's powerful social impulses can be harnessed in the service of education;
3. Vygotsky's demonstration that many children work at a different—and higher—level when doing intellectual work cooperatively rather than competitively;
4. Dewey's incisive critique of authoritarian assumptions in education, a critique whose full implications have yet to be explored;
5. Bruner's contention that education at every level should and can provide an intellectually respectable version of the cultural possessions of a highly civilized adult;
6. the breath of fresh air in philosophy represented by the shift toward ordinary language and non-formal logic, especially as represented by the work of Wittgenstein, and the consequent stress on "reasons" rather than "arguments";

7. the keener appreciation of the analogy between the rules of a game and the laws of a society—again with particular reference to the work of Piaget and Wittgenstein;
8. intensified concern with the rights of minorities and, by extension, with the academic and intellectual rights of children;
9. a shift in the definition of education, associated most explicitly with Dewey and Bruner, from education for learning to education for thinking, with a consequent emphasis on the acquisition of those skills that make feasible the acquisition of new skills and with the claim that nothing sharpens reasoning skills better than disciplined classroom conversation;
10. new analyses of language, meaning, and thinking (in particular, Ryle's effort to operationalize meanings in terms of thinking skills), which have confirmed the relevance and soundness of children's oft-frustrated quest for meaningfulness in education;
11. the work of such philosophers as Dewey, C. I. Lewis, J. O. Urmson, and Kurt Baier in the theory of valuation;
12. the realization that the logic of relations developed by De Morgan, Peirce, and others is particularly applicable to reasoning with differences of degree (e.g., "better than," "worse than") such as are involved in reasoning about values;
13. the recent recognition of the fundamental role of thinking skills in basic skill acquisition by many cognitive psychologists and by the National Institute of Education.

The Components of an Approach to Value Education

It has long been held that one of the virtues of a good society is that such a society promotes the virtue or virtues of its citizens. In some quarters this is interpreted to mean that schools must supplement the efforts of the family to impart values to the child and that the values with which the schools are particularly concerned, as public institutions, are called "civic values." This is not seen as indoctrination but as a cultivation of the society's youthful resources, as an initiation of the young into that which our civilization considers most meaningful and important among its own traditions and ideals.

Such a view has much to recommend it, but implicit in it is the danger of encroachment on parental rights with regard to their children's beliefs and on the intellectual rights of children attending public institutions in a democratic society. Moreover, society itself has a stake in the matter, for its own interest requires that it promote intellectual integrity and excellence along with good citizenship. But is this feasible? Can civic virtue be inculcated without producing intellectual slavishness? Can values education escape the accusation that it must be either conformist or subversive?

It should be evident to anyone observing the educational process at the elementary and secondary school levels that the transmission of values to the younger generation is ubiquitous, although in an informal, random, and unsystematic fashion. In no way can this be avoided, nor would it be desirable to attempt to avoid it. Every teacher, whether of home economics or history or biology, has to make selections as to what is to be taught and has to set priorities as to when it is to be taught. These choices will be based on criteria, on professional standards, on educational policies, all of which likewise represent the outcomes of many processes of valuation. Such choices will also reflect the pervasive cultural outlook as to what is or is not to be recommended to children. The problem that now must be faced is whether professional methods exist for the upgrading of this transmission of values.

If such upgrading is to take place, it must be conducted in a responsible fashion that does not violate the civil rights or rights of conscience of children and their families. This means it will not do if, in the name of fighting prejudice, one set of prejudices is substituted for another. And it further means that the method of teaching will have to be thoroughly consistent with what is taught.

This is why we must be wary of highly touted panaceas that leave only disenchantment in their wake: "Mickey Mouse" courses that promise to alter in a weekend what it has taken a professional lifetime to put together; policy pronouncements without implementation; course title changes that conceal the same stale curriculum; meek submission to mass-media competition masquerading as educational wisdom—so many cures worse than the disease. There is no magic additive that will transform the system overnight. But there are better ways of doing things, even though these ways may not be very glamorous and even though it would take years and years to bring about wide-scale results, despite a vast amount of hard work, goodwill, and good fortune.

Specifically, now, what needs to be done, and how is it to be accomplished? The areas to be dealt with are:

1. the ambiguity of "values";
2. the strengthening of character, particularly with regard to citizenship;

3. the application of reasoning skills to values and the eventual incorporation of value inquiry into all subject areas;
4. recognition that valuation is an aspect of every human endeavor and that craftsmanship in valuation is one of the most excellent attainments of civilization;
5. delineation of the pedagogy appropriate to value inquiry in the classroom;
6. summary and conclusions.

Some of these areas are so complex that treatment of them will necessarily be cursory and sketchy, whereas in other cases it has been deemed advisable to illustrate by means of concrete examples what can be or is being done rather than offer abstract recommendations. Taken together, however, these various treatments are representative of a unified position with regard to education for values. But what *are* values?

The Ambiguity of "Values"

The term "values" is mischievously ambiguous. In its singular form, "value," it suggests the worth or importance of something. Whatever matters, in this sense, is a value, whether it be oil or freedom, security or education, silver or justice, food or beauty. The plural form, "values," on the other hand, generally is used to indicate someone's opinions as to what is important. Our opinions as to what is worthwhile cherishing may in time become cherished opinions, but whether they do or not, the fact that we think something to be of value is no guarantee that we will act to bring it into being or to maintain it if it already exists. About the most we can say is that people are generally disposed to act in accordance with their opinions; if they do not, if a discrepancy arises between what they profess and what they practice, we may well question whether they actually believe what they profess to believe.

The latter point is important for value education, one goal of which is to enable students to recognize what is of worth and another goal of which deals with the improvement of judgment. Presumably, the judicious person is aware of value alternatives and is competent in setting priorities or in making selections among such alternatives.

This suggests a second ambiguity in the term "value." Just as not everything believed is true, so not everything valued has genuine worth. Many things are prized that do not stand up when it comes to scrupulous appraisal. Our valuings often reflect blind impulses, unreflective tastes and preferences, crude desirings, whereas the truly valuable, the truly desirable, is what is revealed to be such by thorough reflection and sustained inquiry. Genuine values are therefore the product of value inquiry in somewhat the same sense that educated persons are the product of education; we should not confuse the raw material that is initially fed into the process with the refined end-products that come out of it. Those things that are merely matters of unreflective interest or desire must be considered to be only apparent or *prima facie* values. They have not yet been tested experimentally. It is not yet known that they will endure and serve—that they *will do,* as Dewey puts it.[4] By examining the grounds and consequences of particular values, value inquiry moves away from subjectivity and toward objectivity in assessing what is important or worthwhile, whether the values in question be aesthetic, political, environmental, ethical, social, or any other of the countless categories into which values fall. It is evident from what has been said that a major thrust of value education involves encouraging children to engage in value inquiry and helping them to do it well.

Values are present in every area of human experience. What was unimportant yesterday may become of urgent importance tomorrow. Thus the conservation of environmental values appears to be called for in the twentieth century with an intensity unknown to previous centuries. Even when we are discussing beliefs about matters of importance rather than those matters themselves, it is obvious that there is no area of human experience where people do not make an effort to distinguish the better from the worse or where tastes and preferences do not prevail in a relatively unexamined state. In every society there is economizing—efforts to amplify the "goods" of life; in every society there are discriminations of what is beautiful as over against what is ugly, of what is tasty as over against what is unpalatable, of what is within and what is beneath the dignity of human beings, and all of these involve value judgments. Education for values clearly cannot be limited to matters of personal conduct, critical though these matters be; instead, such education must extend into any area in which there are judgments of better and worse. Ultimately this will mean that every course will have its value inquiry component and every grade level its value inquiry seminar. As will be seen, this seminar will have an especially important role, for it will be there that students will concentrate their attention on the sharpening of reasoning skills and on the interplay of ideas in our civilization. It is there too that the concept of the community of inquiry will be embodied in its most integrated form, with resultant impact on the charcter of the participants.

The Strengthening of Character

Since children spend so much of their lives in school, it is evident that the school bears considerable responsibility for their socialization. "Socialization" here means the acquisition of behavior characteristic of good citizenship. One of the most pronounced of these characteristics of good citizens is their readiness to consider the good of society along with consideration of their own personal good. They do so with a kind of spontaneity that suggests that their readiness to integrate their personal goals with the common good is a direct expression of their full acceptance of the responsibilities of citizenship. The ensemble of habits that disposes a person to behave commendably—in this instance with regard to civic obligations—is what is called "character." Thus individuals of civic virtue habitually weigh the claims of society against those of self-interest and are unflinchingly critical of imperfections in those claims, while staunchly supporting what is sound in them.

At this point the school finds itself in something of a bind. It is an institution dedicated to teaching and learning, through transmitting the knowledge of one generation to another; such, in any event, is its conventional self-concept. However, it is not at all clear that this is what character development calls for. Indeed, to interpret the school's function in this fashion, from the standpoint of character strengthening, might well be counterproductive.

When it comes to improving any form of practice, we generally learn much more from being shown than from being taught and from doing than from listening. Those who coach us in tennis or singing or bicycle-riding are careful to model for us what they want us to do. Consider, for example, the training of teachers: the professor in the school of education may spend an hour lecturing the student-teachers on the superiority of discussion over lecturing. But when the teachers are doing their practice teaching in the classroom, they will seek to emulate what the professor did and not what he or she advocated: they will lecture. So it is in general that when adults counsel children, "Do as I say and not as I do," they succeed only in serving as models of hypocrisy.

Thus, administrators and teachers, like parents, are models. They show by example how one may act, and children often do likewise. That is, children internalize the forms of adult behavior. They incorporate it into themselves; they make it their own. A child may deem anything an adult does to be exemplary and worthy of such appropriation. That it is done by an adult, particularly by a parent or teacher, seems to be justification enough. Hence the heavy burden of responsibility that adults must endure, for almost anything they do and not a great deal of what they say is going to contribute to that ensemble of internalized behaviors, that ensemble of habits, which is the child's character.

But persons are not the only models for a child. Institutions and institutional practices often serve the same socializing function. Take the game: the child who learns to play a game—say, baseball—comes to see things from the points of view of all the other players in addition to his or her own, for unless one fully understands in a game what the others are doing and why they are doing it, one cannot respond to them meaningfully or effectively. But more—the player internalizes the rules of the game, which become second nature. After all, players do not wonder whether or not to accept and obey the rules of the game (i.e., the laws of the social institution in which they participate). This is what makes them minimally competent baseball players even when they are not highly skilled. What is more, each player comes to take not only the point of view of the other players toward one another, but also their point of view with regard to the game itself. The player who is new to the game comes to prize the game as a "value in itself" and to cherish the rules of the game as valuable because they make the game possible.

Now it is much the same with developing "good citizens." They must come to see that civilization is something prizeworthy on its own account and infinitely preferable to barbarism. Likewise, they must recognize that the social rules and practices that promote civilization are estimable precisely because they serve that instrumental purpose.

Good citizens, like good players, are proud of their integrity. Players who flout a rule will be penalized, but it is for the violation of their own professional integrity that their deeper regret is reserved. In a similar fashion, children come to be honest because they prize honesty and are revolted by its violation rather than because they fear the punishments attendant upon dishonesty. Young citizens must develop an awareness of the need to protect the integrity of their civilization, just as they sense the need to protect their own integrity. They will then be horrified by barbarisms such as genocide rather than be attracted to it as a fascinating source of morbid thrills.

If, then, internalized institutional practices are a major source of the habits and attitudes out of which character arises, what can be done to set before children the kinds of practices we would like them to internalize? As a starting point, we should try to build upon the child's own efforts to contribute positively. We should therefore accept and work with the child's wish to participate, to cooperate, and to inquire. This means the transformation of the traditional classroom into a seminar in which children will be engaged in value inquiry in a participatory and cooperative fashion. They will abide by the rules of academic discussion (or will gradually learn to do so); they will listen to each other, prepared always to offer reasons for their own views and to ask for the reasons of their fellow participants; they will come to appreciate the diversity of perspectives among their classmates and the need to see matters in context. The seminar in value inquiry will come to serve them as a model of social rationality; they will internalize its rules and practices, and it will come to be established in each of them as thoughtfulness, considerateness, and judiciousness. And for children who exist so often among fragments and ruins, among disappointments and frustrations, the formation of and participation in such a community can be a source of hope for a lifetime. All the more reason that these seminars be sequential at every grade level through elementary and secondary school, for only such reinforcement will ensure that their impact will be both cumulative and lasting.

Children develop into rational beings not simply because they are born with their skulls full of brains, but also because they find themselves in families and in societies that are hospitable to rationality. To the extent that our institutions are themselves rational, we foster rationality in the children who grow up among such institutions and internalize their characteristics. But a child ground between two parents whose commands are frequently contradictory or controlled by two institutions with incompatible systems may behave in ways that perplex us with their oscillation between withdrawal and aggression. We should never underestimate the relief and liberation we provide to children when we introduce them to literature and mathematics and countless other forms of rationality, thereby assuring them that the world is not totally incoherent and that in many respects it welcomes and values their thinking.

We have been speaking of character as a set of habits that, as an ensemble, generally guides our unreflective behavior, although this may well occur in accordance with rational procedures that we have internalized. Granted, such a process makes for individuals who are socially adjusted, but will they be reflective and reasonable? Moreover, will any such reflections be capable of affecting the environing social institutions so as to modify and improve them? Here we see the other side of the values education coin. For if—in a social studies course, let us say—the nature of society is presented as immutably fixed, students so taught will be inclined to throw up their hands and exclaim, "Nothing can be done!" But society and its component institutions can be presented more problematically. Thus the guiding ideals of a democratic society, such as justice and freedom, can be presented as goals that the society is committed to move toward and progressively approximate. Such ideals need be presented not as finished concepts but as concepts that are open and contestable, inviting discussion and clarification. Consequently, with the acquisition of the mechanisms and methodology of valuation, students will find themselves capable of appraising the institutions of their society in terms of the manner in which those institutions actually implement and make possible the realization of the ideals of the society. Each ideal then becomes a criterion of evaluation rather than a symbol to be invoked rhetorically and subsequently ignored. In this sense good citizens are reflective citizens, vigorously insistent that ideals not merely be professed but that they be operationalized and implemented. The values education aspect of the educational process can here make an important contribution.

After all, the dangers of totalitarianism are often the result of weird mixtures of rationality and irrationality. One case may be that of a highly organized, methodical, and efficient system operating in the service of insane goals; in another instance, noble goals are pursued madly and with devastating ruthlessness. Either case has a fanatical misunderstanding of the need for the rational adjustment of means and ends and for the harmony of goals and procedures. Unless children are given the opportunity to understand how this can happen, and how ruinous it can be when it does happen, there can be little hope that, when they become adults, they will understand matters any better than we have or that they will endeavor, for their part, to move the world a degree or two in the opposite direction from catastrophe.

In sum, then, schools must prepare students for citizenship by affording them every possible exposure to and participation in the sorts of rational procedures that characterize adult society—in law, in diplomacy, in labor-management negotiations, in corporate organization, wherever people mediate, search, criticize, examine precedents and traditions, consider alternatives, and in short reason together rather than have recourse to arbitrariness and violence. Only by such active participation in democratic and constitutional praxis will young people be prepared to exercise citizenship when they become adults.

Rational social institutions are our best assurance that individual citizens will be reasonable. There is nothing like the knowledge that there is a constitution, that there are laws, and that there is due process—all of which an individual can appeal to in the event of injury—to defuse the impulse toward violent retaliation. We cannot wait for individual citizens to become rational before providing them with an environment of rational institutions and procedures, since it is only the prior existence of such an environment that sets the stage for and produces the reasonableness of the individual. We all respond warmly to rhetorical pronouncements about justice and freedom, but as citizens our confidence is likely to be placed in such well-established proverbs as "no rights without remedies," because we know that persons who have no remedy for wrongs done to them can only loosely be said to have legal rights. On no institution does the responsibility for rational procedures fall more heavily than the school, since it is the institution through which all members of society flow, as sand through the neck of an hourglass. Therefore, a society that wants thoughtful and reasonable persons to emerge from the schools must see to it that the school environment is itself thoughtful and reasonable. To attempt value education in a public institution that prefers to leave its own procedures unexamined may well be an exercise in futility.

The Application of Reasoning Skills to Values

As we know, effective thinking relies on a battery—one might almost call it a battalion—of reasoning skills. Many of these skills represent proficiencies in the use of logic. Only logic contains the criteria by means of which sound reasoning can be distinguished from unsound reasoning; it is therefore a discipline that is unique among the sciences and invaluable to an educational approach that aims at improved thinking.

These reasoning skills do not vary greatly from one domain to another; thus deduction is deduction, whether in natural science or in the humanities. Consequently, reasoning in the area of values does not require special value reasoning skills: it simply means that the same skills—the general reasoning skills—now have to be applied to value problems, such as those in ethics, in an orchestrated fashion. This matter should not escape attention; reasoning skills fostered for the purpose of improving ethical judgment can also be applied to academic matters, and children who are proficient in reasoning academically but have difficulty applying the same skills to problems of value can be taught how to do so. The prospect that reasoning with values should have academic benefits as well as moral ones should be attractive to school administrators as much as to parents.

Talk of "applying reasoning skills to value problems" can be distressingly vapid. How is it to be done? How are the concepts operationalized? Here there is a need for specificity, and nothing else will suffice but that a number of the more important skills be identified and illustrations be given of how they might be used in the area of ethics or of value questions generally. Accordingly, here is an inventory of twenty-seven reasoning skills (see Appendix for illustrations of their application to civic and ethical values as well as to facts). These skills are:

1. drawing inferences from single premises;
2. standardizing ordinary language sentences;
3. drawing inferences from double premises;
4. using ordinal or relational logic;
5. working with consistency and contradiction;
6. knowing how to deal with ambiguities;
7. formulating questions;
8. grasping part-whole and whole-part connections;
9. giving reasons;
10. identifying underlying assumptions;
11. working with analogies;
12. formulating cause-effect relationships;
13. concept development;
14. generalization;
15. drawing inferences from hypothetical syllogisms;
16. ability to recognize and avoid—or knowingly utilize—vagueness;
17. taking all considerations into account;
18. recognizing interdependence of ends and means;
19. knowing how to deal with "informal fallacies";
20. operationalizing concepts;
21. defining terms;
22. identifying and using criteria;
23. instantiation;
24. construction hypotheses;
25. contextualizing;
26. anticipating, predicting, and estimating consequences;
27. classification and categorization.

It is obvious that these are only some of the major reasoning skills and that many others could be cited. It should be understood, however, that value problems are almost always highly complex and are not the subject matter for any one reasoning skill. They require that whole clusters of skills be applied to them in a convergent and reinforcing fashion. So applied, reasoning skills have a cumulative impact far greater than might be supposed from examining them in isolation.[5]

Let us take an example. It supposes a high school classroom in which students are attempting to come to grips with the problem of war. At first there is no agreement on the desirability of peace, since a few students maintain that war is a necessary and healthy international condition. But then it is proposed to put this issue aside for the moment and to *assume* the desirability of peace. The following interchange subsequently takes place:

> JACK: If it's peace you want, prepare for war.
> BEN: If it's peace you want, prepare for peace.

The issue has now been joined in a highly constructive fashion. Alternative hypotheses have been proposed, suggesting diametrically opposite paths for arriving at the identical goal. By tracing out the likely consequences of the alternative sets of means, it may be possible to show that one hypothesis has greater plausibility than the other. Notice, however, the skills that must be properly marshaled and deployed by the participants in the discussion: the concepts of *peace, war,* and *preparation* must be thoroughly understood (13); the interdependence of means and ends must be acknowledged (18); all considerations must be taken into account (17); it must be understood that the question at issue is the operationalization of the concept of peace (20); suitable information from social studies must be employed to lend a sense of context and actuality (25); historical examples must be cited—with care—as relevant examples (11); and other skills will also have to be used to varying degrees.[6]

How can students learn these thinking skills and learn to coordinate and orchestrate them in the ways that are obviously necessary? For what is needed, beyond the skills themselves, is a *cognitive readiness* to employ such skills. This readiness consists in such dispositions as cooperativeness, trust, attentiveness, readiness to listen, and respect for persons. Such tendencies are fostered by the conversion of the classroom into a dialogical seminar committed to value inquiry. There will then be trust that the procedures of the members of the group will be reliable because they are self-correcting; there will be care for the procedures and for the members of the group; and there will be a readiness to appraise and criticize one's own reasoning as well as that of one's peers. As these dispositions become habitual, they lend further support to the individual's character formation, as it has been constructed by internalizing the rationality of social institutions.

The skills needed for reasoning about values are the same skills needed for reasoning about anything. Thus there is not one set of reasoning skills for values and another for facts. It therefore follows that to improve the capacity of students to think about value issues will concomitantly improve their capacity to deal with all academic subject areas. For example, if our emphasis in teaching reading is on the mechanics of the task, such as the grammar or the phonics, and not on the meanings to be inferred from what is read (which is, after all, the incentive for reading in the first place), we cannot expect success in getting children to read well. But reasoning focuses precisely on the meanings to be inferred from the written materials, so that improvement of reasoning skills increases the bonus of meaning, and of pleasure, which children can obtain from what they read.

Meanings are to be found in the relationships of words to one another and in the relationships of language to the world. To reason is to focus on those relationships while holding firm to the criteria of valid inference. For example, consider the question of the meaning of such terms as "fact" and "value." Some say that a fact is a true statement. Some say that a fact is an actual bit of the world, not merely a linguistic expression. And some assert—more plausibly, it would seem—that a fact is both of these in relationship to one another. Analogously, values may be viewed as that which is actually of importance, or as opinions as to what is of importance, but it would seem more plausible to consider them as both, in an encompassing relationship. The relevance of this illustration is that both facts and values are dimensions of meaning, and they are such meanings as children do want from their education. Enhancing their reasoning skills gives them the better education that they want and that we want for them.

A final word on the relevance of thinking skills to values is that it is not uncommon to find negative attitudes among academic underachievers. Since it is frequently assumed that a negative attitude causes the child's lack of academic achievement, efforts are made to change the child's attitude. Such efforts are generally unsuccessful because of a mistake in the diagnosis: it is not poor attitudes that cause children to be underachievers so much as it is underachievement that causes children to have negative attitudes, which attitudes then help to produce unreasonable or unruly behavior. Children who cannot cope with those aspects of their lives that demand reasoning skills—and certainly schoolwork is one of those aspects—can hardly be expected to think positively when they are not offered opportunities to strengthen the skills that would enable them to cope. Of course, there are many exceptions to the preceding generalizations: some who do well in their schoolwork are nevertheless anti-social, and some who do poorly are nevertheless not anti-social. But these exceptions cannot excuse the failure of the society to provide all children with the reasoning skills they need.

Valuation as the Focus of Value Inquiry

Students engaged in value inquiry will discuss and study many things, such as the nature and use of criteria, the relationship of means to ends and of ends to further ends, the role of analogical reasoning in consideration of values, and the influence of context on moral reflection. A most important area of study would be valuation itself—that is, the ways in which people in different walks of life do in fact decide value matters: the role of desires and preferences, the role of evidence, the ways in which priorities are set, the employment of casuistry and of logic, the recourse to due process, the reliance on bureaucratic regulations, and the use of discretion. These are only some of the countless ingredients that come together in the selection of an executive, the choice of a college to attend, the promotion of a technician, the sentencing of a prisoner, the choice of a library book, the decision to enter a certain career, the selection of the family automobile or house—the list is obviously endless.

It is commonplace to remark that democratic societies favor a plurality of values, this being the characteristic outcome of freedom of choice. Be that as it may, it does not follow that there is a lack of consensus when it comes to the practice of valuation. That consensus is reflected in the procedures that are normally employed—indeed, that are virtually taken for granted—whenever a decision is to be made where there is public accountability. So established are these procedures that it would be legitimate to think of valuation as a craft, and as with any craft, there are better and worse ways of practicing it.

Suppose a town finds itself in need of a new town manager or a new superintendent of schools. Very likely a municipal code will govern the selection procedure; there are job specifications to be met, criteria to be applied, interviews to be conducted, and all of this is spelled out carefully in advance. What is more, regardless of the political or religious persuasions of the citizens of that community, the selection procedures themselves will not be challenged, unless they are accused of not being fair enough. In short, there is a body of common practices—due process, rules of order for the conduct of meetings, accepted procedures for hiring and promotion, equal opportunity guidelines, appeal to logic for the drawing of valid inferences, abiding by the procedures of scientific inquiry when the question is one of evidence—with regard to all of which there is a consensus so powerful that any dissident is compelled to appeal to these very procedures or to an improved formulation of them. Schooling in citizenship involves getting young people to realize that it is to such procedures that one automatically has recourse, for they represent the social reasonableness that students must internalize.

It should hardly come as a surprise that value education necessarily involves study of how valuation does in fact take place. After all, we assume that young people who want to go into business would do well to study how people do business and that young people who want to go into music should study how people make music. If they are to learn to make better rather than worse value judgments, where should young people begin their studies, if not with the ways in which people already do make value judgements?

Those who appreciate irony and paradox may feel there is something equivocal in thus urging the development of an empirical subject area of valuation, to be studied by those whose processes of judgment we wish to improve. One cannot go from *is* to *ought:* from the study of the ways in which people *do* make value judgments, one cannot infer how one *ought* to make value judgments. Consider an analogous case, it will be urged: the case of thinking. Psychologists study the ways in which people *do* remember, imagine, learn, recognize, infer, and so on, but surely this descriptive information is not to be taken normatively. From the ways in which children do think, no inference can be drawn about how they would think if they were thinking well.

But the two cases are not analogous, or at least they are not sufficiently so to make the comparison helpful. The ways in which we think when we are behaving casually—associatively, elliptically, disconnectedly, polyphonically—are not generally models of good thinking, such as we find in brilliant arguments, powerful explanations, and intense poetry. The scattered ways we do think are hardly the ways in which we can and ought to think.

On the other hand, valuational practice in a given field—whether apple farming or house construction or book printing—is based on traditions that involve consciously employed and perfected criteria. There are standards for well-constructed homes and books and for extra-fancy eating apples. They may not be ultimate standards: they are in constant need of reappraisal. But the study of what is done in the area of valuational practice in any field where there are craft traditions cannot but be helpful in disclosing what ought to be done. To be sure, revolutions in valuation are always possible, but these involve a shaking of the foundations that announces the presence of art.

Unfortunately, there is at present no concentrated, specialized area of research in valuation. It is a most important area of human activity, deserving of careful study by the behavioral sciences, but the facts of human valuation must be pieced together from anthropology, sociology, psychology, political science, government, economics, and a host of more specialized disciplines. Yet, if social studies courses are to acquaint students with the evidential basis of valuation, these data would have to be derived from an area in the behavioral sciences—the study of valuation—which requires its own academic standing and integrity. This recommendation is made not to multiply university disciplines but to provide curriculum developers and teacher educators the kinds of research and analyses necessary for the construction of value inquiry approaches on the elementary and secondary school levels.

It must be stressed that curriculum development works out of established disciplines. Almost without exception, attempts to develop school curricula that are not based on such disciplines have been failures. One can bring economics to early childhood education, or foreign languages, or government, or chemistry, but whatever it is, one takes an existing area of study on the university level, identifies the major components, sequentializes them, and translates them into ordinary language. What one must not do is try to whip up smorgasbords, with a taste of this and a taste of that, with no integrity whatsoever. Until the study of valuation is a well-developed, university-based discipline, it will be difficult to construct a valuational strand in the social science curricula at the elementary and secondary school levels.

The Pedagogy Appropriate to Value Inquiry

Science educators have long noted that it is less important for students to know facts than for them to be adept at discovering and evaluating evidence relevant to the problem at hand, to know where to look for information when they needed it, and to be versatile in exploring ways in which the hypotheses under consideration might be verified or rejected. In short, what is important is not so much "knowing science" as "thinking scientifically." A comparable example would be the case of history. At best, students will acquire only a tiny sliver of historical knowledge, and this fragment, whatever it is, must be taken with great circumspection and with a very fine sense of proportion, neither of which qualities elementary school students necessarily possess. But students can be encouraged to "think historically" and to have a historical sense that they can apply both to their own lives and to the life of their civilization. They may or may not discover a "cunning of history," but they can attempt to re-enact Jefferson's relationship with Adams or Mark Anthony's with Caesar so as to get a sense of how historical figures might have reasoned, and this thinking about thinking will further contribute to their beginning to think historically. Likewise, students who begin to reason about values will eventually come to think valuationally. They will think "in the language of values," as one who learns a different language at first has to translate from the new language to the old but eventually begins to think in the new language. Such should be the pedagogical aim of value education.

Seminars in value inquiry, whether in senior high school or in early childhood, should be conducted by the discussion method. There are very good reasons for doing so.

First, didactic methods, such as lecturing, are unlikely to have the desired effect and may even have the opposite effect from that intended. The children most in need of value education are usually the least receptive to it when it is presented in a way they perceive to be proselytizing or indoctrinational. Efforts to compel their value beliefs often succeed merely in making them even more skeptical or negative. In contrast, the discoveries of a discussion group are generated by the group itself and do not appear to have been imposed by an alien authority. If we trust children to reason for themselves, we are likely to find that, in the long run, the values they adopt are more acceptable to us than the ones they adopt when we try to command their assent to our adult authority.

Second, children love to discuss, and as educators we should know that we are far better off using conduct that children are already motivated to engage in than trying to find incentives to get them to do what they are reluctant to do. As a matter of fact, there is no better way of sharpening thinking skills than through disciplined dialogue. How fortunate we are that children should want to do in this instance just what we want them to do!

But here a note of caution is in order. Children do enjoy talking about values. They love to deliver themselves of their opinions and to recount their personal experiences. In most instances, there is nothing wrong with this, provided it is seen as the *starting point* of value inquiry rather than as the terminus of it and provided that the objective is the perfection of skills for reasoning about values rather than the mere unburdening of memories and feelings. So-called brainstorming sessions are alleged to have a therapeutic effect when value questions are at issue; be that as it may, educational goals are best met by educational means and by strengthening the student's character and reasoning skills so as to make therapeutic sessions unnecessary. There are seldom hard data about the impact of such sessions. There are, of course, anecdotes about their liberating effect, but there are anecdotes too about how they left children feeling stripped and vulnerable, while others felt justified in adopting the maxim that everything is relative. It would be difficult to see how students in value inquiry seminars, studying the craft of valuation, would be likely to conclude that the better and the worse were indistinguishable.

Likewise, the use of moral dilemmas in the classroom can be quite problematic. Dilemmas are constructed by arbitrarily ruling out meaningful options and by limiting those that remain to those that contradict either one another or themselves. In laboratory settings, this technique is employed to determine how subjects will behave if their reasoning powers are neutralized and they are left to their instinctual or emotional devices. In a classroom, such a technique, if unaccompanied by the exploration of rational alternatives, can be of little educational value.

Education for values can instead take the form of dialogical inquiry in an atmosphere of intellectual cooperation and mutual respect. The conversation that unfolds in a disciplined fashion in such seminars is then internalized by the children. They become acquainted with the other points of view and the other perspectives in the classroom; they become accustomed to challenging others for reasons and to being challenged for their own; they begin to reflect critically and objectively about their own views; they become more confident as they realize that one may be mediocre in spelling or arithmetic yet very impressive in articulating the perspective one has gained from personal experience. This is so important because so many children who "drop out" in the classroom want desperately to "tell their cause aright," and even more desperately they want to be listened to and respected by their peers. By helping children learn how to reason together, we give them a taste of what community can be. If, then, we fail to reinforce it, they may be stuck for the rest of their lives with this weak, impoverished understanding of the genuine merits and benefits of participatory democracy.

Summary and Conclusions

A value is a matter of importance; in this sense, due process is a value, and so is rule by the will of the majority with due respect for minority rights. To understand and appreciate fully the worth of due process, majority rule, and minority rights, one must be able to compare them with the procedures characteristic of non-democratic forms of government. Such comparisons lead to reflections on value, and such reflections lead to beliefs as to what is of civic worth or importance. Often, when we speak of "values," in the plural, it is these beliefs that we mean.

Justice and goodness are valuable, but so are endangered species. Truth and health and happiness are valuable, but so are *Anthony and Cleopatra* and the *St. Matthew Passion*. When we refer to value education, are we doing anything more than speaking honorifically about the ideals of civilized human beings, as well as about the makings, sayings, and doings that we deem excellent? Is value education nothing more than our commending our values to our children, with accompanying injunctions and exhortations, or do we want the younger generation to be more reasonable with regard to values than we have been? Choice of the latter alternative suggests faith in educational progress and in the possibility that certain social policies can be adopted and implemented so as to ensure that each generation will be wiser than its predecessor.

Let value education then be the teaching of elementary and secondary school students to reason about values. This means, in part, teaching them to think more skillfully and showing them how such skillfulness can be applied to value issues.

But reasoning can supply only part of the answer, just as the schools can supply only part of the answer. Of formidable importance is the establishment of conditions hospitable to the development of character. Certainly the most potent institution in this regard is the family, but the family is hardly the only institution influencing character formation. The ensemble of habits that makes up a person's character is shaped by the forms of participation in which that person engages. Briefly put, we internalize the character of the institutions to which we belong, and to the extent to which those institutions are themselves rationally organized, we will be in the habit of acting in ways that are rationally justifiable, even when we act unreflectively. The athlete does not have to deliberate whether or not to obey the rules of the game: acceptance of the rules is second nature to the athlete.

Similarly, if we want children to be responsible when they are adults, we should give them proportionate responsibilities while they are children. If we want them to respect due process and grant it to others, we should accord them the same due process. By engaging in student government procedures, they learn some of the advantages and difficulties that attend majority rule, while at the same time they become accustomed, in their deliberations, to take the rights and viewpoints of others into account. And if we want adult citizens who are rational with respect to values, we should introduce children to value inquiry so that they can discover for themselves that what is of genuine worth is not the object of any desire, however shallow or immature, but is rather that whose claim to being a value is supported by reflection and inquiry. Indeed, inquiry is that institution whose procedures, when internalized, contribute most heavily toward the development of reasonableness in the individual.

We now have two legs of the tripod: reasoning about value issues and a personal character such as disposes one to act in accordance with rationality. The third leg of the tripod is the craftsmanship that enables the individual to integrate habits and reasonings, character and reflection in such a way as to lead to sound value judgments as well as to commendable actions. To learn this craft, we have to turn to those who practice it. Here we find no shortage of teachers, because virtually everyone is a practitioner, although with varying degrees of excellence, as with any craft. But study carpenters constructing homes, teachers grading students, search committees ranking candidates, executives evaluating employees; study how criteria are used in making value judgments, how means and ends are coordinated, how consequences are weighed, how social costs are deliberated, how priorities are set—and not just in our society but in other societies as well. Gradually what will emerge is the outline of the craft of valuation, and it is this craft that must be imparted to children, along with reasoning skills, cognitive dispositions, and habits of good citizenship.

But all of this is empty if the skills are taught by drill, the habits are learned by rote, and the craft is taught by arid lecturing. The context, the setting in which value inquiry is to take place, is vital. It has been shown that the process should be principally one of discussion, with the object of converting the classroom into a community of value inquiry. In such a context, children become proficient in orchestrating the various reasoning skills with which they have become conversant. If one were to identify anything as a specific value reasoning skill, it would have to be this proficiency in utilizing the other skills so that they converge on and reinforce one another. If seminars in value inquiry could be established in which children would acquire cognitive dispositions and skills as have been described here, it would not be necessary to relinquish the ideal of a social and intellectual community as the sort of context in which we would like our children to grow up, learn, and live.

Nevertheless, two academic areas bear an especially heavy responsibility. One is social studies. The study of valuation is an empirical approach to an important aspect of social behavior. As such, its contents properly belong in the social studies, and curricula in that area need to take cognizance of valuation and provide for it. Of course, if valuation is not taught in an appropriately open and participatory manner, students will not be encouraged to seek to improve on existing practices.

The other area is language arts. Because reasoning skills are so closely intertwined with language, the seminars in value inquiry referred to previously can take place as a continuing aspect of language arts instruction. Children's texts in value inquiry can be assigned as "readers," and resultant discussions will in no way be out of place for the purpose of improving meaning acquisition and language comprehension, to say nothing of improving the continuity between reading, speaking, and writing. But a still better alternative is to add philosophy to the curriculum as a sequence of courses required of all students. Thinking reasonably about values requires concept-formation skills which philosophy is especially well-equipped to provide. It is unlikely that children can be taught to engage in ethical inquiry outside the context of philosophy, for ethics is a part of philosophy and of no other discipline.

One of the most valuable contributions philosophy has to make to the conversation of mankind with regard to civic education is the model philosophers offer of a community of inquiry in which the participants are profoundly aware of how much they can learn from other participants with whom they strongly disagree. So long as we think we have nothing to learn from each other, democracy becomes merely a pluralistic *détente*.

6   Ethical Inquiry and the Craft of Moral Practice

It is a widely shared view that the rate of social change is accelerating, causing each older generation to feel decreasingly secure with the moral education of the younger generation entrusted to it. They feel less secure because of doubts that the information previously considered reliable and therefore passed along with confidence from one generation to the next may no longer be counted on to be as relevant as it was under more stable circumstances; less secure because of the realization that younger-generation members nowadays put so much stock in the views of their peers; and less secure, too, because of the sense that any view put forth by members of the older generation seems to challenge the younger generation to espouse views that are directly the opposite. The result is anxiety within the family concerning the adequacy of the process whereby values are transmitted from parents to children and increasingly a turning to the schools to provide the moral instruction that the family feels it has failed to provide.

The schools, however, have their own reasons for being uneasy. They are willing to accommodate the demands to prepare their young charges for eventual citizenship. But they feel hardly ready at all to provide the personal values for which parents had previously taken responsibility. The situation appears to lack viable options. If classroom teachers espouse any particular ethical principles and urge them on their students, they are vulnerable to accusations of indoctrination. On the other hand, if teachers refuse to espouse such principles or openly question them, they are vulnerable to accusations that they are teaching children to believe that values are merely relative or merely subjective. In brief, the schools have no wish to be accused of indoctrination, whether of any absolute scheme of values or of a relativistic approach to values.

What the schools would like to find is a channel—even though it be no wider than a razor's edge—that will enable them to pass between the Scylla of authoritarianism and the Charybdis of vacuous relativism. They want their young charges to grow up to be reflective and reasonable individuals, capable of thinking for themselves. But the demand for moral education apparently urges upon students a commitment to a set of values that are to be embraced whatever the students may think about them. The schools find it difficult to square their obligations as educators to encourage their students to become autonomous with their obligations to parents and to the society at large and to accept a conventional posture with regard to personal and social values. Unless they can thread their way between the twin dangers of authoritarianism and vacuous relativism, they are clearly in a no-win situation.

These opposed alternatives are hardly unfamiliar: they are simply another perennial version of the traditional opposition of authoritarianism and anarchy. Three hundred years ago, Hobbes and his followers bluntly announced that if people wanted a peaceful, orderly society, the specter of anarchy was far more to be feared than the specter of authoritarianism. And yet, hardly a generation later, hope began to dawn in England that the dread contradictories could be defused: if human beings were permitted to reason together, the democratic way would turn out to be a viable one.

Thus the ability to reason has always been the sticking point. Doubt that adults could reason together constituted the most formidable barrier to political democracy. Currently, doubt that children can reason effectively constitutes the most formidable barrier to moral education.

We pride ourselves on being realists, in the mold of Hobbes and Freud. Not for us the sticky sweet, idyllic portrait of childhood bequeathed us by Rousseau and romanticism. We prefer to believe that underneath their mild exteriors, children nurse powerful, if latent, forces of aggression. If, occasionally, some of them mistreat animals, we single this out as evidence of a cruel streak in children; in the process, we ignore the profound sense of kinship that many children feel for animals, their horror at our hunting and slaughtering and reckless experimentation, and our extermination of countless species that could just as easily have been preserved. When we attempt to justify the violence we beam at them through television by claiming that it appeals to and helps to satisfy their innate aggressive tendencies, it is like the proverbial case of holding someone under water and then accusing the victim of drowning. If children express hostility to violence, we sniff suspiciously, seeing in their remarks a ploy to evade punishment; we do not care to be reminded of the high correlation between violence done to children by adults and the resultant anti-social behavior of those children. We even nod our approval at grotesque caricatures of children, such as in William Golding's *Lord of the Flies,* in which adult perversity is projected upon children with the same wild implausibility as when pre-adolescent actors and actresses mimic adult love scenes on the stage.

In short, we mock children's values because we know that children are both physically weak and inexperienced, and we think these are adequate grounds for disparaging the ability of children to be reasonable—that is, to be sensible and rational and to think for themselves. Also, we have found that when we exhort children to be reasonable, they generally fail to comply, and this provides us with still further grounds for believing that the ability to be reasonable is beyond them. It does not occur to us that exhortation is hardly the way to bring about such reasonableness.

The conflict between Hobbes and Rousseau concerns whether children have an innate tendency either to preserve themselves, at whatever cost to others, or to be just, to seek equity, and to love peace. By and large, both Hobbes and Rousseau concern themselves with what the child is innately, instinctively, impulsively. Reason hardly enters in. Even in Rousseau's disciple, Piaget, children seem naturally inclined to be equitable, or else it is the outcome of their experience with their peers; it is from adults that they learn to suffer—and hence to practice—inequity. But once again their capacity for reasonableness, as far as Piaget can tell, is frail and feeble; it will grow and prosper only as the children mature and begin to approximate the realistic understanding of the world possessed by mature, scientifically oriented adults.

Dewey's approach is radically different. Hobbes and Rousseau are both right; children are born with countless pairs of opposed tendencies: to be generous and to be selfish, to be competitive and to be cooperative, to love and to hate, and so on. All of these together constitute the child's diffuse fund of impulsive energies. It is the social structure of the given society into which the child is born that screens out this alternative and filters in the other, which rewards and encourages this but punishes and discourages that. Consequently, the child learns to pour his or her energies into the pattern of conduct of which society approves. These social patterns vary enormously, but whatever people one visits, one will find the same stubborn insistence that their social arrangements play no causal role in shaping people's motivations but merely accommodate that set of instincts of which human nature is thought to be composed. Dewey saw the problem, then, to be to weaken the capacity of adults to impose their unreasonableness on children and to strengthen the capacity of children to think for themselves and thereby be in a position to defend themselves in a world in which irrationality is rampant.

It was contended above that the most formidable barrier to political democracy has been the belief that people would be unable to reason together. But this is assuredly an oversimplification. What circumstances had begun to emerge and had formed the conditions that made reasoning together possible? One thinks of the devising of constitutions, of parliamentary rules of discussion, of due process, of mechanisms for representative government. In short, one thinks of the methods and procedures that had to be contrived and of the institutions that had to be founded so that the political process could be pried open enough to allow the first infusion of rationality to trickle in. Without such methods, procedures, and institutions, reason is helpless.

Likewise, the reason of the child is helpless in the absence of conditions that nurture reflection and in turn are responsive to it. If the school, the family, the teacher, and the curriculum do not foster thinking and do not welcome it when it occurs, the likelihood that the child will be able to engage in ethical reasoning is fairly remote. Equally important, children learn to reason together with their peers, for the only way to deal effectively with peer pressure is not to engage in futile efforts to eliminate it but to endeavor to make it rational, and this can be done by converting the classroom into a reasoning community.

Now the methods and procedures that one must employ in order to be reasonable can be thought of as tools or instruments, and it would be correct to think of what is being espoused here as coming from an instrumentalist perspective. When it comes to ethical reasoning, philosophy is an indispensable method, the subdiscipline of logic is an indispensable apparatus, and within logic there are countless tools (of which the syllogism is an example) that one learns very early to make use of. After all, ethical reasoning need not be thought of as a mere toying with bloodless abstractions, for what is called moral conduct is the practice of such reasoning. Of course, when Jeremy Bentham remarks, "If in the pursuit of *well-being,* it be the province of ethics to take the direction of human conduct, in that same pursuit it is the province of logic to take the command and give direction to the course of ethics itself,"[1] it should hardly be necessary to add that it is the obligation of philosophy to oversee the course of such logic.

We need to examine in more detail these instrumental conditions of ethical reasoning. Nevertheless, before we do so, we had better glance at some of the presuppositions of such an inquiry. At the very least, we should devote some attention to the question of the logical and ontological status of moral conduct, once we presume to consider such conduct to be the practice or practical aspect of ethical reasoning. The logical issue that concerns us is the similarity or dissimilarity that obtains among moral acts. The ontological issue concerns the classification of moral acts—in particular, whether they are to be seen purely as doings or as doings that have so much in common with makings as to represent a fuzzy borderline area where the two categories overlap.

Let us begin by considering the position adumbrated by Stuart Hampshire. To Hampshire, ethics and aesthetics have to do with markedly different domains and entail radically different procedures. A work of art is not an answer to a problem: it is gratuitous—a free, original, and unique creation. There is no need to seek its reasons or to try to establish its justification. Nor can a work of art be repeatable or generalizable. In contrast, moral acts must be justifiable: their reasons and purposes beg to be inquired into, and in the course of that inquiry we may discover the general principles from which such acts have been derived. Moral acts, after all, are the products of consistent policies. To summarize Hampshire's position, we can have recourse to his own formulation: "Virtue and good conduct are essentially repeatable and imitable, in a sense in which a work of art is not. To copy a right action is to act rightly; but a copy of a work of art is not necessarily or generally a work of art."[2]

Hampshire is thus crystal-clear about right actions: insofar as they represent conduct that conforms to a given rule, they replicate one another and are identical. Works of art, on the other hand, are so dissimilar as to be virtually unique.[3] Hampshire's distinction between ethical *doing* and aesthetic *making* could hardly be more categorical and decisive: between doing and making there is an ontological gap that is unbridgeable.

Whether Hampshire's argument is tenable is certainly questionable. Instead of assuming that makings and doings are radically different, one can readily assume that all human products—including what we say as well as what we make and do—have the same ontological status as human judgments,[4] and that the model we select for their explanation should exhibit a range of shadings or degrees rather than a trinity of airtight compartments. At one end of the spectrum might be the extreme of total uniqueness and at the other might be the extreme of total uniformity. Doings, makings, or various combinations thereof might be found at any place along the spectrum. Once we put the matter in this light, we can promptly recognize that making stretches from one end of the continuum to the other and that doing can be seen as the analogue of making. The making continuum extends from the extreme of mass manufacture to the extreme of works of fine art, with products of craftsmanship just about in the middle. The degree of individualization among objects coming off the assembly line is nil, but individualization increases gradually and steadily as we move in the direction of fine art.

If we were to look at moral conduct along the same continuum, Hampshire's "right actions" would correspond to the products of the industrial assembly line: wholly undifferentiated, because wholly unresponsive to differences in context and betraying not the least sign of moral reasoning. And we do have an analogue of such distribution in terms of human conduct, with military behavior corresponding to industrial production. It is hardly an acceptable model for right action, and the other extreme, of highly individualized works of art, is also problematic.[5] But what about the center of the continuum? What is there in conduct that compares with craftsmanship in production? And if right actions do indeed correspond to the products of craft rather than of mass manufacture or art, what implications does this fact have for moral education?

Consider the characteristics of craft as specified by Collingwood:

1. a strict separation of means and ends, in which "means" are not things but the actions by which things are utilized;
2. a distinct difference between planning and execution, in which the result to be obtained is thought out before being arrived at;
3. in planning, the end determines the choice of means, while in execution the availability of means determines the outcome or end; and
4. a raw material is transformed by craft into a finished product. The raw material precedes the work of craftsmanship and is not discovered or invented along the way, as is the case in art.[6]

Several other characteristics provided by Collingwood are not mentioned here, but it is noteworthy that he gives little or no attention to such conventionally cited features of craft as skill, tradition, and utility. It is customary, that is, to think of the actions by which craftspersons utilize their means or materials as skilled actions and to think of these skills as fairly isolable. It is usually assumed, too, that craftsmanlike making follows and respects a tradition of such making, even when it may deviate innovatively from such a tradition. Furthermore, it is generally taken for granted that the useful arts (versus those considered fine) involve the very scope and substance of craftsmanship. On the other hand, Collingwood acknowledges the rational aspect of craft (in its manner of coordinating means and ends) and does not seem to discount its practical aspect, so that on the whole it would not be amiss to portray his conception of craft as an instance of rational practice. If we were tentatively to accept this way of looking at the matter, it would not be at all difficult for us to accept reasoned moral practice as a species of craft.

Now, among the necessary (but not sufficient) conditions for something's being a craft is its ability to be taught by someone to someone else. Insofar as acting or violin playing or pottery throwing or furniture making or ballet dancing or oil painting can be taught by one person to another, what is taught is the craft element. One might be tempted to infer from this that the art component of these activities must not be teachable, but that is not exactly the case. The art aspect one learns for oneself as a result of one's teaching oneself. The acting coaches or painting teachers cannot teach the art to one directly, but they may be able to teach one how to teach oneself. Insofar as the reasoning element in moral practice involves the kind of thinking that one person can teach another to do—or to do better—it is a matter of craft. But insofar as the reasoning element in moral practice involves thinking for oneself, it is not something that one person can directly teach another person. It is something I will have to teach myself to do, but perhaps you can help me by teaching me how to teach myself to think for myself.[7]

If I choose to become an ice skater, a farmer, or a computer operator, I assume that my teacher or coach will be knowledgeable about the techniques, procedures, methods, and other forms of know-how that constitute the traditional experience and the received wisdom in those areas and will pass them along to me or somehow get me to embody them in practice. It will hardly do to merely be handed a table of do's and don'ts and told to enact them, nor will it do to cultivate just that respect in which my approach to ice skating, farming, or computer operation is artistically unique. Not that rote learning is necessarily excluded: the penmanship teacher may still insist that I practice my *g*'s and *k*'s by doing a page apiece. Whether or not such dreary, mechanical labor constitutes a step forward in the learning of a craft cannot be established in isolation but depends on the manner of its integration into the learning process. In any event, brute replicability, so readily acceptable in mass manufacture, may be only barely tolerable to the craftsperson, who would like his or her pupils and apprentices to demonstrate something more than knee-jerk compliance with tradition, with its deadly uniformity of outcome.

To introduce children to the tools and procedures of ethical inquiry is in effect to prepare them to engage in reasoned moral practice. What are these tools and procedures? Constructing an inventory of them presents no great difficulty. The problem is that such an inventory no more represents the craft of moral practice than a farmer's toolshed, with all the tools hanging neatly from nails and pegs, represents the craft of farming. It is, all the same, a way of beginning, a way into the problem, and perhaps the tools can be set forth in a way that does not pretend to be exhaustive.

To begin with, there are various repertoires of skills, like night watchmen's sets of keys, each appropriate for unlocking a single door. Of course, the sets of skills that must be uppermost in our minds at this time are "thinking skills," but this term is far too vague and covers an area that is far too vast. Anything done skillfully can be said to have involved thinking, whether it be a winning pole vault or a raccoon's deft way of getting into a tightly shut garbage can. For our present purposes, we need to focus on those aspects of thinking that are capable of being formulated, capable of being distinguished by appropriate criteria into "better" and "worse," and capable of being taught. Let us therefore focus on reasoning, inquiry, and concept-formation skills.

Reasoning skills. Reasoning skills are proficiencies in such areas as classifying, defining, formulating questions, giving examples and counterexamples, identifying similarities and differences, constructing and criticizing analogies, comparing, contrasting, and drawing valid inferences. Although inductive, informal, and deductive proficiencies are important members of the reasoning skills family, it must be acknowledged that deduction is a fairly mechanical process and qualifies as reasoning only when the drawing of a conclusion is not taken as the termination of inquiry, but as a justification for sending the thinker back to re-examine the premises.[8]

Inquiry skills. Inquiry skills are proficiencies in such areas as description, explanation, problem formulation, hypothesis formation, and measurement. It would also be justifiable to include individual reasoning skills (e.g., classification and definition) whenever they are employed in advanced disciplines, as well as complex combinations of reasoning skills. Taken together, these varieties are sometimes referred to as higher-level thinking skills. It would not be inaccurate to conceive of reading, writing, and translation as special cases of inquiry skills, while recognizing at the same time their enormous importance to the inquiry process as a whole.

Concept-formation skills. The formation of concepts involves skill in mobilizing reasoning processes so that they converge on and identify particular conceptual issues. Furthermore, concepts must be analyzed and their implications explored. When William James compared the movement of thought to a series of "flights and perchings," he was referring to our reasonings and our concepts, for reasonings represent transitions and concepts represent consolidations. (Perhaps it should be added that reasonings are transitions that preserve truth, irrespective of meaning, whereas translations are transitions that preserve meaning, irrespective of truth. Both types of transition are indispensable to ethical inquiry.)

It would be improper to conclude that reasoning, inquiry, and concept-formation skills together constitute the logical equipment needed for engaging in ethical inquiry. To do so would omit an enormous range of mental states and acts that provide the cognitive conditions for the emergence of thinking skills. Indeed, many mental acts can be considered incipient skills, or infra-skills. Some varieties to be taken into account follow.

Mental acts/states. It is not easy to distinguish relatively simple mental acts from those complex combinations of act and state that we can call mental acts/states. Fairly clear-cut examples of mental acts are choosing and deciding. Doubting, believing, hoping, respecting, wondering, and understanding might be classified as acts/states. (Kant, it will be recalled, thought of respect as a "feeling self-wrought by a rational concept," which we may translate into our own usage as a mental state with a cognitive element or germ.) The significance of such acts/states for moral practice should be evident.

Mental acts. Mental acts include such mental performances as supposing, surmising, conceding, remembering, choosing, deciding, comparing, and associating. Although it is not clear to what extent mental acts represent skilled performances, they would seem to represent at least infra-skills or proto-skills, since it is possible that their development can to some extent be fostered and strengthened by education. (For example, some children appear reluctant to assume or to suppose that which is contrary to fact. Perhaps they have been encouraged to believe that the real world is so dangerous a place that they cannot afford the luxury of fantasy or imagination. Yet inhibitions such as these can be overcome if the classroom is functioning as a community of inquiry, where as a matter of course children talk to each other in a reasonable way about things that matter to them.) The need is for a rich profusion of mental acts, each of which can be performed competently. One of the best ways of strengthening children's abilities to perform mental acts is to engage them in the reading of literature, for authors regularly have their characters perform such acts, and to understand what is going on, the reader must imaginatively emulate such acts and even re-enact them at times. (To read that a character in a story inferred *q* from *p* is to be encouraged to infer *q* from *p* ourselves.) The resultant gain in ability to perform mental acts translates itself immediately into a gain in ability to write.

Metacognitive acts. We know that inquiry is recursive, constantly monitoring itself for the purpose of self-correction. We tend to forget that the same is true, although less systematically, with regard to thinking. One thinks often of one's own thinking, reflects on one's own reflections, and makes inferences about one's own inferences. But whenever one mental act is the subject of another, the latter act is metacognitive. Thus we make inferences about other people's inferences as well as our own. Almost any mental act by any person can be the subject of almost any mental act by another person or by oneself. This crisscrossing of metacognition is an important aspect of the fabric of classroom dialogue, just as dialogue is essential to ethical inquiry.

In discussing reasoning skills, inquiry skills, concept-formation skills, and the skill aspect of mental acts, we have not distinguished between these skills insofar as they might be generic to all disciplines and to all inquiry and insofar as they might be specific to ethical inquiry alone. Thus the skills involved in doing formal and informal logic would be applicable in any discipline in which these logics are applicable; it is in this sense that they are generic. On the other hand, certain procedures or tools may be more characteristic of some disciplines or lines of work than are others. (An example would be drilling with metal drills, which is usually associated with oil exploration and dentistry rather than with police science or psychiatry.) Thus a procedure such as universalization, in which one asks, "What if everyone were to act in this fashion?" seems rather specifically ethical in character. Likewise with concepts: some, like right, obligation, and privilege, seem particularly ethical; others, like problem, presupposition, and criterion, appear to be generic to any aspect of inquiry. Still, the difference is loose and flexible and is of value perhaps only to curriculum developers, reminding them that they must give ample attention to both the generic and the specific when preparing the curriculum for any discipline.

Thus in developing curricula in ethical inquiry for children, one must acquaint such students with tools and procedures not usually thought specific to ethics. For example, children need to be introduced to and familiarized with part-whole and whole-part relationships and to be given practice in distinguishing between differences of degree and differences of kind because, as they become more versatile in working with such distinctions, they become more sensitive to the problematic nuances of strictly ethical relationships. Once equipped with the instruments of inquiry, children are very adept at seeing their application to particular moral situations.

This, then, is the narrow pass between Scylla and Charybdis, between authoritarian indoctrination and mindless relativism: to stimulate children to think, to improve their cognitive skills so that they reason well, to engage them in disciplined dialogues with one another so that they reason together, to challenge them to think about significant concepts from the philosophical tradition, and yet to develop their ability to think for themselves so that they may think reasonably and responsibly when actually confronted with moral problems. Trained to think critically, they will no longer be defenseless when efforts are made to indoctrinate them. And yet, trained to listen carefully to others and to take into account other people's points of view and perspectives, they will no longer be an easy prey to mindless, cynical alternatives because they will have come to appreciate the advantages of objectivity.

The foregoing account has been limited to consideration of the instruments with which children must be equipped if they are to be prepared properly for moral praxis. Nothing, unfortunately, has been said about the need to induce in students the realization that such instruments must be loved and cared for, in the same way that all craftspersons love and care for the tools they use and the procedures they employ. The process of dialogue, indispensable to the strengthening of reasoning skills, has also gone virtually unmentioned, as has the process of curriculum development by means of which the philosophical tradition is re-examined for those ideas in which children might have interest. Then these ideas, framed in the simplest possible language, are strewn lavishly across the pages of children's novels so that children may pick them up, as they might pick up a strange stone or a lost toy, talk about them with one another, and turn them over and over in their minds. But these are matters that beg for actual demonstration rather than arid argument. They are among those things that Plato taught us are best made known by being shown.

Omitted, too, in the foregoing account is adequate consideration of the ethical subject matter of children's classroom discussions. A word is in order, therefore, in favor of focusing such discussions on issues that the children themselves are perplexed by rather than those that adults think the children ought to be perplexed by. So often young children are precipitated into discussions of adult problems of war, unemployment, nuclear waste disposal, and the like, when for them the pertinent issues are such matters as friendship, family, and shame. By focusing on these more relevant, personal issues, to which the child brings a real rather than a feigned interest, we can systematically promote the process of moral reasoning, along with the development of a reasonable character in the child. Such a character, prepared in childhood, can later be deployed in confronting the still more profound and intractable problems of adult life and of society. This is not to say that small children should be discouraged if they evince interest in political, social, or economic matters, for whatever is of interest will sustain subsequent reflection. But it is a plea not to embroil children in issues in which they have yet to develop interest, in an effort to evoke from them what we consider an appropriately emotional and moral response. We should try to keep in mind that the adult's lack of interest in philosophy may seem just as outlandish to a small child as the child's lack of interest in adult matters seems to us.

IV

The Impact on the Curriculum

7 Philosophy and Science Education at the Elementary School Level

Philosophy and Science Education

The sciences are incomparable in their expertise in introducing students to an understanding of nature through observation and experimentation. Unfortunately, the pedagogy that science educators have employed to motivate students to observe and experiment has left much to be desired.

Many science educators have taken it as axiomatic that young children are abysmally ignorant about nature but at the same time, fortunately, are incredibly curious and inquisitive. It would seem to follow naturally, such educators have reasoned, that children would be overwhelmingly grateful to be shown the truths about nature that science teachers are so eager to offer them. Unhappily, matters are not quite so simple. For one thing, the inquisitiveness with which most children begin kindergarten must be steadily and persistently reinforced if it is to be retained, and the facts seem to be that by the fourth grade or so, the curiosity about nature that many children had exhibited earlier is now much diminished. On the other hand, by this age children have built up an extensive network of hypotheses and theories by means of which they explain to themselves how the world works. Scientists may look upon these as primitive myths and take it for granted that the children will leap at the opportunity to exchange their myths for the truths offered them by science. As it has turned out, this is simply not the case. Not even experienced scientists readily agree to exchange a new and superficially more plausible theory for a not-altogether-satisfactory one with which they are currently operating, and it is usually a long period of negotiation before advocates of the old and advocates of the new are reconciled. It is not much different with children. If we want them to give up their views about nature, we have to be prepared to discuss frankly with them the reasons why they should do so, and we have to discuss with equal candor their reasons for thinking that we should adopt their views. Without such open discussions, we will not only fail to get them to see the world as we see it, which is a matter of no great moment, for the more important thing is that we will fail to get them to think scientifically and to participate wholeheartedly in inquiry. But these discussions must be logically disciplined and reasonable. We not only have to talk with children about the differences between our conceptions and theirs but also have to reason with them. Because science education has not traditionally provided such a reasoning component, it must be offered as a supplement derived from another discipline. Since philosophy has traditionally provided the aegis for the study of reasoned discussion, it is not surprising that philosophy should be that discipline.

Another point is worthy of mention in this regard: there is general agreement that science education should not be merely a matter of providing answers. The important thing, we say, is that the children themselves should pose the questions. This is all very well, but it remains inadequate. Children may be inquisitive enough to raise questions but may still resist our furnishing them with ready-made answers. They want to be allowed to think these matters through for themselves and come to the answers themselves. It is not that they reject our answers as such: it is that they reject the method we propose for their getting at those answers. They don't want us to think for them; they want to think for themselves. Not that they are wedded to their own explanations, but that they want to participate in the inquiry and share in the experience of discovering how things work. We all are familiar with children's eagerness to "help": "Let *me!*" they insist. And that is all they ask. We needn't fear that they're trying to "take over." They just want to belong, with us, in a community of inquiry. Thus the mere fact that children are inquisitive does not ensure that they will be receptive to the information that is the hard-won product of our efforts, but not theirs.

In recent years, the notion has become familiar in educational circles that for students merely to learn the outcomes of classical scientific inquiries does not ensure that their scientific education has been successful. Success would occur only if students had been taught to think scientifically. But what does this mean, to *think scientifically*? In its most essential aspect, it means to ask oneself the kinds of questions scientists ask themselves, to be alert to the problematic aspects of one's experience the way scientists are, to reflect self-critically about one's own procedures the way scientists do, and to find it of value not just to one's thinking but to one's life that if a distinction needs to be drawn, it becomes urgent that one draw it, and if a connection needs to be made, it becomes urgent that one make it. On the other hand, one is not thinking scientifically when one encounters a discrepant case and is not perplexed by it, or when one fails to realize how one's own reflections as a scientist are in fact internalizations of the conversations one has had and might have with one's colleagues in the scientific community. It is considerations such as these that must guide us in constructing a curriculum subtitled "Reasoning about Nature." Just as the most successful hunters are those who can surmise the ways of their quarry and, when the quarry hides, have a hunch where it hides, so the most successful scientists are those who can outfox, outguess nature, and have a hunch where it hides when it does so. They learn to think how nature works: where a cancer might strike next, the way a shell is made clockwise or counterclockwise, the way a moon is formed. Likewise, the student must think how the scientist works and must think how the scientist thinks. If science education as it is currently constituted cannot succeed in getting children to think in these ways, then the task of doing so must be assumed by other portions of the curriculum. Yet, if this is what is to be done, it must be done in such a way that the reasoning skills children acquire transfer readily to other disciplines and make for that "thinking across the curriculum" that is so widely praised and so seldom accomplished.

Science Education and Thinking Skills

For some time, science educators have been heard to insist that students needed no special cognitive skills training in order to carry out scientific experiments, since these skills could be expected to develop naturally and would be in place when needed. This complacent faith in the convergence of the curriculum with the stages of child development has not often proved warranted. Children's cognitive skills need to be cultivated and in place *before* they are called upon. What is more, they cannot be cultivated in isolation from the disciplines to which they must subsequently be applied. In the process of learning the skills, students must also be familiarized with the procedures by means of which the skills are to be transferred and "plugged into" the various parts of the curriculum. The example of students being taught formal logic on the one hand and natural science on the other, with the naive expectation that they would then be able to think logically and scientifically, is no less absurd than the graduate student who, assigned a paper on Chinese poetry, attempts to prepare to write it by consulting the encyclopedia articles on poetry and China.

Of course, it is not by chance that philosophy is selected as the discipline with which structured inquiry is to begin (even though a case could be made for this having been so historically in our culture). The reason has to do with the accessibility and attractiveness of philosophical topics and methods to children. Philosophical concepts tend to be inherently fuzzy, and decision procedures for defining and clarifying them once and for all are notoriously lacking. Such concepts lend themselves readily to dialogue, with students quickly finding themselves engaged in a tug of war over various interpretations of the concepts under scrutiny. This capacity of philosophical concepts to generate competing lines of argument and a sense of cooperative cognitive inquiry is what makes them appear so meaningful and dynamic to children.

On the other hand, scientific concepts, although generally definable by means of specific criteria and classificatory procedures, tend to appear to the early elementary student as inert rather than dynamic. They do not lend themselves so readily to conflicting interpretations (except in those cases in which a student is skilled enough or sophisticated enough to ask the right questions). That blood is red or that water is colorless are givens that are unlikely to provoke questioning or reflection. But suppose that more information is supplied about actual conditions of observation: the blood is said to be red "to the normal eye," or the water is said to be colorless "in small quantities." Suppose, too, that the students in this instance have already explored in their philosophy classes the "fallacies" of division and composition: they are aware that what is true of the part need not be true of the whole, and vice versa. Such students may well be impelled to reflect and to question whether blood is still red when viewed under a microscope and whether water is still colorless in large amounts. In other words, children with philosophical training in thinking skills will not be prepared to assent unthinkingly to commonplace statements of fact: they will want to know under what circumstances these statements are indeed true and under what circumstances they are not.

Consider another example. The teacher says, "We know that water is colorless. Given this knowledge, can we infer that water is also tasteless and odorless?" No doubt some students will respond, based on their own sense-experience, that their water is not tasteless. But others, equally astute as a result of their philosophical preparation, will likely respond that the taste and odor cannot be inferred logically from the color. Someone may even offer a counterexample, such as, "My mother's perfume is colorless, but it's not odorless!" Still others may say, "It's not the water that has the bad taste: it's the impurities in the water!" Trained philosophically to make careful distinctions, they are beginning to think scientifically.

Thinking Skills and Philosophy

A few people may still think that interest in thinking skills is of recent vintage and be incredulous when told that philosophy has had some experience in this area. Philosophy, of course, is not nearly as well known in the modern world as science is. In general, we may say that the very early stage of an inquiry into a newly discovered subject matter is philosophical. It is a stage in which perplexities abound, as do speculations about how to resolve them. But as the inquiry proceeds into more precise observation, experimentation, and measurement, the philosophical phase yields to the scientific. Not that philosophy disappears, even so, for it lingers on in the form of critique. Every discipline has its "philosophy of"—there is the philosophy of literature, the philosophy of education, the philosophy of art, and the philosophy of science. The "philosophies of" represent critical thinking about these disciplines, utilizing the repertoire of conceptual and analytical skills that form a portion of the philosophical tradition.

Philosophy attempts to clarify and illuminate unsettled, controversial issues that are so generic that no scientific discipline is equipped to deal with them. Examples would be such concepts as truth, justice, beauty, personhood, and goodness. At the same time, in its even-handed way, philosophy attempts to unsettle our minds with respect to those matters we tend to take for granted, insisting that we pay attention to aspects that we have until now found it convenient to overlook. Whatever the topic, however, the aim of philosophy is to cultivate excellence in thinking, and philosophers do this by examining what it is to think historically, musically, mathematically—in a word, to think excellently in the disciplines.

There is, however, something else of significance that philosophy brings to the quest for excellence in thinking, and that is its subdiscipline of logic. Logic is a normative rather than a descriptive discipline. That is, it makes no effort to describe how people in fact do think but offers instead criteria by means of which we can distinguish good thinking from bad thinking. Although logicians may differ among themselves on one issue or another, it is generally recognized that logical considerations are of major importance in determining what it means to be reasonable. Since reasonableness is a prime objective of reflective education, logic has much to contribute to the cultivation of thinking. An outstanding instance is the fact that those seeking a taxonomy of thinking skills can readily begin with the reasoning skills needed to perform the cognitive operations of which logic consists. (Bloom's *Taxonomy of Educational Objectives* virtually ignores these reasoning skills. In the light of this, one must wonder how it achieved the canonical position it has held for the past quarter-century.) Another way of putting this is to say that cognitive psychology provides descriptions of how thinking does in fact take place; logic provides normative canons that tell us how thinking ought to take place; a philosophy curriculum attempts to take both sorts of considerations into account and to show how they are interrelated.

It would be misleading to think of philosophy as all theory and no practice. On the contrary, it is very often something done, with the theory dissolved in rather than separate from the practice. Professional philosophers may do philosophy better than others, as professional athletes play sports better than others, but the difference would seem to be one of degree rather than of kind. If philosophy is what we do when our conversations take the form of inquiry disciplined by logical and metacognitive considerations, we have no right to withhold the term "philosophy" from those children's conversations that have taken on this very same form.

Before considering in more detail the contribution that philosophy can make to the strengthening of thinking skills, we should take into account the ways in which the separate fields of philosophy can contribute to the strengthening of education. The major fields to be mentioned here are epistemology, logic, metaphysics, ethics, and aesthetics. Much of the weakness of modern education can be traced to the elimination from the curriculum of the concerns normally treated by these subdisciplines.

We can begin with epistemology. As is well known, early childhood education has been criticized for dwelling on the need for memorization and recall of mere information rather than getting children to think about that which they are also expected to know. For example, the students may be expected to know that Halley's comet is composed of frozen gases. Now, the thought that may occur to some students is, "How do we know that?" In other words, they want to know by what means this information was obtained and why we think it true. But they may not dare to ask such questions, if their experience has been that such questions are dismissed as irrelevant. Still, the critical-thinking children in the classroom will remain curious about the epistemological grounds for taking the statement as true. That is, when confronted by a series of statements such as:

It is alleged that the comet is composed of frozen gases.
It is thought that the comet is composed of frozen gases.

It is believed that the comet is composed of frozen gases.
It is contended that the comet is composed of frozen gases.
It is known that the comet is composed of frozen gases.
(And so on.)

students are as interested in the first part of each sentence as they are in the second. How can one think critically about what one is told, after all, unless one can inquire into the grounds for such assertions and the criteria employed in deciding what counts for true? And unless students are made aware of mental acts, how can they assess the epistemological value of "it is known . . ." as contrasted with "it is believed . . ."? (Some students may actually think there is no difference in the truth claims of these phrases!)

To be introduced to the grounds and conditions of knowledge and not merely to the knowledge itself is what any epistemologically astute child might request. One could broaden this further by saying that meanings are contextual, and when one suppresses awareness of the context, one suppresses, in effect, awareness of the meaning. (Think of the difference in meaning of the statement, "All men are animals" when voiced by a biology professor and when voiced by a girl coming home from a date!)

Epistemology concerns itself with the grounds we may or may not have for calling something true, and whenever children want to know the reason for calling something true, they are asking an epistemological question. It is at this point that logic takes over. Given that certain statements are known (or assumed) to be true, what reasoning can we legitimately engage in so as to extend that knowledge? As has already been noted, it is logic that provides the criteria for assessing the reasoning by means of which we try to extend the truth and preserve it at the same time. "Does it follow that . . .?" is a prototypical logical question. So is, "How can you assert this and its contradiction?" And so is, "Aren't you assuming that . . .?"

It must be pointed out that the philosophical concerns are not only voiced by the children in the classroom: the teacher may find them equally unavoidable. If, for example, children insist that they see the sun move every day across the sky, the teacher may feel it necessary to wonder if "it only looks that way," and upon being pressed, the teacher may have to amplify his or her explanation of the distinction between "appearance and reality." But this is a metaphysical distinction. It is a distinction that is far too general to fall within the scope of any of the particular sciences, and yet it may very well be presupposed by all the sciences. (The same is the case with such distinctions as art versus nature, life versus art, truth versus beauty, permanence versus change, unity versus multiplicity.) Teachers and children alike must wonder how they can be expected to think and to speak without reference to the presuppositions that underlie the information that is being presented to the class.

Ethics and *aesthetics* introduce children to the reasons people have for calling things "right" and "fair" and "good" and "beautiful." It is difficult to see how the study of such reasons and reasonings should have been eliminated from the classrooms, while continuing to present children the reasons people drill for oil or go to the office each day or get married. The ways in which people make value decisions, and the decisions they make, are among the hardest facts there are. An elementary school social studies program that ignores the social fact that we prefer, we rank, we grade, and we use criteria when we do so must be accounted irresponsible.

Aristotle seems to have thought that one could postpone the application of practical reasoning to ethical matters until one had perfected the process of reasoning itself—along about middle age. But this is absurd. One must learn how to reason and how to apply it simultaneously: if we begin by postponing its application, we will probably never get around to applying it. It is important to introduce children to the fact that human lives take different shapes, and that the shapes they take are often given them by the ideals people hold and the dispositions they have acquired. If children recognize that the question, "How ought life to be lived?" is one that addresses them as much as anyone else, they can begin to work on it and, as a result, may turn into adults who take it seriously, for the question concerns not simply how each and every one of us ought to live, but how all of us together ought to live. This is why *Kio and Gus* differs most radically from the ordinary children's text: it presents people discussing the true, the good, and the beautiful, expounding their views as to what is precious and excellent and perfect, and attempting to find reasons with which to justify their opinions. The program attempts, in this way, to provide a model of what it is to introduce information to children in an atmosphere of reflective appraisal and judgment rather than in an atmosphere of passive and uncritical acceptance, or of unquestioning disbelief.

We can now turn to the question of the specific dispositions, mental states, mental acts, verbal acts, reasoning skills, and inquiry skills that are fostered and strengthened by elementary school philosophy. Although all of these need to be cultivated to improve the major skills of reading, writing, speaking, and listening, they do not necessarily derive from the same sources or have comparable functions. They differ, moreover, in the extent to which we can choose to engage in them: we may decide to reason or inquire and then set about doing so, but we don't seem to decide to have a certain disposition or affective state and then proceed to have it. They also seem to differ with respect to their cognitive complexity: affective states may contain only a cognitive germ, but mental acts, verbal acts, reasoning skills, and inquiry skills seem to be on an ascending scale of cognitive complexity.

1. The dispositions that the *Kio and Gus* program helps to cultivate include those that dispose children to engage in mental acts, verbal acts, reasoning, and inquiry. In particular, one might mention the dispositions to be inquisitive, to wonder, to inquire, to speculate, to be critical, to hypothesize, and to infer. (It should be understood that a disposition is a readiness or preparedness and is not limited to human beings: glass, for example, is disposed to shatter when struck.) The best way to get children to acquire these dispositions is to have them participate in communities of inquiry. Such communities encourage the practices that, in turn, prepare people to develop such dispositions.

2. "Mental acts" is often employed in a catch-all fashion to cover a broad continuum that ranges from affective states through combinations of affective states and cognitive acts and then on to cognitive acts proper. Examples of affective states are despair, dread, and infatuation. The combination of affective state and cognitive act can be exemplified by doubting, wondering, fearing, hoping, admiring, respecting, and believing. More specifically, cognitive acts would show, as instances, supposing, wishing, surmising, conceding, remembering, choosing, judging, deciding, and comparing. (Obviously each of these lists could be extremely lengthy.)

3. Verbal acts are utterances, always with a mental dimension. That is, many mental acts go unverbalized, but no verbal act lacks a mental component. Examples would be asserting, saying, alleging, contending, telling, proposing, hinting, and stating. Since dialogue generally omits explicit mention of verbal and mental acts, we tend to learn about them by reading about them taking place. One of the many great advantages of a literature component in a thinking skills program is the contribution it makes to our awareness of the countless nuances to be found in thinking and speaking. Another is that it gives us models of thinking and speaking people. The ability of children to become such people depends considerably on the availability of models—even fictional models—with which to identify.

4. Examples of reasoning skills would include proficiencies in performing various deductive and inductive operations (such as inferring and detecting underlying premises or presuppositions), as
well as formulating questions, providing reasons, constructing definitions, classifying, seriating, exemplifying, and forming concepts.
(The latter is so prevalent and important as almost to stand alone as
a megaskill.) By and large, the source of precise information about
these skills is the domain of (formal and informal) logic. It should
also be mentioned that skill in translating (which is of great importance for the development of reading comprehension, because it
involves the preservation of meaning from one language or idiom
to another) deserves also to be listed among the more important of
the reasoning skills.
5. Inquiry skills are those associated with the carrying out of scientific
procedures, such as measuring, observing, describing, estimating,
explaining, predicting, and verifying.

Philosophy and the Elementary School Classroom

The initial stage of a philosophically conducted science session engages
children in that combination of reading, speaking, and listening that sets a
stage for the dialogue to follow and at the same time presents the children
with a model of reflective discussion.

The children are then canvassed to determine what they found of interest in the passage they read. This enables the students to nominate
items for discussion: in effect, it allows them to establish the agenda (although it does not prevent the teacher from introducing other topics that
in the teacher's opinion are deserving of discussion). As the dialogue continues, the teacher will introduce at appropriate junctures those exercises
or discussion plans provided by the instructional manual for developing
the points at issue or for strengthening the reasoning skills needed for
extricating the meanings from the passage being discussed.

Where the teacher is looked upon as a font of information and the point
at issue in the classroom is a matter of factual knowledge, the practice of
turning always to the teacher for reassurance or verification is established.
This creates a pattern of teacher-student interchanges that defeats the
purpose of philosophy for children, because it undermines the notion of
community and legitimates instead the notion of teacher as informational
authority and students as ignorant learners. In a community of inquiry,
on the other hand, teachers and students find themselves together as

co-inquirers, and the teacher tries to facilitate this by encouraging student-student as well as teacher-student interchanges.

It should be understood that the teacher, in relinquishing the role of informational authority, does not relinquish the role of instructional authority. That is, the teacher must always take ultimate responsibility for establishing those arrangements that will guide and nudge the class into more and more productive, more and more self-corrective discursive inquiry. The teacher must be always on the alert for illogical conduct among the students, just as a person chairing a meeting must be alert to any possible transgression of the rules of parliamentary procedure. But even here the teacher need not rule with a heavy hand. He or she may ask the other students whether, for example, a remark was, in their opinion, relevant; whether an inference made did, in fact, follow logically from the premises that had been established; whether the most useful method of construing certain terms was being utilized; or whether they agreed with the assumptions that apparently underlay the speaker's assertions.

When the classroom discussion turns on particular terms or concepts, the teacher has an opportunity to introduce an appropriate exercise or discussion plan. In general the discussion plans are used to explore and clarify concepts, while the exercises are employed to strengthen skills. There is, however, considerable overlap in these cases, since the cognitive skills one fosters by means of exercises are also helpful with concept for-mation, and the conceptual clarification obtained by following discussion plans can be also invaluable for providing a framework of understanding in terms of which the building of cognitive skills can make some sense to children and teachers alike.

These are the logical and pedagogical considerations that govern the conducting of a philosophical discussion. But there are philosophical considerations, too, and the children will often nose these out even before the teacher is aware of them. This is because children are quick to detect what is problematic, and if they are innocent enough, they will make no secret of their perplexity. Since they often simply do not know enough to take for granted what adults take for granted, they raise their hands and question points that may seem obvious enough to the teacher but that, upon examination, turn out to be fraught with hidden philosophical implications.

Teaching for Cognitive Proficiency

It is generally agreed that the cognitive foundations of the child's develop-ment are established in the family situation, where logical and syntactical proficiencies are acquired along with the acquisition of language. In the early elementary years, teachers should be concerned to treat the deficiencies that have occurred in the child's logical and syntactical development, and this may occur primarily through the nurturing of the children's conversations in the classroom. In fostering skilled cognitive performances, teachers need to de-emphasize the labels by which the logical operations are identified and to emphasize the successful performance of these operations. It cannot be denied, of course, that to call the operation to the child's attention is to be well on the way to identifying it, but the point is that this is a process that can well be stretched out in time, with the identification following rather than preceding the practice. For example, if students can read the following:

Mary is taller than Joe.
Joe is taller than Tom.
_____

So Mary is taller than Tom.

Mr. A. is the father of Mr. B.
Mr. B. is the father of Mr. C.
_____

So Mr. A. is the father of Mr. C.

and can recognize the reasoning in the first case as sound and in the second case as unsound, this is considerably more important than that they be able to say that "taller than" is a transitive relationship and "father of" is an intransitive relationship. There will be time enough to learn the labels.

Another way of putting this is to say that the early elementary phase of education is one in which cognitive skills are strengthened by practice; in the middle school, children are introduced to the principles that underlie the practice; and in secondary school, children are encouraged to apply the principles to in-school disciplines and out-of-school life. Having learned to reason epistemologically, metaphysically, ethically, logically, and aesthetically, they are now prepared to reason algebraically, geometrically, historically, scientifically, and practically. Nevertheless, no great precision can be pretended here. Children's thinking does not move in a lock-step progression from primordial skills to complex skills. It would seem rather that many or most of the skills are acquired as one learns language, although the acquisition of the more complex ones is naturally more shaky, schematic, and imprecise in this early stage than the acquisition of the simpler ones. Moreover, it is not easy to say just which skills are lower-order and which are higher-order. Bloom's taxonomy, again, is most misleading in this regard. Classification, for example, is engaged in by the most unsophisticated toddler and by the most sophisticated scientists, yet even the classificatory performance of the toddler raises theoretical questions of great complexity. Nor does it offer a complete solution to say that lower-order cognitive skills are "one-step" skills and higher-order skills are "multiple-step" skills.

Here we confront a serious problem of curriculum development. What developmental psychologists tell us about the mental growth of the child is, of course, not to be ignored. On the other hand, we must distinguish mental development observed to have taken place under conditions of minimal intervention from development resulting from deliberate efforts to stimulate and accelerate the mental growth of the child. We want to know not merely what it is that children can effortlessly grasp but what is within their reach, under circumstances that are the most felicitous and intellectually provocative we can arrange. Without experimenting with a variety of curricular interventions, we cannot possibly know the limits of children's cognitive development. Without educational intervention, children's casual cognitive behavior can be dismally concrete, drearily empirical. It is unfortunate that many curriculum developers have concluded that this state of affairs is an unchangeable given and have constructed their curricula accordingly, omitting virtually all abstractions that, it is felt, the child might find "too difficult." Is it any wonder that children, mired in a curriculum that emphasizes perceptions and ignores relationships, are "abstraction-deprived"?

Thus, curriculum-makers may either try to make their curricula conform to what psychologists tell them about child development, or they can devise their curricula as heuristic devices designed to push children's cognitive performance well beyond the level of mediocrity displayed by unchallenged children. An adequate science curriculum aims to challenge children to think—and to think for themselves. But it also seeks to encourage children to be reasonable, and this requires that it provide a model of coherence and reasonableness, however chaotic or complex children's minds may be in fact.

8 Reasoning in Language at the Elementary School Level

A reasoning, reading, and language arts program should concentrate on the sharpening of thinking skills while affording children the opportunity, through cooperative dialogical inquiry, to think philosophically about ideas that concern them. But where is one to begin? One could well begin by approximating as closely as possible the state of wonder and puzzlement that is generally characteristic of early childhood. After all, if education is to begin where the child is, rather than where the teacher is, what could be a better starting point?

When we say that children are perplexed, we commonly think of them as struggling to *explain* the world that surrounds them. But this may very well be a projection of adult puzzlement and is influenced by scientific thinking, for children not only wonder how things are caused but also wonder at the very fact that things are as they are. Thus, for example, children are puzzled by family relationships, with their intricate rules and mysterious origins. Or children will be puzzled by words, and again, it is not the origin of words that concerns them so much as the interaction of words with one another and their reference to the world. Nor are children necessarily more interested in purposes than they are in causes: the child who stares at her own face in the mirror, or who stares wonderingly at her dog's face, may not so much be trying to understand how these things were caused, or what their purpose will be, but simply what they are and that they are. Children wonder at the world. It is an awe of wonderment so profound that if it were to occur in an adult, we might call it religious.

Children wonder, and they are curious. They have an insatiable desire for reasons. When they ask questions of the form, "How can this be?" it is as if they want someone to justify the world to them. Indeed, there may be more than a slight connection between children's inability to tolerate a world that cannot be justified to them and their intense dislike of injustice.

Adults, by means of the enormously powerful scientific apparatus at their disposal, endeavor to understand the universe and, if possible, to control it. The function of intelligence in children may not be quite so instrumental and operational in character. Children process their experience by reflecting on it. The world they marvel at may not be one they wish to capture and control so much as one whose meanings they wish to apprehend. They are trying to make sense of what puzzles them, although they would probably not be happy if the sense were to be any less delightful than the wonder. This is why they love stories so much. Stories make sense of the world, but they do so in a delightful way. The story-teller, in order to enlighten us, does not have to kill the world first and then dissect it.

So reasoning skills are correlated with meaning acquisition. The more skillfully children draw inferences, identify relationships, distinguish, connect, evaluate, define, and question, the richer the totalities of meaning that they are able to extract from their experience. In this sense, experience is like raw ore: the more powerful the refining techniques, the more effectively the pure metals are extracted from the dross. The cultivation of reasoning skills is the most promising path we can pursue if our aim is to help children find out what it is that makes their experience significant.

Reading and Writing as Reasoning

We are all familiar with the fact that virtually all children, while still very young, learn to speak the language of their parents. This is no easy matter. They must learn pronunciation, inflection, grammatical proprieties (such as the incredibly difficult use of personal pronouns), and how to converse meaningfully and intelligently with their families. Yet, for many children, to read the language they speak so readily is a formidable chore, and to write it is still more formidable. Children who love to have a story told to them over and over again may nevertheless balk at reading it for themselves, and children who read voraciously may be just the ones who freeze up when it comes to writing.

When we try to teach children to read, we tend to overlook how mechanical are our techniques, such as those that stress grammar and phonics, and how close these techniques are to what actually blocks the children from reading. Moreover, we seldom seem to be aware of the intimate relationship between reading, conversation, and writing, so that our efforts to get children to write force upon them very often a formal style quite alien to the style in which they speak. And then we wonder why they do not read and do not write.

If, instead, reading and writing are seen as natural outgrowths of conversation, and if conversation is seen to be the child's natural mode of communication, an order of pedagogical priority very different from those that currently exist could be established, one that would be extremely valuable for the construction of an early childhood curriculum.

Ideally, what should a reading, reasoning, and language arts program do in the early grades?

First, it should establish continuity between reading and conversation on one hand and conversation and writing on the other.

Second, it should present the materials to be mastered in the form of a unified experience, on the child's own level.

Third, it should stress meaning rather than form, by giving precedence to the relationships that language has with the world rather than to grammar.

Fourth, it ought to link the child's experience with the literary experience of mankind, so that the child's wonder at everyday life is found to be akin to the marvels of folklore and fairytales.

Fifth, it should stimulate thinking.

Sixth, it should help children make better use of more familiar words, particularly some of the very simple but problematic words that are critical to our use of language—"if," "but," "and," "all," "no," and "like"—rather than introduce them to a list of new words that they will rarely encounter again.

However, we cannot assume that eight- or nine-year-old children are as ready for philosophical discussion as they will be in another year or two. But as they grow, they move toward increased collaborative competence, logical astuteness, and mastery of language and ideas.

If curiosity is the disposition that children and philosophers share, then concern with the nature of similarity and difference is their common intellectual interest. Either we compare things with one another, or we compare them with an ideal standard. The "we" here can stand indifferently for philosophers or children or, in fact, for anyone. We discover similarities and differences by making comparisons, and to make comparisons is therefore to uncover similar and different relationships. Some children are prolific when it comes to producing fanciful or even extravagant associations; others are timid or inhibited. Nevertheless, the objective for all groups must be a craftsmanlike competence in perceiving and expressing similarities and differences; those who use language with an exuberant flair for figurative expression will always feel free to go beyond such competence, whereas those who have been virtually inarticulate will find that practice in the making of comparisons suddenly opens new vistas in the description and explanation of the world around them.

Early childhood is a period in which language is being acquired at an incredibly rapid rate. We are inclined to take an indulgent view toward vocabulary expansion, even when it represents the acquisition of increasingly exotic terms by children whose proficiency in the use of such unglamorous terms as "all," "only," 'because," "same," and "different" is uncertain and unsteady. This indulgence in novelty can be short-sighted and unwise: unless one has a firm command of the basic operations of a language, the addition of new terminology is more likely to aggravate the problem than to alleviate it. Yet the problem is not one that can be resolved by a brisk review of grammar, for the problems the child faces in learning to use language are substantive as well as formal, philosophical as well as syntactic, and practical as well as logical. When the child's syntactic, semantic, and pragmatic awarenesses are keeping pace with one another, vocabulary growth will present no significant problem.

Ambiguity

Learning a new word is not more important, in and of itself, than learning that a familiar word has not just one but a variety of meanings and can have several such meanings in a given context. When children learn about language, people, and the world in general, there is a danger that they will acquire a severely over-simplified view of these matters. They may assume, for example, that people always mean what they say and that things are always what they appear to be. The naive trust of the child in a just and benevolent order must sooner or later come to grief, as the child attempts to impose a grid of orderly understanding on a world that is many leveled, turbulent in its alterations, and frequently absurd. Therefore, equipping children with an understanding of ambiguity is a valuable preparatory discipline that readies the child not only for the puns, equivocations, and double entendres of everyday discourse but also for the rich allusiveness of literature, the double binds of human relations, and the covertness of nature itself.

Moreover, although learning about ambiguity prepares children to deal with the duplicity that frequently characterizes the world around us, it also helps children discover the relationships of words with words, things with things, and words with things. As we encounter the world, terms and things are manifest and explicit, whereas relationships seem to be much more implicit and latent. We perceive the mountain and the valley, as well as the words "mountain" and "valley," but we are slower to realize the relationship that the mountain and the valley have to one another, the referential relationships between the terms and their objects, or the fact that the words themselves are related to one another.

Relationships

It is when we contrast and compare that we discover relationships: faster than, busier than, equal to, later than. We also discover familial connections: mother of, cousin of, grandfather of. Likewise, we find that there are important linguistic relationships: the way some verbs "take objects" and others don't, the way nouns may be modified by adjectives and verbs by adverbs. Out of this potpourri emerges the astonishing and monumental fact of resemblance: of words with one another, of people with one another, of things and events with one another, of words with people and with things. These resemblances we express by means of literal comparisons and by figurative means as well, for example, similes, metaphors, and analogies.

In the preceding account, liberties have been taken with the order of events, for surely small children have a very lively sense of resemblances. They perceive the world physiognomically by analogy of human characteristics with non-human ones. The cup lying on its side is perceived as a "poor, tired cup," and the numerical 10 is perceived as "daddy and mommy." We labor heroically to convince such children that these are "category mistakes" and that things should be compared with things, numbers with numbers, and people with people. Gradually, we succeed in bringing a degree of order into their expressions by making them see that the everyday world calls for businesslike, matter-of-fact literalness, while only the world of literary expression can accommodate their physiognomic experiences and their figurative ways of expressing such experiences. The child's imaginative response to an animate world is replaced by an armory of conventional reflex responses to a prosaic world. Children have none of the elements of deliberate artifice that are invested in adult experience. However, adults must strive for the expression of the creativity they naturally had as children.

In other words, cognitive development is, in one respect, a sorting out of contexts: we learn not to confuse the spatial and the temporal, the auditory and the visual, the physical and the personal. The very young child, having yet to learn the boundaries of these contexts, finds no difficulty in transcending them and perceives houses as having faces, furniture as cheerful or menacing, colors as happy or sad, and shapes as awkward or graceful. Three- and four-year-olds produce metaphors at a breathtaking rate, but so many of these metaphors appear to us to be recklessly inappropriate that we take prompt steps to strengthen the child's critical abilities. As a result, the child may go to the other extreme, where contexts and orders have been clearly sorted out and random crossovers are prohibited. Therefore, the educational process must accept responsibility for the literal-mindedness of so many of the children shaped by that process.

Awareness of ambiguity, then, is the opening wedge of the struggle to establish a dynamic balance between the child's ability to function figuratively as well as literally. In a sense, simile is the inverse of ambiguity. An ambiguous word can have several distinct meanings in a particular context, whereas a simile suggests that two different things have a definite resemblance. So ambiguity sees difference in similarity, and simile sees similarity in difference.

Similes

In simile, comparison is explicit (whether one says "X is like Y," or "X is as _____ as Y"). In metaphor, however, comparison is suppressed. In metaphor, one wishes to call attention not to a resemblance between two things normally taken to be different but to the identity of those two different things. To say "George was angry" is clinical and remote, for it merely tells us that George was a member of the class of angry beings. "George's face was like a thundercloud" has more emotional effect, although it still involves us in the making of a conscious comparison. "George's face was a thundercloud" is still more dramatic because it eliminates the comparison and speaks of the two radically different things as if they were one. Writers accustomed to using figurative language find literal statements like "George was angry" pale and anemic. Writers accustomed to using literal language find metaphors to be examples of linguistic overkill. However, both forms of expression have their purposes, and it is only when used for the wrong purpose that either mode of expression may be found inappropriate.

A simile is a claim that two things normally taken to be different are in some respect similar, an analogy is a claim that two relationships are alike. Such, at least, is the minimal analogy, taking as it does the form "A is to B as C is to D." Notice that analogies, like similes, involve likeness or similarity. Just as similes become radically dramatized when the similarity claim is replaced by an identity claim and they become metaphors, so analogies can take the form "A:B :: C:D," where the relationships being compared are ratios and the alleged comparison is in fact a statement of equivalence. But the equivalence relationship is anything but dramatic: "3:6 :: 12:24" is simply a tautology, another way of saying "1/2 = 1/2."

Not that small children—even those who are only three or four years of age—need to be counseled by us on the creation of similes and metaphors: their fertility in these matters is far greater than that of adults. What they lack, however, is the critical sense that would enable them to judge the appropriateness or the inappropriateness of the figures of speech they can so elaborately construct. The strengthening of that critical sense can in turn help them become aware of whether their own analogical reasonings are being done well or badly.

Analogies

Many thinkers have seen analogy as the mode of reasoning that is shared by creative persons in all fields. When we express ourselves with a simile, it is because we have noted a resemblance between two things that in most other respects are different. When we express ourselves by means of an analogy, it is because we have discerned a resemblance between two relationships (or between two whole systems of relationships). Whether a sense of proportion is what makes for the ability to formulate analogies or whether the ability to formulate analogies is what makes for a sense of proportion is very difficult to say: perhaps each ministers to the other. But it would certainly appear that the early strengthening of so fundamental a skill as analogical reasoning would be a sensible strategy for both cognitive and creative development.

Analogies are often much more complicated than they appear in their minimal formulations (e.g., "Cats are to kittens as dogs are to puppies"), for they may involve entire systems or constellations of relationships being compared with one another. Someone who remarks that "the rulers of present-day South Africa run their country much like the rulers of ancient Sparta ran theirs" is drawing a complex analogy between two whole systems of government. The irony in the critic's remark that "there was considerable analogy between the way the Schubert songs were written and the way they were sung in the concert last night" is the inference that there should have been a unity between the score and the performance, not a mere similarity.

In a striking figure of speech, the physicist Murray Gell-Mann once remarked that our inquiries into nature are so successful because "nature resembles itself." However that may be, it would appear that scientists search for resemblances among differences and for uniformity within diversity. Whether such uniformity is genuine and substantive or simply methodological and conceptual is a matter still debated. But whenever inductive reasoning takes place, some degree of analogical reasoning is probably also involved. On another hand, the use of analogy in artistic construction is of primary importance. Perhaps the best example would be the theme and variations approach used in music, painting, architecture, and probably, to varying degrees, in every form of art. The enjoyment of the listener or beholder is often proportionate to his or her ability to educe the analogies that have been produced by varying the elements but retaining the relationships under comparison or by varying both elements and relationships while retaining barely recognizable resemblances among the different structures. Indeed, appreciation is a form of inquiry in the sense that it compels wonder and thinking, with analogical reasoning very prominent among the forms of thinking involved.

Rule and Reason

Reasons are introduced because they are what we offer when we are trying to justify what we do. Whether or not the reason offered does justify the act in question is what makes it a good or poor reason respectively. It would be well to mention here that, in teaching thinking skills, one does not necessarily begin by teaching rules, axioms, and definitions from which the remainder of the subject is to be inferred by rigorous deduction. Particularly when dealing with children, a holistic approach is more appropriate. The students must discover some generalization that will permit them to judge any particular instance of a given problem. This method is undeniably less precise and less reliable than procedure governed by rules, but it has other advantages. It is quick, and it is not mechanical. It trains judgment and facilitates comprehension.

It is more profitable in working with eight- or nine-year-old children to ask them whether a particular instance of dialogue represents good or poor reasoning than to ask them to learn and then identify the violations of logic that they find. Eventually, the children may be taught the rules that apply to such cases and whose use gives greater protection against error than the more "intuitive" holistic approach does. The holistic approach, on the other hand, permits the student to respond to minute cues or subtle nuances that would escape a mechanical application of the rules. The rules of logic screen out gross violations, but they do not exclude a vast number of linguistic inflections that would be considered improper reasoning in an informal sense. All the more reason, then, to sensitize children first to the look and feel of illogic and to habituate them to search techniques that raise questions of appropriateness, proportion, and analogical fitness. Later they may learn more formal techniques for detecting invalid reasoning. At the same time, to make the transition to the "formal stage" more gradual, there is nothing wrong with introducing some exercises that call for the use of logical rules.

9   Social Inquiry at the Secondary School Level

Preparing Children to Think in the Social Studies

Social studies courses represent, more than any other area in the elementary or secondary school curriculum, the intersecting requirements of school and education. The schooling stipulation is aimed at producing an informed and responsible citizenry, the objective being the child's socialization. The educational requirement has traditionally been understood as a matter of getting children to learn the basic facts of social life and how such facts came about. By putting these two requirements together, one could construct a social studies course that would prepare the child for citizenship and, at the same time, contribute significantly to the child's education.

Such an approach contains serious difficulties on a number of counts. First, by assuming that the child needs to be socialized, this approach is in danger of insufficiently enlisting those social impulses that children bring with them to every educational setting and that can be one of the most liberating and creative contributions to the effectiveness of such education. In other words, to insist that children "need to be socialized" is to underestimate the contribution children are prepared to make to the social processes in which they are involved and to assume that the society is a structure into which they have to be fitted, rather than a flexible and open-textured order that respects, elicits, and makes room for the creative contributions of the individual. Second, the formulation of education in terms of learning rather than thinking again treats the child as passive, rather than active, as a recipient rather than a doer, as someone to be operated upon, someone to be processed rather than as someone capable of making original contributions to the social process. Third, such an approach underestimates the capacity of children to inquire into the social forces with which they interact. It is not that we are unaware that children possess a rich sense of wonder and an active curiosity. But we are inclined to treat these as childish instincts to be outgrown rather than as constructive responses to the puzzling and enigmatic character of the world children experience. That is, from their earliest moments children are aware of the problematic and in many cases mysterious character of the environment, particularly the social environment that we all share.

As adults, we have made our own adjustments to the strangeness and precariousness of social life, and we are not always patient with the child's puzzlement. But the point to be emphasized is that children are puzzled because the world is in fact puzzling. They are often mystified because things tend to happen in baffling and bewildering ways. An adequate social studies course should attempt to amend the deficiencies just noted. It will enlist the social impulses of the child by creating classroom communities of inquiry. It will cease to treat children as passive blotters whose education consists merely of the learning of inert data and will instead stimulate their capacity to think. Finally, it will candidly acknowledge the problematic character of human existence and the tentativeness of our efforts to understand it. It will therefore enlist children's social impulses, children's readiness to think, and their capacity to utilize their doubts in a constructive effort to evaluate the social institutions within which they exist and the roles that they are expected to play within those institutions.

One of the presuppositions of the idea of democracy, at least since the time of John Locke, has been that the members of such a society should be not merely informed but reflective, that they should not merely be aware of the issues but be reasonable with regard to them. It follows that two tasks are laid upon those who venture to teach children in democratic societies. The first is to make students aware of the nature of the society to which they belong by getting them to learn the main strands of its history and the major features of its present-day structure. The second is to encourage them to think about these matters by sharpening their thinking skills and by showing them how to apply such skills to matters of importance. The first task involves getting students to learn; the second task involves getting them to think. There is reason to believe that we cannot effectively perform the first without effectively performing the second, and would not want to: a history course not taught in the spirit of critical inquiry is not a history course.

At this point a chorus of questions can be anticipated. It is all very well to advocate that teachers should teach thinking skills, it will be said, but who is to teach them to the teachers? It is all very well to urge that children acquire rationality, but what are the criteria of rationality? While children are perfecting their thinking skills, what are they to think about? And what is the pedagogy appropriate to teaching to think—is it not the same pedagogy as that utilized in teaching to learn?

Prior to the advent of Philosophy for Children, these questions could not readily be answered. The answers that can now be proposed are as follows: (1) The criteria of rationality are those that enable us to distinguish effective, reliable reasoning from ineffective, unreliable reasoning and are therefore none other than the rules of logic and the principles of inquiry; (2) the literature of philosophy contains countless intriguing issues upon which children are eager to sharpen their growing intellectual skills—issues such as friendship, fairness, truth, and what it is to be a person. That such issues tend to be persistently controversial seems to make them even more attractive to children than matters more easily resolved whose solution represents little in the way of intellectual adventure; and finally, (3) the pedagogy of philosophy involves converting the classroom into a community of cooperative inquiry, where all are democratically entitled to be heard, where each learns from the other, and where the spoken dialogue among the members of the class, when internalized and rendered an inner forum in the mind of each participant, is the basis of the process known as thinking.

Let us suppose that we have assembled the necessary conditions just cited: teachers have been properly trained, a curriculum has been properly prepared, and criteria for successful thinking have been made explicit, so that the classroom can now become a community of inquiry. How does all of this bear upon reflective education?

As a general rule, we may say that we should not present information to children who have not already been prepared to process such information cognitively in an effective fashion. Unless students have preliminary concepts to work with—rough though they may be—they will be at a loss to organize and comprehend the data to which they are exposed. This is something of which children themselves are dimly aware. For example, take the case of science education. We can get children to go through the motions of performing laboratory experiments, but we cannot prevent their wondering about what such experiments presuppose. What is truth? Why the quest for objectivity? What is so important about measurement? Of what earthly use is description? For what purpose do we need explanations? If these matters could be explored in classroom discussions antecedently to or concurrently with the physical experimentation itself, the resistance or reluctance of many students would be tempered or dissolved, for we would have converted their assignment from a meaningless exercise into a meaningful one.

Approaches to the materials of the social sciences require no less intellectual preparation. A reflective citizenry must be prepared to evaluate the performances of individuals who work within social institutions and the performances of those institutions themselves. But this cannot be done unless citizens have a working knowledge of and are conversant with the ideals of the society that those institutions are supposed to implement. There is little point to teaching students how institutions operate, if we do not at the same time help them understand the goals and objectives that must be brought to bear on such institutions. Without a clear understanding of such concepts as freedom, justice, equality, personhood, and democracy, how are students to be able to tell whether elected officials or operative institutions are performing well or badly? We can teach students the laws of the society, but unless they have some grasp of the constitutional issues that underlie the laws, and some grasp of the philosophical issues that underlie the constitutional ones, their attitudes toward the laws will be contaminated by nagging doubts and misconceptions. It is not in the least impractical to begin discussing the philosophical issues concurrently with examination of the factual data. Indeed, unless children can have the opportunity to consider and discuss the guiding ideals and regulatory presuppositions of the society in which they live and whose operations they are being asked to study, the chances are that they will neither study them, learn them, nor accept them.

Several years ago, in a book entitled *Adolescent Prejudice,* Harper & Row published the results of an extensive study conducted in California by Charles Glock and his associates in the Department of Sociology of the University of California at Berkeley. Glock's findings are highly suggestive, even if he does not always draw from them the inferences that seem clearly implied. It would appear from the study that older generations, convinced of the rightness of their values, have a way of insisting to each upcoming adolescent generation that it accept the traditional beliefs, attitudes, and ways of looking at things. But the younger generation has a way of rejecting parental beliefs, whatever these might be—evidently for no other reason than that they are parental. Is there nothing then that parents can do? Is every effort of theirs to convey their values to their children doomed to failure simply because it comes from them? Glock says no. If we could somehow get adolescents to become reflective and critical—and Glock has no idea, apparently, how this might be done—then children might in time discover the right values for themselves, and they would hold on to such values because it was their discovery, not something imposed on them from above.[1]

This suggests that if we teach children to reason, and if the values we ourselves hold are reasonable ones, then our children will eventually, just by thinking for themselves, come to share our values with us.

But what about citizenship education—isn't that something quite different? Isn't there a specific body of facts and beliefs that must be conveyed to all children and that they must, with or without discussion, be persuaded to adopt? Aren't there indiscussible allegiances and commitments that children must be nourished upon if they are to grow up to be responsible citizens in a democratic society?

Since a democratic society is one in which no social issue can ever be put beyond the pale of inquiry, it is difficult to see how any body of social beliefs might be considered off-limits by the children who are being prepared to enter into such a society in a responsible and fully participatory fashion. The problem is not so much to get children whom we are educating for citizenship to know this or that or to believe this or that—although this in no way forbids us from wanting them to be aware, sooner or later, of what we know and believe. No, the problem is simply that the primary criterion of responsible citizenship is—and has always been—nothing other than reflectiveness. An educational system that does not encourage children to reflect—to think thoroughly and systematically about matters of importance to them—fails to prepare them to satisfy the one criterion that must be satisfied if one is to be not merely a citizen of a society, but a good citizen of a democracy. In a word, education for responsible citizenship is reflective education.

But isn't this too glib? What is the relationship between responsibility and reflection? Unless it can be demonstrated, the whole argument falls apart. The connection can be demonstrated, although it cannot be done here in any elaborate fashion. What we need to recognize is that the educational use of these two terms requires that each of them be taken in a more specialized sense than is commonly done. Thus by reflection we do not simply mean meditation or thoughtfulness but proficiency in thinking skills—whether in making, in saying, or in doing. So reflection has a behavioral dimension—people can act reflectively, create reflectively. And it has a social dimension—people engaged in dialogue are engaged in social reflection; indeed, it is the internalization of that dialogue by each participant that comes to be individualized reflection.

Responsibility, likewise, means more than simply accountability. A responsible person is not just someone you can hold to account. Rather, in its more relevant sense in this context, responsibility implies capacity to respond appropriately and intelligently when confronted with a problematic situation. It is only after these terms have been so defined that one can more readily see how an education that prepares individuals to make, say, and do thoughtfully and intelligently is precisely an education that prepares individuals for social responsibility.

But here another danger looms. There are those who will interpret the term "reflective education" as implying something that is all process and no content, all method and no substance, where nothing needs to be learned except how to look things up. But such an interpretation would be erroneous and would be particularly mischievous when applied to education for responsible citizenship. Such education would seem to comprise four specific tasks:

1. Students must become conversant with—if only in outline—the conceptual foundations of Western civilization as these bear upon the relationship between society and the individual;
2. students must be encouraged to develop the ability to grasp and identify the social situations in which they find themselves and to see those situations as instances of the general considerations that govern the relationship between society and the individual;
3. the thinking skills of students must be exercised, sharpened, and constantly reinforced by illustration and application, so that such students develop (a) a strong disposition to look for the regulatory concepts and ideals that are applicable to each distinctive situation, (b) a logical rigor that will enable them to draw the inferences that necessarily follow from the principles they have discovered, and (c) a reasonableness that will compel them to take all relevant considerations—such as possible consequences of alternative modes of action—into account;
4. an adequate social studies curriculum should (a) treat the fundamental concepts of the behavioral sciences as essentially contestable rather than as lying outside the limits of discussion; (b) seek to match and marry specific cognitive skills to specific concepts, so that students will feel cognitively prepared to grasp and analyze the concepts they are expected to discuss; and (c) present factual or empirical materials in a manner that demands student reflection, by requiring that students consider the possible consequences or implications of empirical generalizations, the reasons that may have led people to act in ways such as these, and the possibility of counterinstances.

As was noted earlier, to educate for responsible citizenship, we should engage in reflective education, so as to produce reasonable children. Now the standard used to determine reasonableness may be one with a very narrow, sharp cutting edge, such as the ability to reason logically; or it may be considerably broader, such as the ability to comprehend the meanings of what one reads and hears, as well as the ability to express oneself meaningfully. Another criterion that is not irrelevant is the academic impact of the educational program: does its introduction produce improved academic performance in other areas of the student's academic life? Another criterion is the attitude of students themselves toward the program: do they enjoy it so much that an observer can see the warmth of their response in the way they behave in the classroom and the way they themselves talk about the program afterward? Yet another is the cultivation of critical thinking so as to facilitate good judgement on the part of the student.

Some Themes to Be Considered in a Philosophical Approach to the Social Studies

It would be useful to consider a group of themes that together form the backbone of an approach that young people may take to understanding society and to the comprehension of human behavior in its social aspects.

Criteria

Those who are dissatisfied with existing educational practice customarily deplore what they perceive to be the inability of school children to evaluate the information they are given about the society in which such children live. Students are alleged to be unable to appraise the things they prize; they are accused of holding their values uncritically. If this is so, it should not be too surprising, since we so infrequently assist students in developing evaluative procedures that will enable them to make reasonable and reliable judgments. We generally fail, in other words, to acquaint them with the use of criteria.

When an exact discipline, such as mathematics, is used as a model of the educational process, there is often a tendency to place a heavier than necessary emphasis on the function of rules and a lighter than necessary emphasis on the function of criteria. Mathematics is a deductive discipline, in which rules function with rigorous necessity. When the same model is carried over into other aspects of education, rules are used as the major premises of deductive arguments. For example, it may be taken as a rule that cases of social aggression should be interpreted as indicating a need for inquiry into possible underlying frustrations. ("This is the case of social aggression; it is therefore necessary to inquire as to sources in underlying frustrations.") A deduction of this sort, given the rules embodied in the major premise, is fairly mechanical and reliable. It issues in a conclusion that is much more restricted in scope than the conclusions that follow from the use of criteria in the making of appraisals.

Let us assume that two students are having a controversy over a certain teacher. One student says that the teacher in question is a "good" teacher, and the other student says he is a "bad" teacher. A third student, noting the mounting intensity of the argument, encourages the opponents to state their criteria. The first student then says that the teacher is good, using the criterion of giving attention to individual members of the class. The second student then offers the judgment that the teacher is bad because his knowledge of the subject matter is inadequate. They have now recognized that their disagreement was related to the fact that they were using different criteria. What the third student may now proceed to point out to them is that the use of a single criterion enables one to make a fairly rudimentary value judgment. In this sense, it does not differ greatly from the mechanical deduction referred to above. All teachers who relate well to individual class members are good; this teacher relates well to individual class members; therefore, this teacher is good. The third student can proceed to show the others that the judgment of the effectiveness of the teacher must necessarily involve many criteria other than merely those two.

It is just such methodological considerations that need to be undertaken in every classroom where the matters under discussion involve either estimates of value or judgments of fact. The objective is not to produce students who are "critical" in the sense of being negative and pretentious. The objective is to produce students who approach conceptual issues with a readiness to appraise and evaluate those aspects of such issues that call for judgment rather than for merely mechanical skills.

What bearing does all of this have on the study of social behavior? What we teach students of how society works can never be wholly innocuous, because the way they think it works will in time influence the way it works. If there are ideals by which society guides itself, and if there are practices and institutions and policies that are supposed to move toward and to approximate those ideals, then the education given to children will be a critical factor to the extent to which those ideals will be realized. Unless students can understand the regulative function of ideals and the need to appraise policies and institutions as means rather than as ends, each generation will mechanically accept as necessary and unchangeable precisely that which is most in need of evaluation by each upcoming generation. It is therefore indispensable that experience with the logical function of criteria become a continuous strand of the educational process.

Government

Every society has a way of operating by means of which the lives of its members can be regulated with some degree of coordination. Forms of government vary very widely from highly decentralized approaches, such as are found in feudal societies, to highly centralized ones, such as absolute monarchies, tyrannies, and totalitarian governments. Even those portions of the world, however rare, that have been anarchistic have been able to function to the extent that they have because they presume a high capacity for self-government in the case of each individual citizen.

There are many different things to consider with regard to the nature of government. Some specialists in government emphasize its compulsive role; that is, government as an organized monopoly of the means of violence. Others stress the role of government in coordinating human affairs, providing for defense and prohibiting undesirable forms of social behavior. The characteristics of government in general are therefore numerous and worthy of the consideration of students in social studies quite apart from their consideration of particular forms of government, such as democracy, tyranny, fascism, and dictatorship. Again, however, when it comes to analysis of these particular forms of government, it will be necessary to weigh the criteria by which each is to be defined and distinguished from the other. There are episodes in *Mark* in which the discussions among the students exemplify the kind of dialogical inquiry that takes place when students endeavor to understand what makes one form of government, such as democracy, different from others.[2] At the same time, in the repugnance that they show for authoritarian procedures, the students exemplify how inquiry into public matters can proceed in a democratic society.

One of the problems confronting the social studies instructor is the imprecise understanding that students have of the very terms that the instructor takes for granted that they comprehend. For example, students supposedly know the meaning of terms like "government," "democracy," "association," and "community" but, in fact, are unable to define them adequately. Moreover, in helping students come to a clearer understanding of the basic features of, for example, the democratic process, the instructor will find it necessary to explore to some extent the presuppositions that are generally entertained with regard to that process. Thus, to say that democracy is characterized by public discussion of the issues that affect the society as a whole and that democratic governments are consequently expected to guide themselves by such a consensus is to presuppose that citizens in a democracy have the capacity to understand the complex issues that confront such societies and the rationality to deal with them. This raises the further question, of course, as to whether democratic societies are capable of communicating the nature of these problems to the public as well as a host of problems regarding the nature of rationality. We generally take the easiest course, which is to presume that the students already are familiar with the answers to these questions, and we further presume that no harm will be done by proceeding to a study of the mechanics of the democratic process. But unless there is an airing of the underlying issues that form the context for students' understanding of specific factual matters, they are very likely to misunderstand or misinterpret the information we provide them.

Law

One way in which human beings attempt to govern their own behavior is to impose rules on it. Each society has rules of conduct that are more or less strongly urged upon the individual members of that society. Thus people are urged to be honest, and children take that recommendation as a moral rule. But dishonesty can become a legal matter and not just a moral one when a violation of a law is involved, as when a witness provides false testimony in a court of law. In other words, there are social rules whose violation calls forth the pressures of public opinion, and there are legal rules where the society has empowered the government to take specific steps to punish the lawbreaker. It is not always easy for children to distinguish among prohibitions based on superstition, on custom, on social morality, on local laws, on constitutional issues, and on religious injunctions. But certainly it would be desirable that students have the opportunity to become sensitized to these differences and to be able to make finer discriminations than those that they can make at present.

Certainly it would be desirable for students to come to a better comprehension than they currently have of the relationship between law and morality, of the relationship between constitutionality and law, and of the relationship between the fundamental principles of political philosophy and constitutionality. Enlightened citizens generally manage to avoid knee-jerk reactions when it comes to emotion-charged issues such as offenses against "law and order." They understand the necessity of the legal procedure known as due process and the rights of both accuser and accused. One thing that distinguishes the democratic society is the balance it is able to establish between the capacity of the individual citizen for judgments of conscience and the restraint of the average citizen when it comes to matters that are better handled by fair and objective social procedures.

Social Institutions

Every society establishes arrangements that, generation after generation, guide people into similar patterns of behavior. We think of these persisting arrangements as social institutions. Because institutions are so much taken for granted within each society, the inhabitants of such societies are generally not very much aware of the extent to which such institutions shape their lives. In this respect, institutions and traditions are rather dissimilar. Traditions are also handed down from generation to generation and shape human conduct accordingly. But traditions are intensely meaningful and are often charged with symbolic connotations to which people in that society are very much attached, whereas institutions are more formal in character and tend simply to be taken for granted.

For example, we tend to take for granted that children should be sent to school, that criminals should be sent to jail, that worshippers should go to church, that voters should go to the ballot box, that people should transact their business in banks, and that shopping should be done in stores. Yet in other societies a very different set of institutions may prevail. Or it may be that two societies will differ very much with respect to certain institutions, whereas in the case of other institutions they will be very much alike. Thus, for example, two societies may have very different economic systems but very similar kinship systems.

While students are learning to distinguish between the government of a society and its institutions, they should not be misled with regard to the similarities and overlappings that may take place between these two aspects of society. Certainly, the question comes up very often of how individual institutions are to be administered—whether it be prisons, schools, churches, or families. Likewise, there are times when certain institutions, such as the corporation or the military, may be able to exert influence over the government of that society.

Community

In our discussion of the concept of community, we have echoed themes that have been stressed ever since the middle of the nineteenth century in a vast number of sociological treatises: communities are characterized by face-to-face relationships, by the personal knowledge of each member of the community of all the other members, and by the common acceptance of the traditions and values of the group. We have also stressed the conventional distinction between communities and associations.

However, as we concentrate on the conversion of the classroom into a community of educational inquiry, we are likely to find that the earlier themes are too specialized and too mechanical for our purposes. Thus the nineteenth-century interpretation of community tended to conceive of it as an ongoing repository of human values: individuals receive the values they live by from the communities in which they live, just as surely as they receive their wages or salaries from the employers for whom they work. But a community of shared experience is differently conceived. Instead of thinking of the community as an institutional structure that distributes values and meanings to individuals, one can reverse the matter and say that, wherever experience is shared in a fashion that enables the participants to discover the meaning of their participation, there is community.

Human Nature

We can hardly claim to know what human nature is. We can only treat it in an open-ended fashion and encourage students to recognize that human nature, like freedom, justice, and so many other fundamental philosophical notions, is an essentially contestable concept.

Nevertheless, there is no escaping the fact that a great deal has hinged, historically, on what people have *thought* human nature to be. Thus in a society in which human nature has been thought to be brutal, violent, and unchangeable, the only appropriate political institution for dealing with such intractable human behavior is said to be the all-powerful state. On the other hand, to those who have conceived of human nature as inherently docile and peaceable and educable, permissive social institutions have seemed appropriate.

Finally, where human nature has been conceived as neither inherently good nor evil, an even greater responsibility is placed on social institutions to develop human potentials in constructive directions. Obviously, then, what people have assumed human nature to be has played a key role in the way they have tried to shape the societies in which they live.

By acquainting students with the enormous complexity and yet the enormous importance of concepts such as human nature, we can do such students a distinct service. We can at least prevent them from taking such notions for granted, and from uncritically building on them in ways that cannot be sustained.

Freedom

To an adolescent, few themes can seem more dramatic than the theme of freedom. Adolescence is a phase of development in which freedom is customarily understood as the breaking of shackles and restraints, liberation from childhood ways, and the discovery of autonomy and independence. But to many in an older generation, the child's yearning for freedom may seem a threat to established values and a misguided expression of childish romanticism.

For all of this, the problem of the adolescent searching for ways of living as a free human being, while still technically a minor and not yet considered mature enough for full participation in the society, has a certain analogy with the problem of the contemporary adult searching for a meaning of political liberty that would be compatible on the one hand with the requirements of justice and on the other with the dangers that lack of regulation pose to the existence of society. As adults, we struggle with the latter question, forgetting that we have been involved in it in one way or another since childhood. Childhood, in fact, is a laboratory version of the problem of freedom in social life.

When these considerations are taken into account, nothing would seem more natural or appropriate than the treatment of freedom in a course in social studies. Such appropriateness is further enhanced when we consider how essential the notion of freedom is to the rhetoric and ideology with which politics is discussed in contemporary society. If freedom is to be made a meaningful notion, then we have to be very precise as to the way we spell out the differences between free and unfree institutions. We have to be able to evaluate the institutions within the society in which we live so as to determine whether they do in fact operationalize and embody the ideal of freedom that we claim for them. If children can be accustomed to engaging seriously and persistently in the making of such appraisals, it will be less likely that unsatisfactory institutions will be accepted uncritically and without examination, when such children have grown to adulthood.

Justice

We have already spoken of the importance of acquainting students not only with the workings of the law in society but also with the constitutional issues that underlie the law and with the philosophical issues that underlie the constitutional ones. As these successive levels of the problem come into view, students become aware of the fact that mere legality is not necessarily to be equated with social justice. This discrepancy cannot fail to be a troubling one, for how can one respect the law when it is so evidently an imperfect embodiment of justice in the ideal? However, if we open issues such as these to students in the classroom, we will find that they can take them in their stride. They can intelligently discuss the consequences to a society of the imperfection of its institutions, such as its legal institutions, without creating a serious risk that they will lose respect for such institutions because of their imperfections.

If the aim of the social studies course is to encourage students to develop a mature understanding of the ways in which society operates, and the ways in which they may live within such a society, then it is indispensable for such students to be sensitive to the foundational role of such key concepts as freedom and justice. This is not to say that they must learn how to resolve the tensions that exist among such concepts. It is quite possible that notions as wide-ranging as freedom and justice may not be made compatible without a sacrifice of other values that we do not wish to give up. But it is just such problems as these to which students must be encouraged to address themselves, and it is just such problems as these that go to the heart of social inquiry.

10 Thinking and Writing at the Secondary School Level

How Can We Stimulate Thinking in Language?

Reasoning and Writing

Writing requires thinking. One must deliberate, plan, infer possible consequences, make assumptions, test alternatives, and engage in other mental activities that have to be carefully coordinated. To a considerable extent the criteria for successful writing are the same as the criteria for logical thinking. One example is the standard of consistency. Consistency remains an important consideration for writers, but it is not the only one. As Ronald Berman has remarked:

> Writing is a series of conceptual decisions. Even within fiction it must describe, include, select, compare, define and ascribe, among many other logical responsibilities. It moves from evidence, through reasoning, to conclusion. It can do these things in a thousand different ways, indirect as poetry, heavy as the law. But it does after all have to translate feeling and intuition into statement, and that procedure underlies everything in the life of the mind.[1]

It is foolish to assume that logic can furnish directions for writing. It merely supplies the criteria for distinguishing between better and worse reasoning. Good writing, whether poetry or prose, involves such considerations as grace and surprise, texture and rhythm, passion and intelligence, about which logic has little or nothing to say. Poetry can be examined empirically to determine under what circumstances it uses forms that are logical or contrary to logic.

The relationship of reasoning to writing is perhaps less obvious in the domain of logic than in that of philosophy proper. The common bond between philosophy and the creation of literature is that both are quests for meaning. Both the philosopher and the writer are fascinated with language and concerned with its precise use. Both may be concerned with the same questions. (For example, what possibilities exist in an imaginary, contrary-to-fact universe that do not exist in the world as it is?) Children who study philosophy may be better prepared to write effectively than those who do not.

The Relationship of Aesthetics to Writing

The field of philosophy most relevant to writing is aesthetics. Aesthetics was at one time a discipline devoted to theories of beauty or, in a more specialized version, theories of fine art. At one time, this discipline proposed theories of both artistic creation and aesthetic appreciation. Gradually, aesthetics came to concentrate only on appreciation, and in more recent times, it has been fashionable to define it simply as the theory of criticism.

There is little to recommend this gradual narrowing of the domain of aesthetics. There would seem to be no persuasive reason why the aesthetic understanding of the philosopher cannot be harnessed to promote rather than merely to appraise the creative activities of individuals and their outcomes. The feasibility of this undertaking becomes most obvious when philosophers construct curricula for children. The aim is to establish classroom conditions under which children are encouraged to think independently and to promote the tendencies of children to engage in artistic activities of all kinds. One cannot fully acknowledge the logical connection until one is ready to see painting as thinking in pigments, sculpture as thinking in clay and stone, dance as thinking in bodily movement, and indeed all the arts as forms of embodied thinking. A thinking skills curriculum, if it is any good at all, must wed aesthetics to the practical disciplines.

Of no practical discipline is this more true than in the case of writing. What is it about writing that baffles children? Why do they resist it so strenuously? If their fear or hatred of it rests on conceptual misunderstandings, then philosophy has a responsibility to undertake the necessary clarification.

Philosophy has a way of turning a spotlight on what most of us are content to take for granted. For example, when children are assigned a number of exercises to do as homework, it is taken for granted that they will have no difficulty reading the directions. But often this is not the case at all; students are bewildered by the technical terms and terse explanations that writers of textbooks assume children will find perfectly clear. The same is true with writing assignments such as the following: "Describe your vacation experiences and tell us what they meant to you." Experiences? Meaning? These are extremely broad terms. The child who attempts to explain them to himself or herself prior to writing may never get to write. The aesthetician as educator needs to be enlisted in the removal of conceptual barriers to writing and in the search for incentives.

How Conversation Mediates between Reading and Writing

It is commonplace that children generally have little trouble with expressive activities such as singing, fingerpainting, music, and dance. They seem to enjoy expressing themselves, so much so that adults often say that it comes naturally to them. In verbal expression, they tend to be terse and concise.

Somewhere around the age of eight or nine many children begin to lose interest in artistic activities and, indeed, in most activities that involve independent thinking. Their speech becomes conventional and prosaic. The demands of formal education begin to conflict with their desire to think for themselves. The formal conditions of expression that teachers insist on often inhibit the child. In fourth-grade classrooms one notes less frequently the bright eyes, joyous faces, and unselfconscious demeanor that had been evident in the same children three years earlier.

When children enter middle school, their poetic impulses come into even greater conflict with social demands for consistency and coherence. Such demands seem to be at odds with the more imaginative elements in poetic composition and also with still other demands for conformity or acceptability of the child as a person. These conflicting pressures gradually stifle the poetic impulse as children grow toward secondary school. A program in the middle school years could catch them while their logical powers are in the ascendency and before their poetic powers have gone irretrievably underground.

In addition to the fact that poetry appeals to children's interests, it has the virtue of economy. Unlike the tortuous windings of prose, with its involved syntax, frequent absence of imagery, and tendency to retain obsolete locutions, poetry is often bright, concise, and intense. It has no need to disparage imagery or to employ logical and rhetorical devices. It stays closer to the level of lived experience.

But while poetry uses language economically, it challenges the writer to employ a wide range of thinking skills. It is unlikely that any other literary form demands greater precision, faithfulness to experience, or grace in the arrangement of elements. Poetry places intense demands on the writer's powers of judgment, conceptual and inferential abilities, and capacity to form or interpret analogies. The poet must perform an enormous variety of mental acts in a concerted fashion in order to achieve the maximum effect with the minimal employment of means.

There is good reason to suspect that poetic and philosophical thinking are naturally congenial. When philosophy first emerged in Greece, it did so in poetic form. The earliest philosophers—the pre-Socratics—were poet-philosophers who wrote in a crisp, aphoristic style. One is reminded very much of the terseness of these early thinkers when one listens to children discussing philosophical issues. There is the same condensation of thought, richness of imagery, brilliance of language, and far-reaching suggestiveness. Thus when we hear a seven-year-old remark, "When we are dead, we dream that we are dead," we marvel at the complex cosmology that such a conception hints at, while at the same time we cannot help recalling Heraclitus, in such sayings as: "Those awake have one ordered universe in common, but in sleep every man turns away to one of his own." Or, "Immortals are mortal, mortals immortal: [each] lives the death of the other and dies their life."

Philosophy and poetry are congenial, but what about poetry and logic? Isn't formal reasoning the very antithesis of poetic creation? An answer to this question is that poetic and logical construction are not antithetical but complementary; they actually reinforce one another. Thus formal logic makes it impossible to reverse a sentence such as "All onions are vegetables." The result would be, "All vegetables are onions," which is manifestly false. Yet, although such an inference would be unproductive from a logical point of view, it might be highly fruitful from the point of poetic construction. Imagine what a world might be like in which all vegetables were onions. Would cutting potatoes make one cry? Would carrots have many layers of skin? Thus invalid inferences, whose results are readily discarded in logical thinking, may turn a child's thoughts to counterfactual worlds in which fantasy reigns. So poetic and formal reasoning are two complementary activities, each demanding rigor, discipline, and coherence, each demanding that thoughts be marshaled energetically rather than in a casual, slovenly fashion.

Some children, who might normally have made the transition from poetry to prose rather smoothly, become incapacitated when confronted too suddenly with the demand for expository writing. The formal conditions of written prose, that is, spelling, grammar, and punctuation, place heavy and, in many ways, arbitrary demands on the thinking process. This sobering encounter with arbitrary demands accounts for some of the resistance children manifest when required to write prose. In the *Suki* program, priority is given to poetic models and poetic writing on the assumption that, if children can begin with what comes to them more easily, they might soon make the transition to what they normally find more difficult. This is not to say that students in the program should be limited to poetic forms of expression. On the contrary, they should be encouraged to express themselves in whatever forms they find most convenient. Literary form should not be a Procrustean bed: it should be adaptable to the literary or creative impulse. Whereas children should be encouraged to experiment with all forms of writing, different children may have strong preferences for very different sequences.

Expert prose has about it a highly polished finish, whereas poetry often appears to be rough textured, full of abrupt leaps, puzzling absences of transition, and surprisingly unconventional use of words. People who express ideas in prose accept and abide by conventional linguistic usages. But poetry involves experimentation with language itself, and there is nothing unusual about using poetry to express unconventional thoughts in unconventional ways. Little wonder then that children, with their natural playfulness, would find the more experimental medium more congenial to their native inclinations.

The negative effect on children of placing too great a weight on expository expression and too little on poetic expression cannot be overstated. If children are discouraged from experimentation with words, there is no way to prevent the inhibition from spreading to intellectual experimentation. If teachers want children to engage in thinking for themselves, they should give them ample opportunity to experience the delight of finding verbal arrangements marvelously taking place before their eyes as inchoate states of consciousness are transformed into poetic imagery and language.

It has been said that "nothing great happens without passion." Whether or not this is true for historical deeds, it does have some relevance with regard to thinking. Contrary to the popular notion that good thinking is cold and dispassionate, it would seem that people do their best thinking when they are stirred—and particularly when they are stirred by ideas.

Now, talking and writing are forms of thinking. At the same time, they are activities by means of which thinking skills can be sharpened. What incentives are needed to get children to talk and to write?

As far as talking is concerned, children need little incentive, and teachers spend a good deal of time trying to get children *not* to talk. It would seem that if children cannot find opportunities to talk constructively they will talk aimlessly, pointlessly, and even, on occasion, destructively. So the problem is not to prevent their talking but to stimulate it and to guide it in positive directions.

If children are to think well, they need to be moved to do so. They need to be stirred. How can they be provided with stirring experiences that will in turn lead to their talking and to their writing? Whatever form such experiences might take, they must seem to the child worth thinking about, talking about, and writing about.

Philosophical dialogue represents a generally shared intellectual experience in which a number of isolated individuals are transformed into a community of inquiry. In such a community, the conversations are impelled by the spirit of inquiry and guided by logical and philosophical considerations. The participants discover in themselves a need to be reasonable rather than contentious. In the process they become self-critical and responsible thinkers.

Children's conversations, when organized and disciplined, provide a superlative opportunity for the sharpening of thinking skills, because verbal communication requires that each participant engage simultaneously and sequentially in a considerable number of mental acts.

Another benefit of conversation is that children want to talk and to be listened to. It is better to utilize an activity children like, which also improves their reasoning power and respect for each other, than to attempt to teach them to think by compelling them to perform in ways that they find intrinsically unsatisfying.

To steer the discussions into productive and profitable directions, teachers will find it worthwhile to employ discussion plans. These discussion plans sometimes concentrate on the leading ideas in each chapter, while at other times they explicate certain minor points that are worthy of consideration. Although the questions in a discussion plan may vary widely among themselves, they are seldom of a random nature. The objectives are to help children develop concepts as well as make necessary connections and distinctions. A particular plan may explore a borderline issue, such as the question, "Can you have a friend whom you don't like?" Such questions lead readily to class discussion. Or the questions may be aimed at helping children recognize underlying assumptions, or discover more general classifications, or provide clear-cut illustrations or instances.

Successful classroom discussion heightens interest in the underlying issues and motivates children to want to express themselves further. We would all like to have the last word, and although we can seldom have our way in this regard when many people are talking together, there is nothing to prevent us from subsequently putting our thoughts into written form. It is both a satisfying and an elegant way of expressing ourselves while getting practice in writing at the same time.

Conversation is the great mediator here. In classroom discussions children express themselves articulately and succinctly, because they do not have to worry about the stylistic formalities of written prose. To facilitate the transition from spoken to written expression, a transition that often threatens to be traumatic, children should be encouraged to retain their conversational style. Gradually, as they develop confidence in their ability to maneuver in this strange new medium, they can be introduced to the formalities expected of the accomplished writer. If there is an easy, gradual transition from spoken to written conversational styles, the crisis of confidence that is so catastrophic for many students will be much less likely to occur.

The first steps have been taken by establishing an intellectually provocative environment in which the children can discuss in a free and open fashion themes that interest them. Nor is the atmosphere only an intellectual one: there are many affective qualities that are evoked in such a discussion with one's peers. The different opinions that are expressed are charged with personal feelings, and as more and more views are brought forth, these differences of feeling are accentuated. One begins to find how strongly one holds on to one's values and begins to identify them more clearly for oneself. Yet the spirit of inquiry prevails in the classroom community, and closer ties are being forged with one's fellow students. The classroom discussion thus succeeds in bringing forth from each individual a rich interplay of personal feelings and individual ideas.

One of the most felicitous features of an animated classroom conversation is that it combines a maximum of intellectual stimulation with only a fairly limited number of opportunities to contribute. As a result, most participants find themselves frustrated. Perhaps they had a single opportunity to speak, which they look back on as the high point of the entire discussion. But as they subsequently reflect on the matter, they begin to realize how many things followed from what they had to say and how important it would have been to elaborate on the point of view that had received such a truncated expression. In short, the very limitations and frustrations of classroom exchanges translate themselves into increased motivation for writing.

The teacher aims to create an environment in which the child will begin to say to himself or herself after the daily discussions, "I need to go on—I need to express myself more." Particular stress should be put on encouraging children to put down what they themselves said in the discussion and helping them to reflect on how their original position was broadened, changed, or reinforced by the discussion.

If anyone has been successful in dramatizing the way children can write poetry, it has been Kenneth Koch, as he has related in such books as *Rose, Where Did You Get That Red?* and *Wishes, Lies, and Dreams.*[2] Koch's method is to begin with excellent models, drawn from traditional poetry. The model is discussed by the children, and Koch endeavors to show them that it is an instance of a type. One is an example of poetic boasting. Another is an example of wishing. Still another model illustrates lying or dreaming. Koch does not encourage children to use meter or rhyme, and he does encourage them to use repetition at the beginnings of lines (e.g., I dreamed that. . . . I dreamed that. . . . I dreamed that. . . .). He likes freshness and spontaneity. The poems his pupils write do not generally seem to be the products of a great deal of reflection.

But poems written by Koch's pupils have a strength and sparkle to them that comes from encouraging students to write in their own language rather than in imitation of traditional models. Children tend to express themselves concisely, using few adverbs and adjectives. This is all to the good, because it produces a tough, vigorous, sinewy texture, with little of the sponginess or vapidity of children who are trying to "emote" or "express feelings" on command.

But if Koch can get children to devise poetry out of certain of their mental activities, such as wishing, lying, and dreaming, then what reason is there not to encourage them to explore a much wider range of their mental activities as possible channels of poetic expression? Children love their thoughts and consider them precious. They are proud of the ideas that occur to them, although they disparage such thoughts obediently when adults remark, "Oh, that's only in your head!" Why cannot their original thinking be as much a source of poetic inspiration as their feelings and their perceptions of the world around them?

Now that the students have been engaged in an animated discussion about a few themes in a chapter of *Suki,* the moment is propitious to encourage them to express their thoughts in written form. After all, many of them are probably bursting with things they would like to say but have not been able to introduce into the conversation. They can now look through their exercise books and consider the variety of alternative exercises on themes relevant to their discussion. The teacher can expedite matters by pointing out a number of exercises that seem particularly relevant. Perhaps some of the poetic models that are contained in the exercises can be read aloud during the discussion of possible alternative exercises.

The poetic models in the exercises are there to give children examples of how such exercises might be handled. The models are generally conversational in tone, so that students can be assured that a relaxed mode of expression is at least as acceptable as modes that are more formal and disciplined.

The function of these models is to indicate to the students what it is possible to do. It should be made clear to such students that the models are not to be imitated, although this occasionally can be done. Instead they are instances of types of writing, for which students are expected to provide still further instances, but one instance of the type need not closely resemble the other. For example, literary boasting may take the form, in one case, of a poem inventorying extravagant claims, and in another case it may take the form of a "tall-tale." Such exercises are legitimate devices for limbering up the literary imagination; it matters little whether they take the form of dramas, poems, literary essays, or short stories.

Although the exercises in an instructional manual provide the initial stimulus in getting children to write, teachers can reinforce the process by supplying their own writing exercises. For example, a teacher receives a child's poem in which there is the line, "The rain measles the window pane." She is surprised and delighted by the word "measles," circles it in red, and writes beside it, "Great!" So far, so good. But what has been learned? How can it be utilized for further teaching?

There is a maxim in the philosophy of science that, when a surprising fact is encountered, one should seek a covering rule from which the fact would follow as a matter of course. This is precisely what should be done in writing instruction. Here are the steps:

1. We notice a surprising linguistic usage. It shocks us because of its unconventionality. But the important thing is that it works. (Example: "The rain measles the window pane.")
2. We seek a rule from which the usage in question would follow and of which the usage in question would be an instance. (Example: "Use nouns as verbs.")
3. We construct exercises in which the students are encouraged to gain practice in the application of the rule. (Example: Suggest a series of nouns to be used as verbs. Alternatively, suggest a series of sentences, with verbs omitted, in which nouns are to be used.)
4. We consider, at least hypothetically, the possibility of using variants of the rule. (Examples: "Use verbs as nouns." "Use adjectives as adverbs.")

We have portrayed the movement from reading to talking to writing as having a more or less definite sequence. But we do not insist on this sequence. There is nothing amiss in a child's beginning to write during the reading. What we are saying is that these three components—reading, speaking, and writing—are intimately interconnected and that an effective course in writing should pay attention to that interconnection.

Some Aspects of Aesthetics Relevant to a Writing Program

When aesthetics is used to generate writing activities in the classroom, a number of considerations will in time show themselves to be more than ordinarily relevant. What follows are some guiding comments that may be helpful in treating these themes as they come up.

Experience

One of the reasons children often give for their not writing is that they have had no "experience," and they claim that prior experience is indispensable. This raises the question not simply of the relationship of experience to writing but of the very nature of experience.

The word "experience" has many meanings, at least some of which children have in mind when they use the term. Some of these specialized meanings are conveyed in such phrases as "sense experience," "experienced workers," "an experienced man of the world," the "experience of war," "life experience," and "knowledge by experience." Perhaps the wide variety of meanings that the word "experience" can suggest would be made easier to grasp by means of a basic distinction. This involves the division of experience into doing and undergoing. By "undergoing" is meant what happens when an individual encounters or endures something. "Doing" describes what happens when one contrives, arranges, or initiates. In other words, in anyone's life experience, one is sometimes agent, sometimes patient, and sometimes both. It is not always easy to distinguish those aspects of experience that are actively initiated from those that happen to someone without any complicity on his or her part. For example, is sleep something one does or something one undergoes? When a person has ideas, is it because one invented them or do they merely occur to one?

There is a further distinction that may be of some assistance in understanding the notion of "experience." This is the distinction between experienc*ing* as contrasted with what is experienc*ed*. At this very moment, each of us is experiencing; we are parts of situations and they are parts of us. Each of us is an aspect, at every moment of our lives, of a transaction with the world. These transactions leave their traces. Experience, like money in the form of capital, can be funded. This funded experience, this accumulated backlog of our past that we bring to bear upon every present experience, is that which has been experienc*ed*. Thus, if you are now listening to a piece of music, what is currently happening is a matter of experienc*ing*. But you also bring to bear upon the present moment the whole of your relevant past: your knowledge of music, your feeling for rhythm and melody, the criteria you have devised from distinguishing better works of music from worse ones, and your knowledge of the history of music. All of these latter represent your funded musical experience that is made use of and focused on each living moment of musical listening.

A third set of distinctions that may be helpful contrasts "mere experience," "an experience," and the "aesthetic quality of experience." When things happen in a fragmentary, partial, and uncoordinated way, or when an individual acts in a random and disorganized fashion, the experience that results is so shapeless and disconnected that it appears meaningless and is referred to as "mere experience." But sometimes an ordinary event may have a shape and organization of its own. There is the memorable dinner that proceeds by carefully arranged stages and has a beginning, a middle, and an end just like a story. Or there was that memorable storm that arose, reached a climax, and then subsided. In both cases, as we recall them, we tend to say "that was an experience!" *An* experience is half-way between the fragmentary, meaningless experience of everyday life and the fully developed, consciously contrived cases that we know of as aesthetic experiences. One reads *The Brothers Karamazov* and recognizes that happenings in the novel are not merely fortuitous events. The plot of the novel was carefully arranged by the writer so that the parts fit together perfectly. The reading of the novel therefore is a way of appropriating the aesthetic quality of experience. In at least this context, life experience becomes art.[3]

Relationship of Art to Experience

The problem of the relationship between art and experience echoes another problem traditionally associated with the philosophical theory of knowledge. People have always wondered if their knowledge of the external world was reliable. Knowledge is based on experience, primarily the experience derived from the senses. Can an individual trust his or her own senses? Is the world shaped, colored, scented in a way that precisely corresponds to the shapes, colors, and scents of one's experience? Or do the senses distort experience in some fashion so that his or her knowledge of the world is uncertain and unreliable?

Just as traditional epistemology (the philosophical theory of knowledge) questioned the relationship between the world and an individual's experience of the world, so aesthetics has frequently concerned itself with the relationship between a person's experience and his or her artistic expression of that experience. Do artistic productions accurately represent human experience, and is art under any obligation to either represent experience or refer to the world at large? Thus, in a sense, the aesthetic problem of the relationship between art and experience recapitulates the epistemological problem of the relationship between experience and the world.

Attention

One of the distinctive things about artists is not so much that they have a special kind of experience of life but that they pay closer attention to the experience they do have.

There is an explanation to people's inattentiveness, and to their frequently voiced complaint that the world is dull, arid, and empty. Inattention is often a form of self-protection. For people who are anxious, the way to cope with things that frighten them is to exclude such things from perception.

If students feel they are not being listened to, they may not listen to adults in return. If parents and teachers don't pay attention, children infer that they don't care. Often children will say that they don't care about anything because "nothing matters."

It has also been said that under certain circumstances attention evokes creativity. A boy who feels himself loved may become surprisingly more attractive; a girl who feels herself loved may seem to be more beautiful. Thus attentive care elicits a response from the person cared for, and that response can be sometimes very creative.

Art and Craft

Whether or not the arts can be taught has long been what might be called a philosophical question, that is, a question that remains undecided and subject to further discussion. It is known that some environments are more hospitable to artistic creativity than others, and it is for this reason that those who conduct studios and workshops seek to create a setting in which the creativity of their students can be evoked more readily. But it is not clear whether there are specific teaching techniques that will ensure that students produce works of art.

There is, however, a dimension of every field of art that consists in the technical or technological aspect of that field. This is the domain of craftsmanship; it comprises the knowable and teachable aspects of art.

With regard to writing, there is a great deal that is formal and teachable, for example, grammar, punctuation, metrics, and other elements of the craft of writing. When we seek to encourage students to be literate, we are merely concerned about their mastery of reading and writing as crafts, not as art forms. No doubt there are times when someone with an adequate knowledge of craftmanship is moved to create a work of art. Such happy occasions do occur, but they cannot be commanded. Nevertheless, if we can more or less painlessly acquaint children with the elements of writing as a craft, we may discover that occasional works appear that can be described as art. But if writing does not come easily to children, or if they feel overwhelmed by formal requirements that we place on them from the very start, they will produce neither writing as craft nor writing as art. Every writing exercise is nothing more than an invitation to verbal play, with the specification of a few rules. Children love to play, and they don't mind the games having a few rules. Each rule then becomes a part of their repertoire of craftsmanship.

What intimidates children is the demand that they produce "works of art," whose distinguishing characteristic is thought to be "the expression of feeling." No doubt all children have feelings, and no doubt art is a way of expressing those feelings. But it is also true that whereas some children do respond to the invitation to use art as a mode of expression, a great many other children do not. The idea of putting their feelings into words, can, for many children, have something very unpleasant about it. The stress on craftsmanship is more neutral. Its objective is not to use art as therapy or to compel the children to express what they don't care to express. Its aim is simply the educational one of enabling them to use their powers for their own purposes.

The other extreme is an exaggerated emphasis on formal requirements in the early stages of the teaching of writing. This can have as paralyzing an effect on the beginning student as the demand that the student express emotions.

Perfection and Rightness

In ordinary language, we use the word "right" to indicate that a part fits well within a larger whole. This notion of rightness as being the appropriateness of a part-whole relationship is not the only meaning that the word "right" can have. But it is one that works very well when dealing with art, just as it has considerable relevance in moral matters. Someone can walk into a room and have a feeling that something is not quite "right," then discover that a picture is hanging crookedly on the wall. Or one may hear a piece of music, feel again that something is not quite "right," and later find out that a violin string was improperly tuned. Everyone has had the experience of looking for just the "right" word to put into a certain spot in a paragraph. No other word will do, because no other word will fit the way the "right" word will fit.

If a person has written something that seems to express what he intended to express and that he feels no inclination to change in any way, he has reason to call his work "perfect." It works well and suits his purposes. It is appropriate to call a work "perfect" when all its parts are right.

Aesthetic Relationships

There are many ways in which people may be connected with other people or with things, and of course there are many ways in which things have connections with other things. There are economic relationships, political relationships, personal relationships, and of course aesthetic relationships.

Aesthetic relationships occur within contexts or situations or wholes. Each whole is made up of a number of parts. The relationships of the parts to one another or of parts to wholes are aesthetic relationships. This may, of course, be an oversimplification. It may well be questioned whether, for example, every part-whole relationship is in fact aesthetic. But it would seem that no part-part or part-whole relationship necessarily falls outside the range of the aesthetic. One may think that the relationship of a door to a house is purely functional, but of course it is certainly subject to aesthetic appraisal and one may find that the door is "beautifully" related to the rest of the house. The same would be true of the relationship of a nose to a face or a tree to a landscape. But because much of human experience is fragmentary and does not consist of wholes, strictly aesthetic relationships are lacking from much experience and are encountered only in works of art.

Meaning

In philosophy, there is a running argument as to whether words alone have meanings or whether life and nature can have meaning too. The issue is never settled. But even if the problem of meaning is limited to linguistic meaning, it remains formidable.

A popular theory has it that linguistic meaning is use. In other words, it is possible to tell what a word means by examining the different ways in which it is ordinarily used. Some of those who have considered this problem find the "meaning equals use" formula too broad and eclectic. It embraces too many divergent and exotic usages. They therefore propose that the meaning of a term is to be identified with the rule that governs the usage of that term. But what is the rule? It would seem to be little different from what has traditionally been called a definition. If meanings were to be identified with strictly definitional meanings, the problem would be a fairly restricted and manageable one, since the literature on the logic of definition is fairly well established. But the problem remains that in ordinary language the word "meaning" has a much broader scope than does "definition."

A number of philosophers have been inclined to wonder if meanings could not be relationships. There is an obvious reason why this proposal should be attractive. Whenever anyone looks for meanings in things or in one's perceptions of things and fails to find them, he or she comes to think of the whole enterprise as futile, because "there are no meanings." But if meanings were relationships, the quest would not be futile at all. Relationships are not perceived in the same way things are perceived. But there are few people who would question whether or not they exist. When one thing causes another thing to happen, there is a causal relationship, even though the causal process has not actually been perceived. For example, when one takes aspirin, one's headache may go away, and although one knows that there is a connection, one has not actually perceived it directly. Likewise, there are relationships between forks and knives, trees and apples, parents and children, beginnings and ends of stories, and people to their government. But none of these may be the direct objects of perception. Yet there is no question that these relationships are highly meaningful, and the case can be made that they in fact constitute meaning. In other words, meaning is not some intangible effect of relationships but consists of those relationships themselves. Whatever relationships a thing has with other things and with a particular individual constitute its meaning.

To understand the meanings in a work of literature is to explore relationships to be found among the words and between the words and oneself. On the other hand, to express meanings one must find connections or relationships that will do that job. This is why the creation of works of art, such as poems, has a way of making existence meaningful.

V

**Reflections
on Practice:
Implications for
Educational
Reform**

11 Constructing a Curriculum to Improve Thinking and Understanding

The chief concern of education was traditionally held to be the transmission of knowledge from one generation to another. What the older generation knew was taught to and learned by the younger generation; in the process, the content of the transmitted knowledge remained virtually unmodified. And so long as education was conceived to be the initiation of the child into the understandings of the adult world, the focus of education was on learning what adults already knew or claimed to know.

The great paradigm shift in the history of education has been the redesign of education to have thinking rather than learning as its target. The major philosopher associated with this shift was John Dewey, although he was of course powerfully influenced by Peirce and G. H. Mead. But it was primarily Dewey who portrayed the natural course of thinking in everyday life as a concatenation of problem-solving efforts, who saw science as the purification and perfection of those efforts, and who saw education as a growth-producing, meaning-producing strengthening of the fallible thinking process indigenous to all human beings.

Once better thinking (reasonableness) was accepted as the goal of education, other things began to fall, domino-fashion, into place. The partnership between the adult and child could no longer be likened to that between producer and consumer or between the tribe and the initiate. The teacher could no longer be conceived of as a gardener who can feed and nourish the flowers in the flower-beds, thereby helping them to become the blooms that they were genetically driven to become all along. Instead, the teacher became part of an adult intervention whose intent it was to liberate the thinking process in the student, so that students begin to think for themselves, rather than parrot the thinking of the teacher or the textbook.

The notion that the child's mind is in a state of maximum integrity when it is relaxed and undisturbed is as specious as the notion that a particle of matter is in its true state only when it is at rest. Minds, like particles, are whatever they do, and that includes whatever they can be made to do by experimental interventions. The live and conscious human being thinks as naturally as it breathes, but getting it to think better requires strategies of considerable complexity. For the problem of epistemology is no longer how the static, empty cannister of a mind becomes filled with representations of a static reality but how a fluent and flexible thinking process engages and interpenetrates its environment successfully. The inexhaustible novelty of nature cannot be grappled with by minds that are rigid and mechanical: mere thinking—like mere learning—is not enough. It follows that knowing and understanding are not mental activities that are simply given: they must be constructed, generated. Hence the need for a generative epistemology, in which an initial educational intervention ignites the mind to inquire into the problematic as well as the settled aspects of the world, and all the while that original act of ignition sets off train after train of sparks and lightning-like repercussions within the mind itself. The traditional problems of just what it is we understand (epistemology) and how we have come to understand it (genetic epistemology) are then seen to be inextricably involved in and dependent on the modes of inquiry in which the mind can be taught to engage and the success of those engagements. For once the process of education can be seen to encompass both concept formation and the construction of conceptual schemes of reality, it is no longer possible to disregard the generative role of education for better thinking or the contributions made by the student to the process and products of inquiry.

Nevertheless, the problem remains of how specifically to involve students in the inquiry process, how to introduce them at least as much to the demonstrably problematic aspects of the subject matter under investigation as to the purportedly settled aspects. How are students to learn to engage in inquiry and to work within the specific traditional academic disciplines if they lack the cognitive skills—the reasoning and inquiry and concept-formation and translation skills—which are a prerequisite for such involvement?

One possible approach is to make use of the discipline of philosophy. What philosophy offers is its familiarity with the reasoning process, its scrupulous approach to conceptual analysis, and its own engagement in self-correcting cognitive inquiry. Further, philosophy provides an insistence on the development of a critical stance, on examining the problematic as well as the settled, and on reasonableness in argument, explanation, and dialogue.

Does this mean that elementary school philosophy is an instance of applied philosophy? One could say so only with reservations. There is no inherent difficulty in applying traditional philosophy to problems that emerge in such adult-centered areas as medicine, law, and business. But traditional academic philosophy, with its insistence on technical terminology and the devising of elaborate and intricate arguments, would no doubt be anathema to children. Still, the doing of philosophy is something children might find quite agreeable, if it meant conversing about philosophical topics in ordinary language disciplined by logical constraints. And if children could not readily be introduced to an already existing community of inquirers, what would be wrong with converting the existing classroom into an ongoing community of inquiry? This is applied philosophy in the double sense that it is applied recursively to the discipline to be taught as much as to problems in the world at large.

The objection that insistently surfaces at this point can be put quite concisely: we need thinking, but we don't need philosophy. Thinking can be improved in each and every discipline, so as to strengthen thinking in those disciplines. Why, it is asked, add an esoteric subject like philosophy to an already crowded curriculum?

The reply to this objection can be equally pointed. We recognize reading and writing as fundamental to education, and we know that these skills should be utilizable within each and every discipline in the curriculum. Yet we do not entrust the study of reading and writing to the various disciplines. We recognize that reading and writing are not merely technical skills, for through them we acquire and express our most fundamental values and forms of life. We therefore entrust the teaching of these skills to the humanities and specifically, in this country, to the teachers of English literature because we know better than to confuse mere literacy with quality education. Similarly, the cultivation of thinking should take place within that discipline, philosophy, which is best prepared to improve the child's thinking and to provide pathways by means of which it can cross over to the other disciplines. Indeed, more than a few philosophers have conceived of philosophy as simply excellent thinking, and even if this claim is an oversimplification, it suggests that the analogy between good writing as literature and good thinking as philosophy has considerable plausibility. We are now in a better position to understand the claim of philosophy to be the discipline that prepares us to think in the disciplines.

If children can do philosophy, then presumably they can do metaphysics, logic, ethics, aesthetics—and epistemology. And if they can do epistemology, then presumably this will result in a proliferation of epistemological meanings and understandings that the classroom discussion of epistemic issues has engendered and has subjected to critical analysis. Nevertheless, whether the topic under consideration be epistemological (or logical or aesthetic or whatever), the communal inquiry into it takes into account its ramifications into other branches of philosophy. Just as one cannot ignore the epistemological and logical aspects of ethical issues, so one cannot ignore the ethical, logical, and other philosophical aspects of epistemological issues.

At the same time, it must be said that a children's community of epistemological inquiry does not exclude a concern for the traditional domains of epistemology proper and genetic epistemology. That is, the children in the community can be quite alert to their own efforts to justify their knowledge claims by assessment of supporting evidence or sustaining reasons, and they can be most perceptive when it comes to detailing how they happen to know what they know.

Consider these alternative approaches to children's understanding. The first, the Piagetian, aims to trace the limits of the child's intellectual grasp by posing a series of problems (e.g., "Are there more flowers than roses here?" or "I like onions but they make me cry so I don't like them.") and determining at what age the child can cope successfully with them. This information is then accumulated and organized so as to produce a series of stages of comprehension. The second approach, the neo-Piagetian, notes that the questions that perplex the child are often syntactically ill formed or obscure, as a result of the inquirer's deliberate ambiguity or vagueness. (Thus the question, "Which is greater?" assumes that the adult's criterion of greatness is correct and the child's, if it differs from the adult's, is incorrect. But the term "greater" is inherently vague and can accommodate a variety of criteria, not just one.) The second approach would therefore remove the obscurities from the inquirer's questions so as to determine more accurately the child's comprehension capacity. The third approach, the generative, contends that the discussion between the first two approaches is merely over whether or not to tailor the questions to the child; neither approach attempts to strengthen the child's intellectual capacity so as to deal with either type of question, should it be asked. The third approach therefore involves sensitizing children to instances of ambiguity and vagueness, while strengthening their questioning, reasoning, and discussion skills, so as to enable such children to cope with the perplexing aspects of natural language that they are bound to encounter in daily life. The generative approach contends that the choice is not between posing more or less intellectually taxing questions but between neglecting or strengthening the child's capacity to inquire. It is not a matter of staking out the cognitive limitations of the child, but of increasing the child's cognitive powers. The remainder of this chapter will consider more concretely how this can be done.

The seven programs in the Philosophy for Children curriculum propose a myriad of philosophical problems for children to ponder, as often epistemelogical in nature as logical, ethical, or metaphysical. For example, the novel *Pixie* (in a program for the same age level as *Kio and Gus,* but stressing reasoning in language rather than reasoning in science), after raising countless questions about classes, families, rules, relationships, and analogies, concludes on the last line with Pixie suggesting that the great unresolved mystery is how we know anything. But if *Pixie* is concerned most insistently with relationships (particularly similarity and difference, and especially those instances of recondite similarities among things manifestly different and recondite differences among things obviously similar, for it is sensitization to precisely such relationships that helps strengthen the child's distinction-making and connection-making skills), *Kio and Gus* tends to concentrate on concept formation—in particular, the analysis, clarification, and interpretation of scientific concepts drawn from zoology and ecology. But both programs seek to strengthen the child's capacity to reason, whether about relationships or about concepts.

To see just how this is done, it will be necessary to consider briefly the strategy underlying the construction of the curriculum as well as some of the presuppositions of that strategy.

Presupposition 1. The child's lower-order and higher-order cognitive skills are not acquired progressively with age but are in formation in the pre-linguistic stages, and this process of formation is much intensified and accelerated in the phase of language acquisition.

Presupposition 2. Children can and need to deal with abstractions long before the onset of the so-called formal stage.

Presupposition 3. Cognitive deficiency of persons of any age may be due to lack of relevant experience, feebleness of reasoning powers, or both. Whether a person thinks well is to a considerable extent dependent on how much experience he or she has had and how well he or she utilizes that experience. It follows that cognitive maturity is not to be arbitrarily defined by limiting its characteristics to skills that adults, owing to their greater experience, can perform better than children. For example, generalizing requires a multiplicity of experiences, but giving examples or counterexamples or reasons can be accomplished with only limited experience. Generalization may therefore be easier for adults, but this is hardly a good reason for taking generalization to be more a hallmark of intellectual maturity than the other skills. (Likewise, the fact that children are more fluent and fertile producers of similes and metaphors cannot be discounted on the grounds that figurative language is inherently of less importance than literal language.)

Presupposition 4. Children taught different subjects in isolation from one another cannot be expected to synthesize those subjects. To teach a course in logic and a course in botany provides few grounds for expecting children to think logically about botanical matters.

In the construction of the Philosophy for Children curriculum, the following strategies were employed.

Strategy 1. Thinking skill performance can be improved by (1) giving children practice in the skills; (2) introducing them to the rationale underlying the skills; and (3) providing opportunities to apply the skills. This means, in effect, that the early elementary school curriculum stresses cognitive skill practice with a minimum of explanation; middle school children study the underlying system of explanation—that is, the logic of the language in which they speak, read, write, and think; at the junior high and secondary school levels, students are shown how to apply to the problems of adolescent and adult life the skills that they can now both use and understand.

Strategy 2. Given the three stages of curriculum development just noted, the second stage, conscious logical proficiency, may be taken as of pivotal importance. (It corresponds roughly to the beginnings of the so-called formal stage of child development.) Reflection on the program (*Harry Stottlemeier's Discovery*) produced for this stage shows the skills required to deal proficiently with this portion of the curriculum, as well as the concepts taken for granted (more or less as "primitive terms") within this program. It then becomes possible to prepare the programs for the younger students, building into them those skills and concepts to be needed in the subsequent program. For example, *Harry Stottlemeier's Discovery* takes for granted such notions as class, relationship, and rule; these notions are dealt with in the earlier book, *Pixie*. *Pixie* in turn takes for granted various concepts and skills that can be discussed or fostered in still earlier programs such as *Elfie,* which is for grades K-2. (*Elfie* concentrates on distinction-making, connection-making, and comparison, skills that prepare the way for the more sophisticated treatments of classification and comparison to be found in *Pixie.* Note, by the way, that it is the curricular treatments that are sequenced and nested, not necessarily the competencies.)

Strategy 3. As can be readily inferred from the discussion of the previous strategy, the educating of young people to become reasonable entails the crafting of a logically sequenced curriculum. Such a curriculum contracts sharply with empirically sequenced curricula, each portion of which has been devised to correspond to already existing stages of cognitive development derived from descriptions of children's behavior in non-educational contexts. If we accept the value of logicality as a component of reasonableness, then logicality has a normative value in the construction of the curriculum. It stipulates how the curriculum is to be organized, and such organization functions paradigmatically for students seeking to discover how they ought to think.

Strategy 4. The curriculum must display affective as well as cognitive continuity. The confrontation between the child and the curriculum must produce excitation of a kind that invites reflection and inquiry. There must be intellectual challenge, but so presented as to be emotionally stimulating. It is this provocation that motivates the children to inquire into the situation in which they find themselves; yet it is the curriculum that sets the tone, so to speak, and provides the situational quality that guides the resulting inquiry. This requirement is met, in the Philosophy for Children curriculum, by providing texts in the form of children's novels.

Strategy 5. The fictional children in the novels are bound to serve as models, and therefore they cannot be merely energetic, playful, but essentially thoughtless children, nor yet can they be children whose sole curiosity is to find out what adults already know. Rather, they are fictional models of children who are intrigued by what is problematic in their experience and sufficiently provoked by it to want to inquire into it. And yet, delicious as the acquisition of the sought-for knowledge may be, it is the process of inquiry itself to which the fictional children find themselves committed, by virtue of their huge enjoyment of it, rather than to incidental outcomes in the form of knowledge increments. Moreover, the portrayal of the children in the novel is of thinking children, children engaging in mental acts and wondering about those very acts, so that what is characterized is the life of thought itself—or the life of youthful thought, at any rate—in all of its dialectical complexity and with a fair amount of its illogicality and irrationality.

Strategy 6. The instructional manuals provided the teachers seek to maintain the inquisitive momentum to which the novel gave the initial impetus. They do this by means of a profusion of questioning and discussion plans, so designed as to raise still more questions rather than pave the way for explicit answers. Thus the manuals aim to foster dialogue and reasoning about the issues raised in the novels.

Strategy 7. Inquiry is necessarily a self-correcting process, and the correction involved is not only the correction of errors but is also the correction of partiality. To correct the partiality of what is gained by observing from a single perspective, we must take into account what is to be observed from other perspectives, and still others. The greater the number of perspectives, the greater the comprehensiveness of information and evidence, and the more we move in the direction of impartiality. Thus inquiry is necessarily perspectival, social, and communal. When a class moves to become a community of inquiry, it accepts the discipline of logic and scientific method; it practices listening to one another, learning from one another, building on one another's ideas, respecting one another's points of view, and yet demanding that claims be warranted by evidence and reasons. Once the class as a whole operates upon these procedures, it becomes possible for each member to internalize the practices and procedures of the others, so that one's own thought becomes self-correcting and moves in the direction of impartiality and objectivity. At the same time, each member internalizes the attitude of the group toward its own project and procedures, and this translates into care for the tools and instruments of inquiry as well as respect for the ideals (e.g., truth) that serve both to motivate the process and to regulate it. For the purposes of generative epistemology (or of a generative approach in any other discipline or subdiscipline), the creation of classroom communities of inquiry is quite indispensable.

These then are the presuppositions and the strategies involved when philosophy is to be employed on the elementary school level; they therefore apply equally well to the utilization of epistemology at that level. Let us consider how this may be done at the early elementary school level.

By and large, the textbooks elementary school students use expose them to conclusions rather than to evidence, to verdicts rather than to testimony. Children are considered incapable of sifting the evidence for themselves or of offering alternative hypotheses that could be entertained by even the most widely stretched imagination. They will be told, for example, that "the moon always presents the same side of itself," but this statement of fact has been achieved only by sifting through a spate of epistemological preambles, such as

It is claimed that the moon shows us only one side of itself.
It is believed that the moon shows us only one side of itself.
It has been observed that the moon shows us only one side of itself.
It is known that the moon shows us only one side of itself.
It is thought that the moon shows us only one side of itself.

Now, unless students are introduced to the epistemological conditions that are prefaces to any statement of fact, they cannot assess the warrant for that fact. Likewise, if they are inexperienced in comparing the cognitive reliability of the various mental acts (e.g., believing, knowing, supposing), their capacity for such assessment is further compromised.

Take another case. Students are told that Newton developed the theory of gravitation after having observed an apple falling from a tree and after having used the theory to explain the rotation of the moon around the earth. But unless the students can grasp the generalization Newton engaged in, his formation of a hypothesis, his testing of it in the case of an apparent counterinstance (the moon), while yet recognizing the legitimacy of the analogy between the apple and the moon—unless students are already acquainted, in other words, with the reasoning and inquiry procedures Newton employed, they can hardly be expected to appreciate his achievement.

These examples point to the desirability of preparing children, at the very least, to observe the hygienic precautions associated with good reasoning prior to exposing them to the subject matters of specific disciplines. For example, suppose children have been through one of the early childhood Philosophy for Children programs and have come to recognize, through various opportunities for practice, that "what is true of the part is not necessarily true of the whole, and what is true of the whole is not necessarily true of the part." (This is, in any event, how they would characterize the fallacies of composition and division.) Now suppose that, as part of an ecology lesson, they encounter the statement, "Water is colorless in small quantities." Immediately they are on the alert. "Does it follow that water is colorless in large quantities?" they ask, and they proceed to answer their own question, "No," they say, "and the proof is that the sea is blue." Now suppose that someone in the class asserts that water is colorless, so it must be odorless. Again they are alert and critical: must it follow? And again they may argue the matter until someone offers the counterinstance of her mother's perfume, which is colorless but "smells wonderful." Yet, without such practice in the making of reliable perceptual inferences, these students might have all too readily agreed that, if water is colorless, it follows that it is odorless. (These questions are derived from an exercise in *Wondering at the World*, the instructional manual accompanying *Kio and Gus*. Other questions raised in the same exercise have to do with whether, when freezing water expands, there is actually more of it, and whether water is a gas since its components are gases.)

As children discuss the circumstances that would be required to make a given assertion true (or false), they begin to realize in considerably greater depth the actual meaning of that assertion. And when they discuss the notion of truth, they begin to realize the complexity of a notion they may earlier have taken for granted. What philosophy teaches us is the risk of taking for granted what we should have more carefully attended to, as well as the possibility of discovering, beneath everything prosaic and ordinary and routine, a universe of extraordinary richness and variety, at which we can only marvel.

The prospect of elementary school epistemology may boggle some minds, but only in an unreflective education—which is perhaps no education at all—would students be expected to know and understand without having a critical appreciation of what knowing and understanding are all about. If we expect them to examine any natural phenomenon in terms of its conditions and consequences, we can hardly exempt knowing and understanding, which are no less natural, from being examined in terms of their conditions and consequences. No indictment of existing education is more serious than the charge that it fosters uncritical rather than critical dispositions. It is difficult to see how the addition of anything but epistemology—and even more important of philosophy in general—can remedy that deficiency.

12 Preparing Teachers to Teach for Thinking

If grade-school philosophy has an Achilles' heel, it would seem to be in the area of teacher preparation. The construction of curriculum materials for children is not an obstacle, for the primary sources already exist in the form of the basic writings of the philosophical tradition. All that is needed is their translation into a form suitable for children, and it has been amply demonstrated that this can be done successfully. But what about teacher education?

The teaching of philosophy requires teachers who are disposed to examine ideas, to engage in dialogical inquiry, and to respect the humanity of the children being taught. Present modes of teacher preparation are not conspicuously noteworthy for developing these teacher dispositions. Indeed, it may well be that the only teachers who fully possess these dispositions are those who had brought them half-formed to the schools of education they had attended. And indeed, those who have worked in the area of teacher education in philosophy for children have found that there is little difficulty in working with teachers who are already "half-way there"; much less receptive are those would-be teachers who are little inclined to enjoy free-wheeling intellectual discussions and who do not suffer gladly children's tentative, unsophisticated, and uninhibited explorations of their mortal lot. On the other hand, the very existence of grade-school philosophy exercises a magnetic attraction for those who do possess the necessary dispositions but who would not ordinarily have considered elementary school teaching within the range of their career alternatives. Needless to say, the accomplishment of a turnover of teacher applicants in the field in which the trickle of those with intellectual sparkle and vitality swells to a steady flow is likely to be the result of a long and arduous process of reform in teacher education, along with the steady growth of intellectual excitement in the classroom, as the ever-present incentive. But it can be done, and it will have to be done if those who currently teach for rote learning are to be replaced by those who teach for active, energetic, and excellent thinking.

As mentioned, the problem of curriculum development in grade-school philosophy is to translate traditional philosophical works into materials children can readily understand and discuss. The problem of translation is also at the heart of the teacher education process. Professors of education tend to employ a restricted gamut of teaching styles. At one extreme, they lecture in their own language, and the would-be teachers must devote themselves assiduously to trying to understand what is being said in that language. At the other extreme, professors of education speak the language of the teacher (which they somehow assume to be the language of the classroom). Seldom do professors of education attempt to educate teachers in the same language as teachers are compelled to employ in educating children. Their failure to do so places the entire burden of translation on the teacher, but they provide the teacher with few clues as to how it is to be done. The teachers do the best they can: they do what they have been trained to do—they teach as they have been taught. This in turn places the burden of translation on the child, who must not only struggle to understand what is being taught but must first translate it from some unknown scholarly language into his or her own.

The only way to avoid this exercise in futility is for professors of education to translate the contents of their disciplines into the language of the classroom and then, using that language, educate candidates for teacher certification in the same language and using the same pedagogical methods as those teachers will later employ themselves with children. Such an overhaul is a big order, obviously, but if it entails junking the lecture method, except for certain specialized purposes, so be it. If it entails going through the curriculum with the teachers in the very same manner as the teachers will go through it with the children, so be it. We cannot continue to place on the teacher the entire burden of translating a scholarly curriculum into children's language, for we know what will happen: the teacher will deposit that entire burden into the lap of the child.

There is another problem with the traditional approach to teacher education, and its historical roots go very, very deep. At one time it was taken for granted that to teach a subject required nothing more than that one possessed the knowledge—or some portion of it—amassed in that discipline. This made for generation after generation of teachers who may have known their subjects but did not know how to teach them. In time, the pendulum swung to the opposite extreme: teachers who had been drilled in "methods of teaching" but who did not know their subjects. The time is long overdue for the pendulum to swing back, although perhaps no more than half-way back, to teachers who know enough about their disciplines to teach them and who are skilled enough in instructional methodology to be able to teach them well. In other words, it is time to strike a balance between instructional methods and educational content.

Given the present state of things educational, this is an appropriate occasion for initiating suitable reforms in teacher preparation. There is a general sense that the content of the knowledge bases of the individual disciplines is rapidly becoming obsolete as far as the rapidly developing disciplines are concerned and increasingly irrelevant as far as the students are concerned. On the other hand, there is no corresponding improvement taking place in pedagogy that would compensate for the declining importance of sheer knowledge as an educational goal, in the way that refineries resort to higher-grade processing technologies as they must contend with lower and lower grades of ore. There is a limit to how often we can "go back to basics." If there is to be a genuine shift of emphasis to "teaching for thinking," it is unlikely that the pedagogical techniques that were far from successful when the stress was on memorization will be any more successful with this change in educational objectives. It will take more than increased wait time, better eye contact, and more frequent use of "why?" to make education truly reflective. It takes more than the fine tuning of standard classroom management techniques to get students to be thoughtful about their culture and its possibilities.

The problem is, where are we to find a paradigm case of teaching for thinking that will have a bearing on the way teaching might be conducted in all the disciplines, whether occasionally or consistently? Is there any discipline whose very subject matter demands teaching for thinking and can be satisfied with nothing less? The answer is that all of them do, but it may be more difficult to get away with *not* doing so in philosophy than in any other discipline. Philosophy and thinking—or perhaps philosophy and the quest for better thinking—go hand in hand. What this means for the topic under discussion is that the methodology of teacher education in philosophy is likely to be highly instructive for the development of patterns of teacher education generally. This is more true of the preparation of elementary school philosophy teachers than that of college philosophy instructors, since the latter receive little or no pedagogical enlightenment during their course of studies. What will be discussed here will therefore be restricted to the education of future teachers of grade-school philosophy and is more a description of present practice than a proposal for future implementation.

We begin with the fact that a philosophy curriculum for the elementary school exists: it is not just on the drawing boards or in the minds of educational theoreticians. It is not just for one grade level but spans the entire length of the K–12 sequence, with more than enough material for each grade level. This does not mean that it is now complete; perhaps it will never be complete. But the fact that it exists means that teachers can be prepared in their seminars and workshops to do what they will actually be doing on a day-to-day basis with children. The materials are already accessible to children; there is little need to translate them into something thought to be even more accessible.

We should not underestimate the extent to which teacher educators are dominated by the curriculum materials produced by commercial publishers. Such materials are prepared by teachers and curriculum developers with considerable classroom experience, and the materials reflect the conservative, traditional nature of that experience rather than the work of those at the frontier of educational exploration. There are, of course, concessions to what is considered to be trendy, as "thinking skills" are "in" at the moment. And there is great to-do about building a certain "user-friendliness" into the materials. Unfortunately, teacher education can be no better than the materials used in the teacher-training process. Dumbing down the curriculum need not lead to dumbing down the way teachers are taught to teach, but it generally does. Texts and tests are the engines that drive the schooling operation. The professor of education is a prisoner of the same system as that in which the teacher is incarcerated, even if, in the long run, it is the children who suffer most from that system.

Current teacher-education practice in preparing grade-school philosophy teachers takes place in four stages.

The preparation of teacher educators. The candidates for such training are drawn from the ranks of those who have a strong philosophy background: college philosophy instructors, holders of doctorates of philosophy, and those of comparable educational background. (Outside the United States, for example, teachers in lycées or gymnasia frequently have as rich a background of course work in philosophy as do recipients of the doctorate of philosophy in this country.)

It has been speculated that, as far as a philosophy background is concerned, the high qualifications demanded of the prospective teacher educator constitute a major potential bottleneck as far as the future dissemination of Philosophy for Children is concerned. In response, it must be said that (1) this hasn't happened yet: the production of trainers has kept pace with the demand for them; (2) philosophers are more likely than non-philosophers to have the necessary background in logic, which trainers must rely on to teach reasoning successfully; and (3) philosophers usually have the background in epistemology, ethics, and aesthetics that provides the common bond, or mortar, for holding the separate bricks of the educational edifice together. On the whole, it is easier to look for philosophers and prepare them to be teacher trainers than to look for professional educators and prepare them in the ways of philosophy. As for the alleged scarcity of philosophers, the answer is the same: the demand can be expected to create the supply.

Prospective teacher educators attend a ten-day workshop in which they are exposed to the curriculum, can conduct individual sessions, and discuss salient issues at length. (Examples of such topics are moral education, the relationship of Philosophy for Children to traditional philosophy, the teaching of reasoning, and procedures for working effectively with school districts, including the use of reasoning tests and the relationships to be established with school administrators.)

Subsequently, the prospective teacher educator serves as a "philosopher in residence" in a classroom setting for four to six weeks, so as to gain experience in working with children, a prerequisite for establishing credibility with teachers. Whenever possible, the novice works for a time in tandem with a more experienced trainer before launching on an independent career.

Preparing teachers: The curriculum exploration stage. A teacher education workshop usually consists of fifteen or twenty teachers and a teacher educator. (Some of the more intensive workshops, which continue for five or more consecutive days, are so arduous that two teacher educators are needed. It is not unusual for one of these to be a non-philosopher.) These curriculum-examination seminars range from three to fourteen days. The shorter ones deal with but a single program, such as that for fifth- and sixth-graders. The others generally deal with two programs, such as a third- and fourth-grade as well as a fifth- and sixth-grade program. This provides several advantages: it prepares each teacher in greater depth, a highly desirable benefit, and it enables the school system to select teachers with greater flexibility, so that the workshop may be composed of, say, seven third- and fourth-grade teachers and seven fifth- and sixth-grade teachers, rather than fourteen from the same level. Each teacher then teaches the program appropriate for his or her level but is also acquainted with the other program. The more widely acquainted teachers are with the entire curriculum, the more astutely they are likely to approach any portion of it.

By and large, teachers are expected to experience this stage in much the same way that their future students are to experience it. They begin by taking turns reading the assigned section aloud. This gives them experience in hearing the language of the text as well as in listening to one another. Taking turns is an exercise in moral reciprocity, and the collective effect of the ensuing discussion is a sharing of the meanings of the text through their appropriation by the group as a whole. Thus, even in the very first stage of exploring the curriculum, the members of the seminar begin to experience themselves as members of a community of shared experience and shared meanings, the first step toward becoming members of a community of inquiry.

Some teachers object to having to read aloud, or to having their students read aloud—what is known in the classroom as round-robin. They favor silent reading, just as they prefer paper-and-pencil exercises to classwide discussions. But these classroom management moves can be self-defeating, if their net effect is to isolate each student from the other students and the variety of meanings they attain from their own reflections. To pen up the individual student in private practice is in effect to deprive that student of the vital experience of intellectual cooperation, of building on one another's ideas, of savoring the freshness of one another's interpretations, of defending one's ideas when criticized, of enjoying intellectual solidarity with others, and of sensing one's own intellectual integrity when revising one's views in the light of new evidence.

It is not uncommon to confound thinking *by* oneself with thinking *for* oneself and to be under the mistaken impression that solitary thinking is equivalent to independent thinking. Nevertheless, we are never so moved to think for ourselves as when we find ourselves engaged in shared inquiry with others. The way to protect children from uncritical thinking in the presence of others is not to compel them to think silently and alone but to invite them to think openly and critically about contestable issues. For this to happen in the classroom, it must first happen in the teacher-training seminar. It is only when teachers have had actual experience of a community of inquiry that they can foster the development of one with their own students.

Following the shared reading of the text, the teacher educator invites the class to propose the agenda for the discussion to follow. The formulation of this invitation will differ depending on the age of the students. With older students, one might ask, "What *puzzles* (or perplexes) you about this passage?" so as to focus attention on what is problematic in the subject matter rather than on that which is settled. With younger students, one might ask, "What *interests* you about this passage?" so as to ensure that questions and comments emerge out of a genuine student involvement with the issues. With very young students, these ways of issuing the invitation may be unsuccessful, because small children are unused to being asked for their opinion by adults and may be somewhat bewildered. It is better simply to ask, "What do you *like* about this paragraph (or page)?" and move from there into the discussion.

As student comments are received, they are written on the chalkboard as close to verbatim as possible. (Every change by the teacher educator or teacher risks deviating from the student's intended meaning, with consequent loss of the student's sense of ownership.) It is customary to identify by name the student (whether teacher or child) who has contributed the statement or question, for this is tangible evidence to the student that his or her participation and originality are respected.

The form of the student's contribution may vary considerably. Some raise questions; some note contrasts or dichotomies (such as real versus artificial, art versus nature, or life versus art); some simply indicate that there is a single concept (e.g., truth) that they would like to discuss.

The instructor has several options at this point. A favorite technique among teachers but probably of lesser interest to students is to group the contributions that have been written on the chalkboard. The grouping, although having some value as practice in cognitive classification, also tends to be abstract, tedious, and time-consuming. Another strategy is to poll the students in the classroom for the question they would most like to discuss first. Still another is to ask a student who has hitherto been silent to select a question for discussion. Or, one can ask the original contributors to expand on their contributions or to criticize someone else's or their own. Finally, one can sometimes have recourse to random techniques, such as picking a card or using a spinner. The task of the instructor is to keep alive the interest generated by the reading and to help it carry over into the discussion, animating it further when it appears to flag and striving always to generate student-student rather than student-teacher dialogue.

In preparation for the class session, the instructor has reviewed the instructional manual and has selected a group of promising exercises and discussion plans. As the discussion proceeds, one or another of these exercises can be introduced, so that the discussions can be better focused philosophically and so that the texture of philosophical practice alternates between free and open discussion on the one hand and specific applications on the other.

Preparing teachers: The modeling stage. It cannot be taken for granted that the practice that teachers engage in during their workshop will be so deeply etched on their consciousness that they will have no difficulty carrying it over into their respective classrooms. Often they feel troubled and defensive about their limited knowledge of philosophy in contrast to that of their trainer, and this may lead them to compensate by being overly assertive about their authority in precisely those situations that call for them to profess ignorance, or only limited knowledge. Moreover, the trainer's pedagogy with adults may strike them as quite difficult to transfer to classrooms with children. For such reasons, trainers must actually enter the individual classrooms, take over the lesson for the day, and demonstrate to the teacher, with his or her own students, how the trainer would like the material taught. These modeling sessions usually occur about six weeks after the teacher has begun to implement the program in the classroom. They provide that modicum of hand-crafted, personal attention that sharply separates this mode of teacher education from campus courses that require the professor merely to tell (rather than actually show) how the students are to be taught.

Preparing teachers: The observation stage. About six weeks later, trainers return to the classroom to observe and evaluate the progress of the teacher's implementation of the program. The evaluation may be oral, written, or both. The trainer may ask the teacher important questions, such as "What did you see me do that you didn't do?" Or the trainer may review such matters as the lack of follow-up questioning or the teacher's failure to involve all members of the class. (Trainers use checklists of criteria for gauging teacher performance, and teachers are encouraged to learn these criteria so as to become more critically self-evaluative.)

Because they are formally similar, the preparation of trainers and the preparation of teachers have been treated together in the preceding discussion. But there obviously are differences, particularly in the fact that the trainers are professionally conversant with philosophy and the teachers have had little (and sometimes unpleasant) exposure to that discipline. One of the things teachers are most eager to know is how to distinguish a philosophical from a non-philosophical discussion. They feel they should not be criticized for failing to foster philosophical conversation if the trainer has never bothered to make clear what such conversation entails. This is not something the trainer is likely to be able to do overnight. It is usually necessary to show teachers the difference between normative and descriptive approaches to the teaching of reasoning (so that they can understand why, say, the learning of the syllogism is so very different from having teachers in training read psychological case studies). It is necessary to introduce them to the distinction between reasons and causes (more formally, between justification and explanation). It is necessary to show them the applicability of philosophy to the unsettled, problematic aspects of any area of knowledge. It is necessary to explain to them how problems seen from within a discipline provide a different kind of understanding from that which is obtained when a discipline becomes an object to itself and looks at itself from a point outside itself. It takes time for these points to be made and to sink in until they form an essential aspect of the teacher's daily practice. But with proper training and practice, the teacher's awareness of the philosophical dimension of human discourse is heightened almost imperceptibly, day by day, until the difference between a philosophical and a non-philosophical discussion has become so evident that one no longer asks to be shown it. This does not mean, in itself, that the teacher has become a philosopher, but it is evidence of the teacher's competence in guiding a philosophical discussion, in faithfully observing the cardinal rule not to block the path of inquiry but rather to follow the inquiry where it leads.

13 Twelve Sessions with *Pixie* in P.S. 87: A Classroom Log

Early in 1982 I decided I needed some firsthand experience in the teaching of *Pixie*. *Pixie* had been published the previous year and was already in use in several school districts. Since I was not getting much feedback from the teachers, I decided to offer an abbreviated course in *Pixie* to some fourth-graders. The school I selected was P.S. 87 in Manhattan. The principal, Naomi Hill, was receptive to the idea, and the classroom teacher, Gloria Goldberg, made me feel quite welcome. I promised to arrive at 9:00 A.M. every Thursday, and to stay for thirty or forty minutes. I knew I could hardly accomplish much in so short a time: *Pixie* would normally be offered in forty-five minute sessions three times a week for the entire school year. In all, I managed only twelve sessions, during which time we read the first six chapters and the last episode in the seventh.

Being from the West Side of Manhattan, the fourth-graders were a highly diversified group. A few struggled with the reading, whereas others read with the pacing and expression of adults. Several were just becoming familiar with English. Some were bold and outspoken, and others were timorous or silent. Indeed, on one occasion in which we were going around the room with a series of questions, one frail, anxious little girl burst into tears when it was finally her turn to answer. But generally there were lots of hands up during discussions, and I felt satisfied that they understood the material in *Pixie* and that most of them seemed to enjoy it.

The accounts of each session were written from memory after each session, and since no audio tapes were made, it would be difficult to check their accuracy. But this is of little importance: what matters is whether regular classroom teachers succeed in using *Pixie* to cultivate the thinking skills of their pupils and generally to enhance their students' powers of reflection. Having tested the waters a bit, I concluded the experiment feeling encouraged. What follows is the journal I kept during this period.

160

January 7, 1982

We read page 1, discussed it at considerable length, and then read the remainder of the chapter. Each child reads a paragraph. Open-minded discussion of Pixie's age: they were interested in the problem that different readers might be of different ages, which would raise a question about the truth of Pixie's statement, but were willing to let the mystery remain unresolved. They have a nice *tentativeness* in this respect. Virtually all the children read well—with expression, in many cases; but it's not a gifted class.

January 28, 1982

Class read Chapter 2 from beginning to end. We then discussed it a page at a time. I would ask, "What interests you on this page? Is there anything written on this page that you'd like to talk about?" In either case, the comment is put on the board.

The exercises matched the conversation very well. The first problem raised was that of possibility, and they were interested in noting that everything was not possible but that it was possible to think about things that were not possible—at least some things.

The passage about Pixie's foot falling asleep was cited. Conversation went like this:

—Can your foot be asleep but you remain awake?
—Yes.
—Can both your feet be asleep but you remain awake?
—Yes.
—Can both your feet and both your arms be asleep but you remain awake?
—Yes.
—Can your whole body be asleep but your head be awake?
—Yes.
—How about the other way around? Can your head be asleep and your whole body awake?
—Sure, when a person is sleepwalking. [boy in back row]

Another conversation proceeded in this fashion:

—On page 2, line 4, Miranda sees the cat chasing its tail. When you look at yourself in the mirror, is that like a cat chasing its tail?

—No, the cat's chasing its body, but when I look in the mirror, I see the *appearance* of my body [Natasha?].

—Well, okay. But how about this? Is a cat chasing its tail like a kite flying in circles?

—The kite has a tail, just like the cat [girl in middle].

—They're not the same, because the cat chases its tail *intentionally* [boy at front table].

February 4, 1982

Class read whole of Chapter 3. Good discussion of first half of chapter. We talked about "reading faces." They claimed that you could read someone's face and tell what that person was feeling. I asked if what the person *said* was ever different from what could be read in that person's face. Yes, they agreed. In that case, I asked, what do you do? One girl answered, "In that case, I always trust what I read in the face."

We also discussed whether unicorns were make-believe or extinct. They generally held that unicorns were make-believe, but several students said they were real. We then proceeded to talk about ambiguity. I wrote the word on the board, and Mrs. Goldberg reminded them of the importance of *context* in grasping the meaning of a word.

We talked about relationships that could be observed and those that could not be observed. They were clear about family relationships (that being a cousin or a nephew was not observable) but less clear about the perceivability of "being taller than" or "far from."

We did an exercise on family relationships. One child was taken in by the question, "If two brothers each have a sister, does that mean they have two sisters?" However, other members of the class explained the correct answer to her.

Finally I asked, "If your parents had no children, does that mean you probably won't have any?" One student said (with agreement from several others), "If your parents had no children, you wouldn't exist." To which one student responded, "You could if you had been adopted." Shows their ability to examine a question carefully, to see what it presupposes, and to give counterexamples.

February 18, 1982

Today, for the first time, there was meaningful pupil-pupil dialogue rather than pupil-teacher dialogue. Someone (Natasha) said, "I don't agree with what Ashaki said," and before the session ended, this had happened three times. With encouragement it could easily develop.

Thoroughly lively discussion on a variety of issues, mostly from page 25, dealing with excuses and reasons.

Q: Is an excuse just a poor reason?
A: No, there are good reasons and poor reasons, and there are good excuses and poor excuses, but you just can't say that an excuse is a poor reason.

We discussed whether "because I felt like it" could ever serve as a reason, whether children *had* to be younger than their teachers, and under what circumstances was it appropriate to ask questions and not to ask questions.

Q: Would a sore throat be a good excuse for staying home from school?
A: [Guardedly]: *How bad* a sore throat?
Q: Very bad.
A: [In chorus]: Yes, sure.
Q: If you wanted to stay home from school, would it be possible to develop a sore throat?
A: [Chorus again]: Of course!

February 24, 1982

Today students returned their homework (writing the beginning to a story whose ending had been given to them). We then read pages 29-31 and discussed page 29.

Many theories of what happens to the light when you turn off the switch. Does the light "go out"? If not, what happens to it? I asked if dark was the absence of light. Puzzlement. I asked if cold was the absence of heat. More puzzlement. I asked if dark was to light as cold was to heat. Some tentative assent. I contrasted that sentence (written on board) with "hands are like feet." I asked how hands were like feet. (They said fingers, toes, etc.) I asked them to complete the sentence "Hands are like feet as _____." Here a flock of hands went up:

As one nostril is to the other nostril
As elbows are to knees
As your upper lip is to your lower lip
As your left hand is to your right hand

(Notice that most of them are similarities of appearance; the elbows to knees comparison is a similarity of *function.* This one came from James.)

I didn't identify "simile" and "analogy" as the names of the two types of comparisons, but we contrasted them, and they seemed to understand the difference. Molly said that the analogy was a statement that said one relationship was like another.

We then considered the word "mean" on page 29, line 10. "What does 'mean' mean?" I asked. Sam said it could mean like mad, or it could mean that you were planning to do something (meaning to do something), or it could be like the meaning of a word in a sentence.

I then offered an example (without using the term "standardization") of how you could tell whether two contrasting sentences meant the same thing. I wrote "All the students in this room are smart" and "Only the students in this room are smart" on the board and asked what they meant. Someone said the first sentence meant "Each student in this room is smart." But the second baffled them; I think its *scope* bothered them. One student said, "It means the students in this room are smart, but not those in the rest of the school." I asked if it might mean "not those in the rest of the world." They seemed to find that very far-reaching indeed.

We tried two more: "All oaks are trees" and "Only trees are oaks." But this example collapsed when Natasha confused "oaks" with "yolks."

So I used "All cats are animals" and "Only animals are cats." They again had trouble with the "only" sentence, but this was partially the fault of the examples I offered. "Could a fish be a cat?" I asked. "Yes," someone said, "a catfish." At this I agreed out loud that a bird might be a catbird. Obviously we were in trouble with examples of birds and fish that the children could consider "animals." So I asked, "Could the closet be a cat? Could the floor be a cat?" This helped us understand what it meant to say, "Only animals are cats." (And give them practice in counterinstances, it might be added.)

I then explained to them the standardization rule for statements beginning with "only" and gave them an exercise to do. Since "all" and "only" confusions were among those that were most prevalent in the pre-test they were given, this was part of our prescriptive reinforcement.

Overall, the session was the most didactic one we have had, but I think the alternation of loose discussion and tight didactic learning of logical principles is a productive one. The rules give a sense of intellectual security and cognitive power that the more philosophical discussions disclose to them they need.

I think we have to learn to live with a fairly loose fit between the *Pixie* readings, the sequent classroom discussions, and the work on exercises. We would like them to follow in proper sequence, but this doesn't always happen. Sometimes an exercise out of sequence is necessary, and if it is pedagogically unsound that time around, it still may be necessary to prepare the ground for the *next* time around, because I'm beginning to think that *Pixie* should be read twice in one school year, slowly building up the skills, the first time around, with which to penetrate much more deeply into it the second time around.

March 4, 1982

As we move into the difficult chapters of *Pixie* (5 and 6), the inadequacy of one meeting a week is very obvious. I have slowed down the reading of episodes, so that today we took only one episode in Chapter 5.

—What interested you on page 32?
—Chita's comment that two numbers of the same size would be the same number.

We discussed various things Chita might mean by that remark. She might mean, someone said, a number 2 drawn six inches high would be the same as a number 2 drawn two feet high. She might mean that the number 2 is the same as 1 + 1. She might mean that "two" in English is the same as "two" in German or French or Italian or Spanish (these translated terms were all offered by the children). But, I pointed out, you could not just exchange the words from the language to the other: "zwei" means in German what "two" means in English, but "zwei" doesn't mean anything in English. It could also mean that two or more examples of the same number could be found. The child who said this seemed clearly to be arguing for a token-type distinction, whereas others were using the example of dogs and animals, arguing for a genus-species distinction. I did not want to get into the technical terminology and was too bewildered with the variety of theories about Chita's comment to do more than write them on the board and explain the differences.

We then talked about different types of relationships referred to on page 32. Someone said, "Things have relationships, like the relationship between a tabletop and its leg."

—What is that relationship?
—The legs hold the table up [Sam].
—They don't always do that. You could suspend a table by wires from the ceiling [James].

Inspired by James, I offered the opinion that legs don't always hold one up: a fly may be suspended from the ceiling by its legs. No comment from class. One student noted that "multiplication tables don't have legs."

We spent the remainder of the hour reviewing the "all-only" distinction and taking up contradiction.

Since they had had trouble with one of the items on the reasoning test that involves an illicit process syllogism, I moved from the "all-only" discussion to something similar:

All boys in this class are boys who pinch girls.

Jimmy is not from this class.

I first asked if any conclusion could be drawn from these statements, and after a moment of disagreement, there was agreement that no conclusion was in order.

I then asked what change could be made in the first premise that would make it possible to draw a conclusion. Someone, Molly I think, said, "Change the 'all' to 'only'." When I asked what conclusion would then follow, several students said, "Jimmy doesn't pinch girls."

Heartened by this, I showed them how to tell statements that were opposite one another. "How would you prove someone wrong who said, 'All apples are tasty'?" They agreed that all that would be necessary would be to find one apple—or some apples—that weren't tasty. So I wrote:

Opposites

All apples are tasty.	Some apples are not tasty.
No apples are tasty.	Some apples are tasty.

I pointed out that if either one of a pair of opposites was known to be true, the other had to be false. I also emphasized that the sentences in the left column were *not* opposites, nor were the sentences in the right column.

All pretty didactic. But this was a touch of logic for kids who will probably never have *Harry*.

March 11, 1982 (no class)

March 18, 1982

Class read the last episode of Chapter 5. "Is there anything on page 33 that interests you?" "Yes. 'Far' and 'near' are space relationships." This launched a lengthy discussion of the way a relational term might mean a relationship in the way that a noun might mean a thing.

Writing the word "cat" on the board, I asked "What is this?" "A cat."

"A cat? Does it have fur and claws and does it purr?" "No, it's the *word* for cat," they said.

I drew a cat on the board. "What's this?" "A cat." "Is it?" I asked. This time they're more cautious. Someone says, "It's a *picture* of a cat!" "Oh," I said and drew a frame around the illustration. "So what's this?" "That's a picture of a picture of a cat," they said.

We then discussed whether names *describe* the things they *stand for* or *refer to* or *mean.* We took up classification relationships, ranging from animals through cats through (their suggestions) calico cats and tiger cats and so on down to individually named cats. We discussed "being a kind of" as a relationship.

The session ended with a consideration of a comparison of relationships (puppies are to dogs as kittens are to cats) contrasted with a comparison of things (puppies are like kittens) and with my identifying the two kinds of things as respectively *analogies* and *similes.*

March 25, 1982

After reading episode 1 of Chapter 6, we talked about Pixie's trying to put herself to sleep with seriation problems. We took up a number of such problems, the students having no difficulty with them, for the most part. But when I asked "What day would it be two days before six days from now?" one student observed, "You don't have to count forward six days and then go back two. You just subtract two from six, and then count forward four days."

We discussed Pixie's getting her shoes confused in the dark, and we did the "Pixie's shoes" exercise, which went well. They generally agreed that Pixie's new shoes were probably larger than her old ones, but Sam got in a battle with the class because he insisted that the statement "All four of Pixie's shoes are the same size" is not merely "probably true" but "true." We never found out why he felt so sure of this.

We divided into pairs and did the finger identification game. They explained that twisting one's hands like that "caused the messages from the brain to one's fingers to get mixed up." We also did the game (from the *Harry* manual) in which two people put their palms together and then stroke a pair of fingers. First comment: "It feels weird." Second comment: "It feels dead." Third comment: "It's like there's just one body there."

Finally we talked about Pixie's comment, "Momma, are you in there?" "A person isn't *inside* her body, she *is* her body," said Natasha. I asked whether their friend is in the room with them when their friend's voice comes into the room through the telephone. They said yes; one said that we go as far as our senses. I asked, "Do we go as far as our drawings and paintings? Are they part of us too?" "Yes," they said. But Saskia proceeded to remark, "There are two things here. There's the you that's your body, and there are the things you make or do."

April 1, 1982

Sometimes a discussion will take off in an unexpected direction and go so well that you forget to follow up some of the more obvious leads, with the result that the discussion, for all its exhilarating quality, lacks the proper cognitive closure. This happened today when we read and talked about episode 2 of Chapter 6.

Actually, all we managed to discuss in thirty-five minutes was one quote that one of the students pointed out on page 40. Isabel said, "There may be model boats and model airplanes, but there are no model children." I asked what was meant by the phrase "model children," thinking that it was likely to be familiar to everyone. What was curious was that no one seemed acquainted with the expression, even after about ten minutes of discussion. First they suggested that "model children" were young people who modeled clothes for advertisements in magazines. I asked if such a child was a "model child" or a "child model." They agreed it was a child model. So what's a model child? They pointed to a model of a man on the window ledge. "It's like that, but of a child. Not made of flesh and blood, but of plastic." I asked if it was a "model child," a "model *of* a child," or a "child model." A "model of a child," they agreed. So what's a model child? The discussion continued until Mrs. Goldberg raised her hand, was called on, and offered her interpretation of the meaning of "model child," at which point some of the students concurred.

Afterward, I was annoyed with myself for not having followed up the question of whether children are models of adults, since children would seem to satisfy Isabel's stipulation that "the parts are the same and their relationships to one another are the same." But we did spend considerable time on what it meant for the relationships of the parts of the model man on the window ledge to be similar to the relationships of parts of a living person. The exercise on page 40, called "What are relationships?" proved very useful in getting the students to identify relationships, contrast them with one another, and distinguish them from terms. The most fruitful discussions emerged from the first two items:

(1) What is the difference between the relationship between a rider and her horse and the relationship between a driver and her car? And (2) What is the difference between the relationship between a doctor and a patient and the relationship between a buyer and a seller? I had thought the students would have had more trouble with such complex examples (these are, after all, *disanalogies* rather than *analogies*), but they took them very much in stride. It confirms a long-standing hunch: the students can handle the *logic* of analogy and disanalogy, but they may sometimes lack the worldly experience and information with regard to individual *terms* (such as "model child").

We concluded the session by doing the exercise on page 42 called "Constructing Analogies by Sentence Completion." They seemed to enjoy this sort of thing very much; almost everyone in the class participated by volunteering an example. They particularly selected some of the more odious variations, such as "When I watch TV, I feel like a slimy pickle"; "When I am angry, I feel like a purple firecracker"; "When I eat spaghetti, I feel like a weary dragonfly"; and "When I dream, I feel like a constipated lobster." Is there a lesson in this for us?

Oh, yes, back to the disanalogies. When we were discussing the differences between the driver-car and rider-horse relationships, someone said, "They're different in the way you make them go faster." "What do you do in the case of a car?" I asked. "Give it more gas." "What do you do in the case of a horse?" Someone said, "Give it more water." "Giving it more water will make it go faster?" "If you don't give it water it won't go at all," I was told.

May 6, 1982

The last meeting with the class was five weeks ago. Two sessions were missed because of holidays, one because I was called away at the last moment, and one because the class had to have an examination. Yesterday Mrs. Goldberg had the class finish reading Chapter 6 and do some of the analogy exercises. She said it did not go too smoothly.

We script-read pages 40–42, and after some discussion of the individual examples of analogies given in the chapter, we proceeded to the "review exercise" called "Evaluating Analogies." This went very well. I can't help feeling that, *pace* Benjamin Bloom, things go much better if evaluation *precedes* the straightforward memorization or learning of materials. The exercise requires that given analogies be graded (the letter grades they are familiar with are E, G, F, and U). I think the requirement that they *judge* the excellence of the analogy is something they relish and contributes to their understanding of analogies. Folklore tells us that we should first understand the facts, and then make judgments, but Nelson Goodman is more correct when he notes that the only reason to prize the evaluation process is because it leads to better perceptions: evaluation is not the end, but a means to an end.

Anyhow, I asked the members of the class what they thought of "Thoughts are to thinkers as shoes are to shoemakers." Most of them thought it a good analogy. Thinking to play devil's advocate, I asked what shoemakers made shoes out of. "Leather, rubber, and glue," they said. "And do thinkers make thoughts as shoemakers make shoes?" I asked. Mollie said, "Sure—out of other thoughts." I told her her answer was wonderful.

At this point some students wanted to get some clarification on "what an analogy is," and we reviewed the difference between analogies and similes. James offered his example, remembered from almost two months back, that knees are to legs as elbows are to arms. The class agreed it was a good analogy. I asked why. Because, Ashaki said, you flex an arm at the elbow and you flex a leg at the knee.

"Giggling is to laughing as whimpering is to crying" was adjudged good because "it was soft to loud on each side." "Pins are to pinning as needles are to needling" was rated poor, but the students didn't quite know why, since they didn't know what "needling" was.

"Bread is to puddles as butter is to rain" was considered unsatisfactory; Sam said it should have been "Bread is to butter as puddles are to rain." We tried that and likewise rejected it: rain causes puddles, but butter doesn't cause bread.

Given a good rating was "Words are to stories as seeds are to flower-beds," because, someone said, the words bloom in your mind.

And "Trying to get someone else to think is like walking a dog" was rejected because the two things were not similar; however, there was some difficulty in saying just why—surprisingly. At this point, one student raised a perceptive question. Some analogies involve the relationship on the left (between two terms) being compared with the relationship on the right (between two terms). But "trying to get someone else to think" and "walking a dog" do not seem to involve relationships between two terms. I suggested that one person tries to get another to think, and a person and a dog are related when someone walks a dog. But, of course, the questioner is right: some analogies compare one *way* of doing something with another *way* of doing something and involve verbs rather than nouns.

The family of analogies is not a simple one. But the "doing A is like doing B" analogy seems to me reducible to A is to B as C is to D, or at least is comparable to it, as in "Putting sauerkraut over your pizza is like putting chow mein in your milkshake," an example we didn't quite get to before the forty-five minutes was over.

May 7, 1982

Today we spent a couple of minutes at the beginning of the hour reviewing the "all-only" distinction. I drew a picture of a set of turnpike tollbooths with all lights on (i.e., all gates open) and with a sign over the three center booths saying "passenger cars only." Then I drew long lines of cars going only to the center booths. "What's wrong?" I asked. Rudy said, "They think they can't go in the other booths, but the sign doesn't mean that."

We then script-read the last episode in Chapter 7 (about Adam). They said they were interested in the notion of "the unbelievable." I asked if they could give me an example of something unbelievable. Nora, the little wisp of a girl in the front with straw-colored hair, replied, "War." This fairly staggered me, so I asked her to explain. "It's just so horrible," she replied, "it's just more than we can—." Is what she was trying to formulate this: that war is *unthinkable?* I failed to follow it up because this interpretation did not occur to me at the time.

It is worthwhile pointing out, in passing, how often the first comment from the children is the most dramatic. The other comments so often take the lead of the first but in a less novel way; the first often has a breathtakingly original quality about it.

We worked some more on whether unbelievable stories could be true and whether fictional stories could be true ("fictional" was their word). One student brought in the notion of "tall-tales," and we talked about Baron Munchausen a bit. At first, one or two students insisted that Adam would find the theory that we have grown *more* plausible than the one that we have shrunk. But we discussed the difficulty of this, considering such examples of the possible truth of implausible ideas as that "the sun doesn't rise." What I found difficult to elicit from the class was the notion that one doesn't select among ideas on the basis of their plausibility or implausibility but on other grounds. What other grounds? It was not until the end of the hour, the very end, that Sara proposed "evidence." I figured that was close enough.

May 14, 1982

This was our last meeting, and I didn't conduct a *Pixie* session. Instead we had a birthday party for Pixie (having first agreed that, since she was everybody's age, she could celebrate her birthday any day she liked). Upon being opened, an enormous box revealed a huge birthday cake inscribed "Happy Birthday, Pixie," and although I thought it much too large, it managed to disappear somehow, somewhere.

They hadn't realized that today would be the last day, but after a while they began to drift over to the corner to which I had retreated, murmuring thanks in some cases, or simply sidling up like affectionate cats, as if mutely asking for that which would allow us to go our ways knowing that what had to be done—and what we wanted—had been done.

June 24, 1982

Returned today to pick up the post-tests. Since it was only 8:30 A.M., most of the students hadn't yet arrived. But as I passed the playground behind the school, I saw a baseball game in progress, and there on first base was the indomitable Ashaki, wearing a bright-colored headband. As I turned away it came over me once again, but more powerfully and affectingly than ever, how little we know of children's intellectual capabilities and how sure we are of their limitations.

14 Philosophy and Creativity

What I have to say in this chapter will touch upon the convergence and intersection of four domains: the philosophy of creativity, the philosophy of art, the philosophy of education, and the philosophy of philosophy. At the risk of overkill, I might easily add a fifth: the philosophy of childhood. I do not wish to stray too far from the issue, yet I must admit that a very plausible argument for what I want to say would involve most or all of these domains. Thus I might want to assert the following propositions. Philosophy is a form of art. Philosophical behavior is therefore artistic behavior, and artistic behavior produces works of art displaying creativity. Children can behave philosophically, and when they do, it follows that the products of such behavior will display creativity.

Unfortunately, I do not find this argument satisfactory. Some of the assertions are debatable; some of the leaps that connect the assertions are quite tenuous. It will be necessary to examine some of these issues more carefully.

Like all thought, philosophic thought has its allegros and adagios: its rapid movements are probative and speculative, in quest of coherence and comprehensiveness; its slower movements are critical and analytical, in quest of conceptual integrity and responsibility. The guiding ideal of philosophical endeavor is reasonableness or judicious rationality, even where the objective is to find the limits of such rationality. The three quarries of classical philosophy were the Good, the Beautiful, and the True, but the light was soon shifted away from these goals and toward the forms of inquiry employed to seek them out: the practical, the productive, and the theoretical, rendered colloquially as doing, making, and saying. One might do worse than retain these three parameters, so that one definition of philosophy might be "the self-correcting examination of alternative ways of making, saying, and doing."

Since we are to consider the alleged philosophical behavior of children, insofar as it bears upon creativity, it will eventually be necessary to examine the possibility of children's philosophical making, saying, and doing.

We will have to touch upon whether such behavior is a natural accompaniment of children's development, occurs naturally but in a rudimentary form that needs strengthening, or occurs only as the result of careful, specific, and deliberate educational interventions. If such interventions are required, whether to produce the desired behavior or merely to foster and strengthen it, how are they constituted and under what conditions are they likely to be successful?

Before taking these questions up, however, it would be useful to inquire into the possibilities of either incompatibilities or necessary connections among the domains to whose "philosophies of" I have already alluded: childhood, education, creativity, art, and philosophy itself. I hope that in this fashion some conceptual ground can be cleared away and some conceptual space prepared so that the remainder of this inquiry may more readily take place.

Some Conceptual Issues

One of the things associated with the philosophical tradition is that its practitioners have tended to restrict the profession to those whose sex, age, and ethnic origins were more or less like their own. Outsiders were kept outside by means of criteria such as "maturity," "objectivity," and "rationality," which were employed in a fairly self-serving fashion, for it was obvious that these were thought to be the very characteristics that the insiders possessed and the outsiders lacked.

I do not wish to comment extensively here on the monopolization of professional opportunities, but rather to point out that any such opportunity calls for a clear set of specifications (or "specs") of the job to be done and a clear presentation of the relevent credentials of the applicant. Now, what specifications can be provided for performing the work of the philosopher? A host of criteria immediately presents itself as candidates: analytical precision, metaphysical imagination, and so on. But I shall put these aside for the moment, because the phrase "the work of the philosopher" is blurry and needs to be brought into focus. For example, is there a real disjunction between the teaching and the writing of philosophy, or is it only my astigmatism that blurs their relationship?

It may be useful here to note that some philosophers consider such phrases as "to be artistic" and "to be philosophical" as referring to *actions* rather than to processes.[1] Thus an action is something I perform; a process is something that happens to me or in me. I can say "I sketch," "I wonder," or "I intend," but I cannot say "I circulate my blood" or

"I gravitate," except in a metaphorical sense. What is interesting in this distinction for our present purposes is that it leads to a distinction between artistic behavior and work of art that is not exactly a process-product distinction. Similarly, it leads to a distinction between the creativity in the artistic behavior and the creativity in the work of art. Artistic behavior contains creative acts; works of art display creativity. I shall return shortly to the question of the relationship between creative acts and creativity. For the moment I want to pursue the notion of philosophical behavior (embodying philosophical acts or moves) in the hope of explicating some of its specifications.

What do we mean when we say that someone exhibits philosophical behavior? Presumably, we mean that she or he (or it?) exhibits behavior containing a significant number of acts that *prima facie* resemble the moves characteristic of philosophers. Surely we would do the same for athletes, chess players, businesspersons, and doctors: there are ways in which they characteristically behave, and so anyone behaving in ways in which businesspeople typically behave can be said to be businesslike. (I am not attempting to rule out innovative forms of behavior; I am simply reporting conventional usage.)

Of course, one can be businesslike without actually engaging in business, just as someone can act like an athlete without being an athlete. One can approach virtually anything in a businesslike manner or method—sport, love, war, even business itself. Similarly, one can approach virtually anything as if it were a game—love, war, business, even games themselves.[2] So there is a difference between one's approach to a thing and the thing itself, a difference corresponding to the difference between method and subject matter, for one can employ different methods on the same subject matter or the same method on different subject matters.

It follows that one may behave philosophically about anything, including philosophy itself. Likewise, one may, without truly behaving philosophically, engage in acts that resemble philosophical acts (i.e., acts that are characteristic of philosophers) as when, for example, one acts the part of a philosophy professor in a Stoppard play, thereby producing a facsimile or semblance of such behavior.

We must grant the possibility, therefore, that children might be able to mimic or ape philosophical behavior without actually engaging in it, in the same way that a child might strut about in an adult's clothing without thereby becoming an adult. On the other hand, precocious children have been known to be capable of manifesting very mature behavior indistinguishable in certain contexts from that of grown-ups: indistinguishable, indeed, from that of the most poised and reasonable of grown-ups.

Could it not then be the case that children might at times *appear to be merely mimicking or imitating* philosophical behavior when they were in fact actually engaging in it? How are we to distinguish merely apparent philosophical behavior from genuine cases (merely apparent imitations) of such behavior? (It was some such puzzlement that, it may be recalled, Henry James set himself in *The Sacred Fount:* how to distinguish genuine from merely apparent or forged sagacity.)

A boy actor in an Elizabethan play may feign the passions of a female adult, but we have only to observe the same boy for any length of time offstage to recognize the onstage behavior as a discrepant event. Likewise, with parents who claim to love their children: we have only to observe them regularly when they do not know they are being observed. Now, if performance were only a matter of craft and craft were only a matter of skill, there might be no such thing as a forged performance. Collingwood would be right: one would have only to possess the skills of the performer in order to imitate her successfully.[3] But performance is not just a matter of skill, or even of the skill of orchestrating a set of skills. The *interpretation* of the performer is based on her *conception* of the work to be performed, and this provides the creative element missing in the performance of the copyist.

Let us return to the question of characteristic acts or moves. Are such moves identifiable quite in themselves and apart from their employment in a special occupational context? That is, are there moves that a baseball player makes when not actually playing baseball, that a ballet dancer makes when not actually dancing, and so on? Of course there are: they are the very moves that constitute the practice sessions that these individuals usually engage in prior to their actual performances. Baseball players will toss the ball around from base to base and practice batting and fielding; dancers will run through their litany of movements at the bar; singers and pianists will rehearse challenging little exercises. Each group's exercises are fairly distinctive. Thus solfeggio is a preparatory technique employed by vocalists but not by businesspersons, baseball players, or barbers. (Wittgenstein has noted that barbers keep in practice by working their scissors even while they are not actually cutting hair; he found this similar to the practice of philosophy.) And each group's exercises are representative of the group's distinctive behavior. That is, if we were to visit a community and note a person picking up a ball rolling toward him, another singing something aloud, and a third asking that her companion acknowledge having rested his case on an unacknowledged assumption, it might impress us as representing nothing in particular. But if the first person persisted repeatedly in scooping up ground balls, the second persisted in singing solfeggio, and the third persisted in uncovering presuppositions, we would more likely be moved to infer that this might be a baseball player, a singer, and a person engaged in philosophical behavior.

Seeking to expose underlying assumptions is, of course, only one of a great many moves that are characteristic of philosophical behavior, and one could as well specify asking for reasons, seeking to determine the validity of inferences, constructing arguments, interpreting meanings, clarifying concepts, evaluating the coherence and explanatory power of theories, and so on. But the baseball player does not engage *only* in preparatory practice: eventually he plays the game, just as the singer eventually has done with her solfeggio and takes on Schubert. Not that we need restrict ourselves here to performers, for the poet and the artist are no different. An Auden keeps himself poetically fit by lightly tossing off a verse at a moment's provocation, and just as lightly crumples it up and tosses it away, but he is always engaged with the corpus of traditional literature as a Picasso is with the corpus of traditional art. So with the philosopher: there is that engagement always with the philosophical tradition, even when no one so much as breathes the names of Aristotle or Peirce or Ryle.

It would seem then that being a baseball player involves making the moves characteristic of such players (this is where method comes in) together with playing the game they characteristically play (this is where subject matter comes in). One who meets these requirements is a baseball player (although not necessarily a good one). We are concerned here only with classification, not with evaluation. If, similarly, there are those who persistently make the moves characteristic of philosophical behavior and thereby become engaged with the issues—the aesthetic, ethical, metaphysical, epistemological, and logical subject matter—associated with the philosophical tradition, what grounds would we have for denying that they do what professional philosophers do? Perhaps they may not do it as well, but this is irrelevant. Perhaps they are younger, but this is also irrelevant.

Nevertheless, it will be argued, what ultimately disqualifies children from performing philosophically is not their lack of years but their lack of experience. When experience of the world is of minimal significance— as in the case of chess, perhaps, or of mathematics—children can be prodigies. But one cannot be judicious without experience, and it is here that children's inexperience tells against them. The response to such an argument is simply that it considers only the quantity of experience a young person may have and ignores the quality. The very intensity of childhood experience could well compensate for the handicap of not having confronted the world over an extended period. The aim of such a response is not simply to allow for the possibility of a philosophical prodigy, as to allow for the possibility that someday millions of children will be engaged in workmanlike philosophical performances as they practice their philosophical skills and apply them to the other aspects of their education.

Thus far I have been concerned with what it might mean to say that a person is engaged in the philosophical behavior. Here the impatient listener may interrupt with, "Yes, yes, but do get *on* with it! So what if children can be shown to engage in philosophical behavior? Can they produce philosophy and will it be creative? That's what *I* want to know!" This is, I agree, a somewhat different matter but an equally important one, and I hasten to address it.

Let us first consider creativity in a more general sense, as it is involved in all of art and not just in philosophy. Kennick has suggested that, with regard to creativity, the relationship between artistic behavior and work of art is not a convertible one. All cases of creativity in works of art are *necessarily* the result of creative acts, but it does not follow that creative acts will result in creative works of art. Indeed, he contends, even if all cases of creative behavior were found to eventuate in creative works of art and all works of art were found to have resulted from creative acts, we would still want to say that the first relationship is contingent whereas the second is necessary.

Kennick proceeds to conclude that creativity is not a psychological concept: "We can know whether a work of art is creative . . . while knowing nothing about the psychology of creation."[4] I do not think Kennick means to impugn the legitimacy of psychological work in the area of creativity any more than he would disparage work in the psychology of reasoning just because it had little to do with the principles of logical validity. He simply wants us to see that the conceptual aspects of the problem of creativity are not likely to be resolved by purely empirical studies.

For the moment, let us tentatively accept Kennick's paradigm and apply it to the relationship between *philosophical behavior* and *works in philosophy*. Such an application would mean that a person's engaging in philosophical acts would not guarantee the production of philosophical works, but the existence of a philosophical work would necessarily entail its having philosophical acts as its cause. This means that children might exhibit many characteristic philosophical acts *and* be engaged with ideas drawn from the philosophical tradition (so that they can be said to be "playing the philosophy game"), and still their behavior would not necessarily culminate in the production of philosophical works.

But this is not the end of the matter. We had agreed to work with Kennick's approach on a tentative basis to see where it would lead us. What we did not do was ask about the applicability of his approach, given the definition of philosophy with which we began: "the self-correcting examination of alternative ways of making, saying, and doing." And it is here that we discover a bit of a problem.

It is generally agreed, I would think, that philosophy is itself a matter of making, saying, and/or doing. It is when we speak of *doing philosophy* that the problem emerges, because in this instance there is no easy way of separating the doing from what is done in the sense that we can easily separate the making from the made and the saying from the said. The creative doing of an act is not readily distinguishable from the creative work that has been done. It is difficult to imagine how one might engage in noble behavior without having, in the process, performed a noble deed, for to perform the behavior *is* to perform the deed. Kennick's claim that the relationship between acts and works can only be a contingent one fails to allow for the case of ethical creativity, where act and deed are one and the same. And what is true of ethical doing is true likewise of creative doing, as in ballet, where "one cannot tell the dancer from the dance." It is true, too, of philosophical doing, of doing philosophy. If one can be said to be doing philosophy by reasonably discussing philosophical issues in a college classroom, one must also be doing philosophy when reasonably discussing philosophical issues in an elementary school classroom. And if—whether at a philosophical conference or in a kindergarten—the doing of philosophy is creative, then the philosophy that has been done will necessarily manifest creativity. Thus consider the following interchange:

INSTRUCTOR: Can there be thoughts no one has thought of?
STUDENT: There are problems to which we don't as yet know the answer, but there *is* an answer, so that's a thought no one has yet thought of.

This is only a mini-dialogue, but it does seem to be the case that the participants are doing philosophy and that the student is doing it rather creatively. That, as it happens, the student was only eleven years old is irrelevant to the issue, like the psychological data dismissed by Kennick.

If anyone should insist that only the production of philosophical works of publishable quality can be a criterion of philosophical respectability, the case of doing philosophy can be readily cited as refutation. That children should behave philosophically should be sufficient. They have the capacity to immerse themselves in philosophy (as Socrates immersed himself in it as a form of life in which activity and end result were all one and the same), not as preparation for something yet to come, but as praxis here and now. When we encounter children in communities of inquiry, intensely involved in philosophical dialogue, we should be sensitive to how closely they approximate that Socratic paradigm.

Philosophical Creativity

In a recent article, written in response to the despair voiced by John Hospers at the unlikelihood of our ever being able to recount the origins of creativity, Carl Hausman has suggested that Hospers's problem is rooted in his inability to liberate himself from his deterministic presuppositions, that explanation must always be in terms of something logically or temporally antecedent. As an alternative, Hausman suggests that a better understanding of creativity might come through the study of metaphor:

> Taking the metaphor as a model, we might attempt what may be called an "account" of creativity. When accounting for something, we do not necessarily expect to find the necessary and sufficient conditions for it; nor need we expect to be shown that it is predictable. Our expectations are more liberal. . . . An account can circumscribe, so to speak, what is accounted for, and it should do this by drawing on the resources of deterministic explanations to the extent that they can be applied; yet it should also propose descriptions which themselves exhibit creativity through the incorporation of figurative language—analogical as well as metaphorical.[5]

And Hausman cites Peirce as an example of a philosopher who rejects determinism and employs metaphorical language to account for the irregularities and lawlessness of the evolutionary process.

Now, this excursion into Hospers, Hausman, and Peirce may assist us in understanding philosophical creativity in general, so that we may then proceed to assess the possibility of creativity in the case of children doing philosophy. It will be recalled, for example, that Peirce distinguished between two general kinds of reasoning: explicative and ampliative.[6] An example of explicative reasoning would be deduction, for the conclusion of a deductive argument is at least implicitly present in the premises and merely needs to be explicated. Ampliative reasoning, on the other hand, goes beyond what is given. An inductive or analogical argument cannot be limited to what is given or antecedently construed as determined: it bursts the bounds of the known and breaks the barriers that our literal knowledge imposes on us. Ampliative reasoning corresponds to an evolving world as explicative reasoning corresponds to a stable one. Metaphors and analogies represent enlargements rather than equivalences. Such enlargements are not of truth merely, but of meaning in general. Ampliative reasoning can be said to carry us beyond actual experience to a domain of possible, related experience.

If metaphors and analogies are models of the amplification of meaning, and if the amplification of meaning is essentially what is involved in creativity, then perhaps metaphors and analogies, in addition to what they actually refer to, are in an illocutionary sense, metaphorically representative of creativity in general. Notice that we are no longer concerned to talk about creation *ex nihilo*—the movement from vacuity to meaning, but the amplification of meaning—the movement from a lesser to a greater degree of meaningfulness. For when it comes to meaning, as Anaxagoras might say, there is no least.

The meaning of every work of art is inseparable from its being; the notion of a meaningless work of art is self-contradictory. Every work of art adds meaning to or amplifies or revises the meanings already present in the art world. When we credit artists with insight and imagination, we mean that their works enable us to comprehend more effectively the meanings to be found in our own experience. Every aesthetic appreciation enlarges us in this sense, but the appreciation of the creativity in a work enlarges in some mysterious way our capacity for such enlargement: it makes grow our power to grow.

In relating these thoughts to the question of children's philosophical creativity, we should not fail to consider the fact that children are extraordinarily prolific when it comes to the production of similes, metaphors, and analogies, a point well established by Howard Gardner and others. The frequency with which children employ the term "like" suggests that as they proceed from stepping stone to stepping stone, moving beyond the known into the unknown, they have continual recourse to comparisons that point up resemblances to the already familiar. Asked about something unusual like a unicorn, we attempt to classify it in a way that makes it unsurprising, as with the response, "It's a mythical creature." But the child is more likely to reply, "It's like a horse, only with a horn coming out of his forehead." The first part of the child's response likens the unfamiliar to the familiar; the second part acknowledges the novel, the different, the unclassifiable. This same subtle difference underlies the adult's totally inclusive "humans are thinking animals" and the child's partially inclusive, partially exclusive, "humans are animals, only they think."

So much has been written about the powerful role played by metaphor and analogy in science, art, and philosophy that I would only be laboring the point if I paused here to elaborate further on this aspect of the topic I am concerned to examine. Perhaps it will be sufficient then to suggest that "ampliative reasoning" is the middle term between doing philosophy and exhibiting creativity. Insofar as children are proficient in ampliative reasoning, this should be good grounds for suspecting that, given the opportunity to do philosophy, they would do so creatively.

This is not to say, however, that reasoning deductively or explicatively is irrelevant to creativity. Children taught to distinguish between valid and invalid deductive inferences are often stimulated to imagine the kind of world that the invalid deduction implies. Given the example of conversion—"All onions are vegetables, but not all vegetables are onions"—children will proceed to ask, "Yes, but what sort of world would it be, in which all vegetables were onions? Wouldn't it be one in which one cries when one slices the carrots, and one has to peel layer after layer of skin from the potatoes, and so on?" Many children are so comfortable with such counterfactuals and with the exploration of possible worlds that there can be little doubt that they make very creative use of the mechanics of explicative reasoning.[7]

A Novel Experiment: Project Design and Implementation

Thus far our inquiry has explored the murky boundaries and overlappings of the philosophy of creativity, the philosophy of childhood, and the philosophy of philosophy, and we have found that, yes, these domains do overlap. Good. Does anything more need to be said? Surely the conclusion—that the notion of children doing philosophy is not self-contradictory and that children may conceivably behave creatively when engaging in philosophical behavior—is not likely to appear particularly momentous to anyone.

Nevertheless, are we really compelled to leave the matter at this point? Could we not *do* something—make up a questionnaire, perform an experiment—something, anything, to determine whether children might somehow be brought to behave philosophically? Is there no way of applying what we have learned? Some, no doubt, will be aghast at such a proposal. Our job as philosophers, they will say, is to interpret the world, not to change it. Others will see the proposal as a further effort to water down professional standards and will decry the prospect of precocious toddlers conducting university seminars in epistemology or metaphysics.

Such caricatures aside, perhaps the call to action is more propitious and meritorious than it might at first appear to be. What if we were indeed to perform the experiment alluded to a moment ago—what would it involve?

The hypothesis would be that, with the help of a specially prepared curriculum and specially trained teachers, children could be induced to engage creditably in creative philosophical behavior. One welcome spinoff of such a change in behavior might be significant improvement in the children's *educational* behavior, but the initial hypothesis could be verified whether or not this particular outcome was observable. Another outcome might be an increase in the quantity and quality of the creative (but not necessarily philosophical) expressions of the children involved.

The testing of the hypothesis will involve a fairly elaborate project, consisting of a variety of components and going through a series of stages. The components follow.

A curriculum for children. Such a curriculum would represent central themes from the history of philosophy but would be translated into ordinary language. The curriculum would be made available at a number of levels, corresponding to the ages and grades of the children involved. It would also be sequential, so that successive stages would amplify old themes and introduce new ones, present new points of view, and provide for a critical look at other disciplines. Special attention would be given to sequencing the logical elements, so that these develop in a cumulative fashion. In addition to being representative of the history of philosophy, the curriculum would have to be impartial with respect to any particular philosophical views. The overall impression to be derived by students should be rational inquiry, of which each of the components should provide some sort of model or paradigm. The readers for the children themselves should be primary rather than secondary texts. One way of doing this is to devise philosophical novels interesting enough so that children would want to read them independently of their didactic value.

A pedagogical methodology. Since the objective is to induce philosophical behavior and since children have a strong propensity for verbal expression (to the point of sometimes seeming a bit language-intoxicated), the appropriate format should be discussion-centered rather than lecture centered. The teacher must accordingly be philosophically self-effacing (always on guard against being unwittingly indoctrinational) and yet pedagogically strong (always fostering the discussion among the children and encouraging them to pursue the inquiry in the direction it suggests).

The pedagogical methodology should remain consistently dialogical from kindergarten through grade twelve, but there should nevertheless be some significant shifts of emphasis. Thus the younger children (ages five to nine) need practice in reasoning and concept development, with relatively little stress on the learning of principles. In the middle school years (ages ten to thirteen), children are in a better position to grasp the principles of valid reasoning, and in the later school years (ages fourteen to seventeen) they can be helped to apply these principles, plus their improved practice, to the issues in school and in life with which they must deal. This does not mean that very young children should be deprived of abstractions and have their attention focused always on the perception of their physical environment. (We are now slowly emerging from a half-century of such misplaced emphasis in the classroom.)

Instructional materials for teachers. As the notion of doing philosophy with children becomes more popular, one will hear it urged that the Socratic model be hewed to quite literally: "no texts for the students and no manuals for the classroom teachers." For the present, this is quite an unworkable model. Children (like college students) need primary texts, and teachers need prepared exercises and discussion plans. Even though the need for instructional manuals may be conceded, it is still sometimes urged that these can be prepared by classroom teachers with little or no philosophical background. This is also undesirable, because classroom teachers greatly need professional guidance from practitioners of the discipline; they are in no position to give such guidance to other teachers, either as curriculum writers or as teacher trainers.

The training of teacher trainers. Only skilled and experienced philosophers should be teacher trainers, and even they require preparation. This preparation involves a ten-day seminar, in which the participants work through the curriculum in the same dialogical way that teachers and children would be expected to work through it, and a period of working directly with children.

The preparation of classroom teachers. In-service teacher training generally entails five hours per week (half seminar, half practicum) for twenty-eight weeks. A second year's training is often desirable. When this format is not possible, a series of three-day intensive workshops may be adequate to initiate and continue the program.

The benefits of educational research. Experimentation on the involvement of children with philosophy is desirable in order to determine its impact on their reasoning, creativity, social attitudes, motivation, and educability. It would also be useful to discover the extent to which children find philosophy intrinsically interesting, quite apart from its instrumental values.

I shall not continue to pretend that this experiment has yet to be performed. The curriculum, consisting of seven programs for elementary and secondary school, is now virtually complete. Philosophy trainers and classroom teachers are being prepared on a regular basis. Almost two dozen experiments, involving thousands of students, have now been carried out. Most of these studies revealed that children exposed to philosophy improved significantly in reasoning proficiency. There was significant improvement in reading comprehension in the three studies where this was measured, and significant improvements were found in each instance in which efforts were made to detect improvements in creativity, using measures of ideational productivity, fluency, and flexibility. Equally reassuring has been the warm reception accorded philosophy by the children themselves and by their parents (with whom they apparently talk philosophy incessantly). These are some of the reasons for expecting philosophy gradually to become a regular part of the school curriculum.

Can We Expect Children to Produce Philosophical Works Displaying Creativity?

If we can get children to engage in philosophical dialogue by presenting them with stories in which philosophical issues play a significant role and having them examine such stories as a community of inquiry, can we also get them to produce creative works beyond the classroom dialogue itself? And is it possible that such works can display genuinely philosophical creativity?

We must realize, at the outset, that were we successful in such a project we would have had to transcend the conventional limitations of aesthetics. Aestheticians, on the whole, have been inclined to limit their study to aesthetic reasoning, criticism, appreciation, creation, education, and similar topics. It must be conceded that many of these studies have had a generative as well as an exploratory aspect. That is to say, aestheticians have evidently often felt an edifying impulse amounting at times to an evangelical sense of mission, to encourage aesthetic appreciation and discourage philistinism, to facilitate criticism and aesthetic education, and generally to promote the arts in the esteem of humanity. However, the success of aestheticians in generating understanding and appreciation has been incomparably greater than their success in generating creation. One possible explanation of this may be simply that a generative aesthetics is not feasible. This is a falsifiable hypothesis, and one objective of doing philosophy with children can be to falsify it, if not by finding a ready-made set of counterinstances to it, then by generating one.

Now, a crucial component in any generative effort is the role and function of the model. Children acquire facility in talking by listening to adult conversations, identifying with the speakers, internalizing their linguistic behaviors, and simultaneously grasping the logical and syntactic structure of the language they employ. It is in this respect that deaf children are so desperately disadvantaged.

Thus children learn to talk by talking, having been exposed to models of conversation. They may learn to tell stories by being told stories, and they may learn to write poetry by first seeing models of poetry. Models are indispensable, whether or not they are emulated successfully.

Unfortunately, an inherent problem in the use of models is that they may inhibit rather than engender emulative behavior. We know this from our university experience, for we are all familiar with those brilliant faculty members whose lectures were works of art and whose students were in consequence virtually paralyzed with admiration. The same situation is the rule rather than the exception in the case of parents telling stories to their children. The stories written by professional story-tellers are often so charged with imagination and excitement that children find them overwhelming and demand to hear them over and over again. Such stories can be sheer delight, but they may also be so impressively constructed and told as to be intimidating to children who might otherwise use them as models for their own story-telling. Even when it is the parents who invent the story rather than have recourse to one that is ready-made, the joys of creativity and the pleasure of seeing the rapt expressions on the faces of one's captive audience prevent one from realizing that the children are identifying vicariously with the adult's creativity rather than experiencing the liberation of their own.

Needless to say, attempting to do philosophy with children without the model of conversation in a children's community of inquiry that a story can contain is likely to be the hard way to go. On the other hand, the use of such a model can be counterproductive if it is presented as a finished end-product, to be studied with reverence, rather than as a spur to further inquiry and as an illustration of how it can be done.

If we want children to be thoughtful, we must present them with models of thinking children. This does not necessarily mean surrounding them with representations of Rodin's *Penseur,* that isolated male adult with the tense posture and troubled physiognomy. We must somehow portray the thought process itself as it occurs among children, and for this purpose, the ideal medium would seem to be literature—but not existing children's literature. Most children's stories involve fictional children who are happy or sad, beautiful or homely, obedient or disobedient, but seldom are they portrayed as thoughtful, analytical, critical, or speculative. Moreover, it is literature that introduces us to the depicted performance of specific mental acts. Jane Austen's characters infer, presume, speculate, guess, and consider. Henry James's characters "hang fire," "take in (some information)," weigh, deliberate, and ruminate. A curriculum that aims to induce children to give thought to their situations and their lives must likewise depict fictional children giving thought to *their* lives as well as to the world that surrounds them.

At this point we begin to discern what has led publishers and editors to exclude thoughtfulness from their depiction of fictional children. Adults can be shown as actively thinking because the texture of their experience is inescapably problematic, so that they must think and choose as well as act, if they are merely to endure. But children are thought to inhabit a world whose security is ensured by adults, a world into which the threat of problematicity does not intrude, with the result that, under such circumstances, active thinking on the child's part is hardly necessary. The portrait of an inevitably happy childhood is simultaneously a portrait of childhood purged of anything that might be problematic or perplexing, and therefore cleansed of anything that might necessitate reflection. Children's readers, further are not expected to dramatize the plight of the vast numbers of children around the world who suffer from undernourishment, neglect, battering, unwantedness, or condescension and humiliation. But surely such readers must be recognized as bearing a heavy responsibility if they fail to depict children as thinking beings, for the image of the child that children's literature projects has much to do with the image of themselves that children internalize and the self-concept they retain in adulthood.

By means of fictional models, it is possible to show children that they themselves can think more reasonably and more creatively, for we want both to stimulate them to think and to stimulate them to think better. If the reading of the text is followed by critical and interpretive discussions about the ideas hidden between the lines of the novels like treasures in a treasure hunt, students will eagerly vie with one another to express their views, and if they cannot express such views orally, they can be induced to express them in written form, whether in essay form, dialogues, short stories, or poetry.

Thinking, of course, seldom occurs in accordance with the conventions of expository writing: it tends instead to be highly condensed and elliptical. Our thoughts tumble about in our heads, often simultaneously and seldom consistently. Discussion with a sympathetic community of inquiry can help us sort out these thoughts and neaten them up a bit, but to put them down on paper, something more is still needed. Here it is useful to expose students to poetic models that seem to be so casual, conversational, and artless that they seem to be almost like thinking out loud. It is a rather long and difficult journey from thinking to expository writing, but from thinking to the writing of poetry is only a step. Little wonder, then, that children's philosophical thinking, when precipitated into a product, may take the form of a poem.

I have not attempted to identify the variety of examples in the Philosophy for Children curriculum in which children are represented visiting an art museum, discussing aesthetic questions, or engaged in painting or sculpting and discussing problems in the psychology or epistemology of creation, or even in conversation with their parents and grandparents about issues in the philosophy of art. These are, after all, mere contrivances, and they will mean the meanings they generate, as the meanings of the dialogues Socrates held with young people are to be found in the works of his students and in the works of the students of those students, generation after generation, until we arrive at the young people in today's classrooms awaiting their first encounter with philosophy, like bottles in a wine cellar just waiting to be uncorked.

VI

Epilogue

15 The Philosophy of Childhood

The compartmentalization of philosophy reflects and responds to certain differences among specific skills and among specific dimensions of human experience. The skills in question are primarily the varieties of reasoning. The dimensions of experience include the aesthetic, the moral, the social, and the religious. A few philosophers might question the objectivity of the latter domains, but few are likely to contest the objectivity and universality of childhood. It would seem, therefore, that childhood is a legitimate dimension of human behavior and of human experience and that it is entitled to philosophical treatment no less than the other dimensions for which philosophies already exist. Perhaps its chief claim to philosophical uniqueness might be the fact that it is the forgotten—if not actually repressed—aspect of experience.

Although it is not the case that every child is a philosopher, it is generally granted that (except in a few rare instances) every philosopher was once a child. And if recent years have helped to demonstrate to us that the experience of philosophy need not be incompatible with childhood, so it may turn out that the experience of childhood—or at the very least, the perspective of the child—need not be incompatible with adulthood. That we are biologically of different ages no more makes us mutually incomprehensible than that we are biologically of different sexes. Indeed, the situation of adults vis-à-vis children is a bit better than that of males vis-à-vis females, for the latter distinction is symmetrical, neither having ever been the other, whereas adults have once been children, even though children have never been adults. Moreover, just as the differences between male and female perspectives constitute no insuperable barrier to their being experientially shared, so the differences between child and adult perspectives represent an invitation to the shared experience of human diversity rather than an excuse for intergenerational hostility, repression, and guilt. For example, were childhood to be a less closeted and more openly acknowledged dimension of human experience, we might expect more candor from philosophers in admitting the extent to which their "mature" views were systematic embellishments of their firmly held childhood intuitions and convictions. Yet even those philosophers who might take the opposing view, contending that their views as adults differed totally from the opinions they held as children, might acknowledge the extent to which the development of their later outlook represented a reaction against childhood convictions that were no less philosophical than the ones that replaced them.

The question will nevertheless persist as to what there is about childhood that entitles it to become an area of philosophy. The answer to this question would seem to be that, to deserve a philosophy, a subject area should be rich enough in implications as to contribute significantly to other areas of philosophy. Specialized studies in the field in question might in turn have value for metaphysics, or for logic, or for epistemology, and practitioners in these areas might find that they ignored the new field at their peril. The question, then, is whether childhood meets this requirement. It would indeed appear to be the case that developing philosophies of childhood hold promise of meaningful implications for social philosophy, metaphysics, philosophy of law, ethics, philosophy of education, and other philosophical areas. The purpose of this chapter is to identify certain of these areas in which work is already being done or needs to be done.

Projects are already under way, or need to be undertaken, that would be responsive to the following questions (to name only a few):

1. Do children have a right to reason, and what implications, if any, are thereby relevant to the philosophy of law?
2. Can children engage in ethical inquiry as a meaningful alternative to their being subjected to moral indoctrination? If so, what are the implications of such ethical inquiry for the general field of ethics?
3. How can the roles of children in any theory of community be of value to social philosophy?
4. In what ways does the question "What is a child?" throw light on the question "What is a person?" so as to contribute meaningfully to the metaphysical import of the latter issue?

We can here examine each of these issues in a bit more detail.

Do Children Have a Right to Reason?

It is well known in philosophy that considerable attention is currently given to children's rights. The flourishing of this interest is, of course, gratifying, but there is a signal need for a greater focus on the child's right to reason, especially that aspect of the problem that Bertram Bandman, in a recent article, has called "the child's right to inquire."

When we employ a catch-phrase such as the "right to inquire," we are in danger of overlooking the ambiguity that is prevalent in the use of the term "inquire." This is especially true in the case of children, since we all know how tirelessly children can direct questions at adults, whereas we know of few, if any, cases of children engaging in inquiry in the Peircean sense. So it is not surprising that our initial understanding of the phrase "right to inquire" should be in the sense of the child's right to ask questions, particularly of adults, and with regard to matters that adults may not care to discuss with children, either because they wish to protect children from such knowledge or because they wish to protect both the children and themselves from the irresponsible use of such knowledge. In this sense, the child's right to ask entails the further issue of the adult's right not to respond.

As we know, the fact that every answer has a question does not mean that every question has—or is entitled to—an answer nor that every challenge is entitled to a response. Hobbes points up an analogous situation when he argues that there may be certain things that the citizen, though justly commanded by the sovereign, can justly refuse to do. Likewise, there may be times when, although the child is within his or her rights in asking certain questions, the adult may without injustice refuse to reply or may properly choose to reply evasively. Evidently there are times—and here Hobbes is instructive—when one person's right to command does not necessarily imply another person's obligation to obey. It is in just such a jurisprudential no-man's-land that the examination of children's rights might turn out to be most rewarding.

But whatever the merits may be of examining the child's right to inquire in the sense of "asking questions"—presumably of those who "know the answers"—the more important issue continues to remain unexamined, and that is the matter of the right of children to engage in cooperative inquiry. Such a possibility seemed remote as long as there was no such thing as philosophy in the elementary school. But now that it has been firmly established that there are sound academic grounds for the institutionalization of philosophy as an integral portion of elementary and secondary education, we cannot turn away from the fact that the question of academic freedom can no longer be limited to the college campus. In the years to come, the counsel of philosophers will be increasingly needed to deal with the emerging issues of the academic freedom of children, as these proliferate under a variety of headings, such as the child's right to know, to reason, to doubt, and to believe. (Let us hope that a separate legal struggle will not be required for every mental act.)

Finally, it should not be overlooked that the denial to an individual of the right of expression is simultaneously the denial to others of the right to learn what the individual in question might have expressed. It is in this sense that, if children are to be "seen and not heard," their silencing deprives the rest of us of their insights. To the objection that children's views are seldom insightful, it would not be improper to suggest that an assay of adult views might also seem largely unprofitable.

Can Children Engage in Ethical Inquiry?

The discovery that children can do philosophy—and that they do so competently and with relish—points up in other ways the need to develop philosophies of childhood. For if children can reason as they begin to speak, and if they can do philosophy as they begin to reason, the present alliance between philosophical ethics and developmental psychology will begin to show welcome signs of strain. Should it be the case that at every stage of their growth children can engage in ethical inquiry, ethics need no longer be tainted, as it now is, with that indoctrinational manipulation of children's moral views and attitudes, which calls itself "moral education." Those who make use of philosophy in order to indoctrinate are deplorable; just as deplorable are those who make use of philosophy in order to undermine grounds for certain beliefs, with the excuse that only by doing so can they liberate children from dogma and superstition. For this, in effect, could be the indoctrination of relativism, or some other "ism."

Those who champion developmental theories of childhood tend to make two crucial errors. First, they frequently assume that childhood is a preparation for adulthood and is to be viewed as only a means to an end, or as an incomplete condition moving toward completeness. Adults know and children don't know; children must therefore acquire the knowledge with which grown-ups are so richly endowed. Thus the first mistake is to assume that, if children are not moving in the direction of what we adults know and believe and value, there must be something wrong with their "development." Such a view ignores the possibility that childhood is no more incomplete without a subsequent adulthood than adulthood is without a prior childhood. It is only together that they make "a life."

Second, the proponents of the developmental thesis are always careful to select those criteria that will reinforce the case they are trying to make, while ignoring other criteria through whose use that case might be weakened. Educational disciplines that have been organized in a simple-to-complex sequence are proposed as models—mathematics would be a good illustration. As children master such disciplines, their progressive development is thought to be taking place step by step and "true to form." But those who uphold the development thesis make sure not to select such criteria as artistic expression or philosophical insight, for to do so might make their case seem less compelling. Why do children create such impressive paintings while in early childhood? Why do they ask so many metaphysical questions while still young, then seem to suffer a decline in their powers as they move into adolescence? How can children learn the terms and syntax and logic of a whole language—indeed, often, of several languages—while they are still toddlers, a feat beyond the scope of most grown-ups? What would education have to be in order to *sustain* the child's development along the meteoric lines with which it begins, rather than let it lapse, as it now so frequently does, into apathy and bitterness? It would seem that for every criterion that supports the development thesis, another can be found that goes against it. And for every aspect of the child's growth where there seems to be a natural unfolding, there is another aspect wherein development occurs only by sustained intervention—education being a prime example.

In short, the philosophy of childhood would be much enhanced by fresh work in ethical theory. Such work would take into account the capacity of children to engage in rational dialogue, to offer reasons for their conduct, and would not treat children patronizingly or condescendingly by assuming that their behavior is necessarily more selfish and less idealistic than the behavior of adults. Such work would also recognize that the developmental approach has achieved a dubious plausibility by comparing children with adults primarily in terms of adult knowledge, rather than in terms of other criteria whose employment might lead to children appearing much better and adults much worse. A theory of ethical inquiry is needed, but those who devise such a theory ought to keep firmly in mind that the ethics they are engaged in is part of philosophy and not part of science. For an ethical approach to claim to be "scientific" would ensure its demise in a school setting about as surely as if it were to claim to be guaranteed by "religion."

Can Children's Roles Be Useful to Social Philosophy?

Another area in which work needs to be done is social philosophy. The philosophy of childhood needs to address itself to those respects in which childhood has been indicted for traits that should be treated as problematic rather than taken for granted. Typical of such indictments is the charge that, unlike their parents and grandparents, young people find work repugnant. Now, the point has been made by Dewey that, in a certain sense, laziness is a modern invention, since it is the response one would expect to those aspects of modern factory work that make such work obnoxious. But this is probably not the explanation for the observed change in children's attitudes, and if it is not, what is?

If one listens to the complaints of parents, one hears the problem formulated as a lack of intergenerational symmetry: our parents worked hard, and we learned to do so from them; why haven't our children learned to do so from us? Like our parents, we love work; why do our children hate it so?

A good reason for considering this a problem in social philosophy is that it is an example of the decline of community. Only a few generations ago, the basic work unit of the society was not the individual or the factory, but the family. The family was a working community, in which individuals of all ages had their tasks to perform. But as the drive for personal success replaced the normal process of generational succession, the work-oriented children of such communities struck out after their own goals and worked for them as wholeheartedly as previously they had worked within the bosoms of their families. They became professionals, whose work ethic was personal rather than social. Their work—as doctors, scholars, accountants, administrators—was something they could not share with their children, because the family was no longer the basic work unit to which they belonged. The child's efforts to participate were rebuked with such comments as, "Don't bother Daddy, he's busy!" or "Please go out and play; can't you see Mommy's working?" Soon the child caught on: what came between him and his parents or between her and her parents was this hateful thing called work. Perhaps the parents could not be disliked, but what they were doing could be.

Here, obviously, we need guidance. Do we accept this change in attitude as a fait accompli, or do we wish to attack it or circumvent it? If our choice is to attempt to reconstruct the work community, how is this to be accomplished? Could the creation of communities of inquiry in which adults and children participate together as equals be a step in that direction?

It is not unusual to see people's eyes light up when they hear of children engaged in inquiry. There is more uncertainty in their response when the notion of community is broached. But it is difficult to conceive of inquiry that does not take place in a community setting, and if this is generally the case with adults, how much more true is it in the case of children! The recourse to shared and objective procedures, openness of evidence, the challenging of poorly drawn inferences, the consideration of the consequences of suppositions and hypotheses—all of these help to form the fabric of a community of inquiry among children as well as adults. When these and allied procedures are internalized by each participant, the result is critical reflection. More than critical, for it is also self-critical. One becomes accustomed to asking oneself the same hard questions one levels at one's companions in dialogue. Needless to say, those who are able to engage in cognitive self-criticism are in a good position to being able to exercise behavioral self-control. The internalization of the procedures of the community of inquiry thus has a moral as well as a dialogical or theoretical dimension.

Furthermore, the formation of childhood communities, where candor and trust mingle freely with wondering, searching, and reasoning, provides a needed social support during those critical years in which children are loosening the ties that bind them to their families and endeavoring to establish themselves as mature and responsible individuals. We should not forget the warning voiced repeatedly by Margaret Mead that we must learn to devise social mechanisms that will smooth the transition periods for growing children. Otherwise, these periods become moments of childhood crisis.

Children and Persons

Finally, there is the problem of the child as a person. We generally think of personhood not as something given at birth but as something gradually achieved. No one seems able to say just what the normal age is for becoming a person, but we suspect that, compared with ancient times, the starting point of personhood is now put at an earlier age and the beginning of maturity at a later one. Yet, although there has been some shrinkage in the period of one's being a non-person, or a not-yet-person, we have continued to believe that one must give behavioral evidence of deserving to be called a person before the appropriate rite of predication can be performed. The same may be said for acknowledging that the child has a self, or is rational. There is generally sound warrant for any reluctance to employ terms honorifically, but such warrant may not be sufficient to justify withholding personhood and rationality from young children.

Now, ordinarily, a clear-cut distinction must be made between achievement and ascription. Achievement terms are based on observable behaviors and are to be accorded only upon the actual manifestation of such behaviors (in the sense that those who write are called writers, those who run are called runners, and so on). But ascription terms endow their object with properties (such as prestige and charisma) independent of any observed behavior, since these properties exist wholly to the extent to which people are willing to ascribe or impute them. In between these more clear-cut cases is a host of knotty issues, in each of which it can be debated whether the predications are or are not gratuitous.

However, the achievement-ascription distinction is rather like a set of cards that has a joker in it, and the joker lies in the fact that the application of the distinction to cases where *meaning* is at issue may be somewhat different from its application to cases in which *truth* is at issue.

It sometimes happens, C. I. Lewis tells us, that the subject must bring certain conditions to an experience in order to understand or comprehend the object correctly, and whatever the subject must in such fashion bring along in order to grasp the meaning of the object belongs to the object and not to the subject.[1] Were this claim of Lewis's to be accepted, it would follow that concepts like "person" and "rational," whose ascription makes meaningful what otherwise was not meaningful, deservedly belong to the object of such ascriptions. We are therefore pragmatically justified in considering the behavior of young children to be the behavior of rational persons, in that we can comprehend such behavior as being more meaningful than if we refuse to engage in what we consider to be unwarranted and gratuitous ascriptions.

To impute rationality to a child is further warranted on the grounds that doing so has so often resulted in evidence of the child's rationality. This is therefore not to be confused with the judicial postulate that people are not to be considered guilty until they are proved guilty. Treating accused persons as not guilty does not confirm their innocence; treating children as rational tends to produce evidence that confirms their rationality.

Whether or not these particular arguments will be found persuasive, the issue of the child's personhood and rationality will remain to haunt the philosophy of childhood. And here another aspect of the problem appears to require a pragmatic formulation. For if we refuse to acknowledge the rationality of children, we cannot satisfactorily engage in philosophical dialogue with them, because we cannot accept their utterances as reasons. If we cannot do philosophy with children, we deprive their education of the very component that might make such education more meaningful. And if we deny children a meaningful education, we ensure that the ignorance, irresponsibility, and mediocrity that currently prevail among adults will continue to do so. Treating children as persons might be a small price to pay, in the long run, for some rather substantive social gains.

Appendix

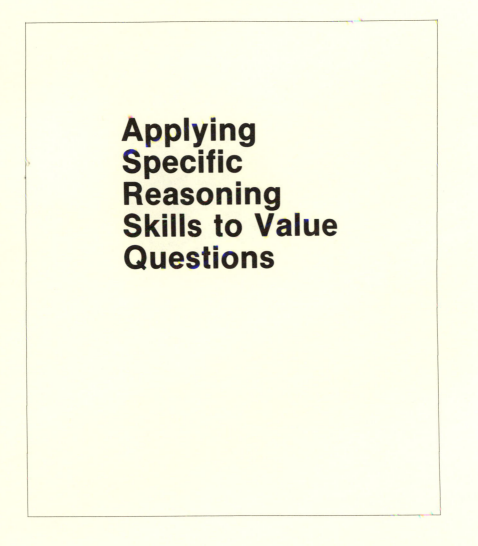

Applying Specific Reasoning Skills to Value Questions

Applying Specific Reasoning
Skills to Value Questions

**Illustrations of how specific thinking skills may be applied to
value questions**

A curriculum for values education would attempt to develop specific
reasoning skills and to apply them to specific value issues. The following
examples are simply intended to show how this is done; it is not intended as a
paradigm but as a set of typical instances, for use in this case at the middle
school level. (Some examples may be more appropriate for early childhood
or secondary school.)

Accompanying each reasoning skill is a brief explanation or rationale, in
some cases phrased as behavioral objectives. Also given is an application, as
exhibited in a fictional children's conversation. In the actual classroom, this
bit of dialogue forms a portion of an exercise, the doing of which brings
about the learning of the rule. In other words, the fictional illustration
becomes the basis of classroom discussion, so that the students participate
actively in the process, progressively discovering the rule embedded in the
illustrations.

**1. Drawing inferences from single
   premises**

Students should be able to perform
logical conversions and know the
rule governing valid and invalid
conversions. (That is, they should
know, for example, that "Some
bullies are students" can be validly
inferred from "Some students are
bullies" but that "All people are
bullies" cannot be validly inferred
from "All bullies are people.")

FRANK: Some Europeans are French, so it follows that all Frenchmen
are Europeans.

RITA: Sorry, you're wrong. If some Europeans are French, what follows is that *some* Frenchmen are Europeans.

FRANK: But that's ridiculous! Everyone knows that *all* Frenchmen are Europeans!

RITA: Some Europeans are Russian. Does it follow that all Russians are Europeans?

2. **Standardizing ordinary language sentences**
Students should be familiar with and able to apply elementary rules of logical standardization. For example, a sentence beginning with "only" should begin instead with "all," but with subject and predicate reversed.

LINDA: All novels are works of fiction.

GENE: So it follows that only novels are works of fiction.

Note: Gene's wrong. What follows is, "Only works of fiction are novels."

3. **Drawing inferences from double premises**
Students should be able to draw correct conclusions from valid syllogisms and be able to identify by inspection at least some instances of invalid inference. It should be remembered that syllogisms are sound only if they are formally correct (valid) and if the premises are true or assumed to be true.

a. SAM: I read in a book that all Vulcans are stingy.

MIKE: Well, I must not be stingy, because I'm not a Vulcan.

Note: Sam didn't say that *only* Vulcans are stingy.

b. MARCIE: Boys are aggressive.

WALTER: The girls on the volleyball team are all aggressive, so I guess that means they're boyish.

Note: Even if it were true that all boys are aggressive, it wouldn't follow that all aggressive people are boys. It should be obvious that there is a logical underpinning to prejudice. Exposing the faulty reasoning underlying ethnic and sexual stereotypes may not remove the prejudice, but it might be helpful.

c. HENRY: Some criminals are fascinating.

DORA: You must find the Zilch brothers interesting, because they've just been convicted of bank robbery.

Note: Henry didn't claim that *all* criminals are fascinating. Had he said so, Dora's inference would have been correct.

d. ANDY: All cruelty is wrong, and stepping on a cat's tail is cruel.

MARIE: So stepping on that cat's tail was wrong. Gee, and it happened completely by accident!

Note: If Andy's premises are true, Marie's conclusion must be true. But her further remark suggests there may be a question about the truth of Andy's second premise.

e. TED: Giving much-needed assistance is always right. If you help me break into this store, you'll be giving me much-needed assistance. So helping me break into this store will be right.

SID: Giving assistance *isn't* always right.

Note: Sid questions the truth of Ted's first premise. In cases d and e, further discussion of the truth of the premises will involve additional reasoning skills such as defining terms, recognizing contextual aspects of truth and falsity, and using criteria.

4. Using ordinal or relational logic

Students should be conversant with rules governing transitive and symmetrical relationships and should be able to distinguish valid from invalid instances of relational logic.

a. GLEN: Washington was a greater president than Harding.

HAL: If that's so, then Harding wasn't as great a president as Washington.

b. JOAN: In writing, verbs are as important as nouns.

TRISH: So it follows that, in writing, nouns are as important as verbs.

c. TRISH: Ophelia was in love with Hamlet.

JOAN: That means Hamlet must have been in love with Ophelia.

Note: The reasoning in a and b is correct. But in c, Joan's reasoning is faulty. The relationship "being in love with" is not symmetrical.

d. GLEN: Sparta was stronger than Athens, and Athens was stronger than Thebes.

HAL: So it follows that Sparta was stronger than Thebes.

e. TRISH: Germany is next to France, and France is next to Spain.

NORA: So it follows that Germany is next to Spain.

Note: The reasoning in d is all right, but not in e: "is next to" is not a transitive relationship.

5. Working with consistency and contradiction

Students should be able to recognize the consistency or inconsistency in a given narrative or description. They should also be able to formulate and apply the formal rules of contradiction. (Two statements are mutually contradictory when, if either one is true, the other must be false.)

PHIL: No countries are democratic.

LIZ: Well, I know some that are, but I guess we could both be right.

Note: The statements of Phil and Liz contradict each other. Therefore, they *can't* both be right.

6. Knowing how to deal with ambiguities

In trying to understand textbooks and other sources of information, students need to be wary of ambiguities. They should be able to distinguish the ambiguities of words with several meanings in the same context from sentences whose grammatical arrangements make diverse interpretations possible (i.e., semantic versus syntactic ambiguities). Students should also recognize that some ambiguities (especially in literature) are valuable rather than mischievous.

a. The judge stopped drinking after midnight in the town tavern.

b. The director didn't like the way the dog behaved in that scene, so he shot it again.

c. SUZY: I loved that Mozart concert! I'd forgotten just how great music can sound!

d. The visiting anthropologists watched the Indian dance.

e. The actress with a broken leg was in a huge cast.

f. There was room for only one more student in the art class with the live model, so we drew lots.

7. Formulating questions   Students should be familiar with some of the defects with which questions are frequently contaminated, such as that they may be vague, loaded, self-contradictory, nonsensical, or based on incorrect assumptions.

HORACE: Fred, have you stopped cheating on exams?
FRED: I never started.
Note: If Horace knows that Fred *has* been cheating on exams, there is nothing wrong with the question. But if he does not know anything of the sort, his question is just a fishing expedition and therefore illegitimate.

8. Grasping part-whole and whole-part connections   Students should know how to avoid part-whole mistakes—that is, assuming that if a member of part of a group has a certain feature, the entire collection has that feature. Also to be avoided are whole-part mistakes in which a feature of the whole is attributed to the part.

a. TANYA: The members of the police force in our town are quite small.
   TINA: It must be a small police force.

b. GIL: The police force in our town is wide awake twenty-four hours a day.
   JOSH: Those poor police officers! How do they manage without rest?

Note: In the preceding examples, a is a part-whole fallacy and b is a whole-part fallacy.

9. Giving reasons   When students behave in questionable ways, we often ask them to *justify* their actions with reasons. We also ask them to cite reasons in support of questionable opinions. Students should be able to distinguish between giving reasons and giving explanations—the latter do not justify, but both employ the term "because."

LARRY: On this take-home exam, I need to explain Japan's attack on Pearl Harbor.
SUE: I guess you could talk about the way Japan and the United States were rivals for military and economic control of the Pacific.
LARRY: Maybe that explains the attack, but it doesn't justify it.
SUE: Of course not! Causes aren't reasons.

10. Identifying underlying assumptions

Students should be able to specify the assumptions that underlie a particular statement, where the truth of the statement is contingent upon the assumption. Such assumptions may also underlie questions, commands, and exclamations.

a. GRACE: Look at these pictures of concentration camp victims.
CINDY: Yes, it makes you wonder what terrible things they must have done to have been treated that way.

b. NAT: If the Mississippi reaches flood stage, will it endanger Cairo?
TRACY: Yes, assuming that the Cairo you're talking about is the one in Illinois, not the one in Egypt.

c. SALLY: The world's oil reserves will last for another thousand years.
JANE: What rate of depletion are you assuming?

Note: In a, Cindy's comment exemplifies the illegitimate assumption of a cause—in this case, that victims must be guilty of something.

11. Working with analogies

An analogy is the citation of a resemblance between two relationships—for example, "Kittens are to cats as puppies are to dogs" or "Sawing is to furniture as chiseling is to sculpture." The ability to put oneself in another's place often involves analogical reasoning and is sometimes termed "moral imagination."

a. When someone accidentally dropped a wastepaper basket on Neil's toe, Isabel tried to remember how it felt when she got her thumb caught in the car door.

b. Tommy's father has lost his job, and his family is having a hard time.

Jenny says, "I can't imagine what is must be like! My parents have *always* had jobs!"

c. Chita's brother steps on the cat's foot by accident, and the cat lets out a loud screech. Chita picks up the cat and hugs it, saying to her brother, "You hurt it!" "Oh, no," he replies, "animals can't feel pain."

d. Kate speaks lovingly every day to her plants. Her sister says to her, "Why bother?" "Funny," Kate replies, "that's the same thing people say to our teacher about the way he treats *us.*"

Note: Analogies can be expressed in a great variety of ways, but they always involve a resemblance between two relationships or a resemblance between two systems of relationships. Analogies are highly important in science (especially in induction) and in poetry, but it should not be forgotten that, in music, variations are analogical. Training in analogical reasoning is especially important in value inquiry, since the validity of judgments often depends on whether the experiences cited are comparable.

12. Formulating cause-effect relationships

Students should be able to identify and to construct formulations that suggest specific cause-effect relationships. They should also be able to identify the "after this, because of this" fallacy.

a. AL: The stars come out after the sun goes down.
HORACE: Sure, but do the stars come out *because* the sun goes down?

b. GLORIA: General Grant drank a lot and won the war.
GLADYS: Yes, but did he win the war *because* he drank a lot?

c. TAD: The League of Nations was formed right after World War I, and within a couple of years, Fascism and Nazism developed.
SETH: But did the formation of the League of Nations *cause* the rise of Fascism and Nazism?

d. BEVERLY: The second word of every sentence *always* follows the first, and the second word of every sentence *only* follows the first. Therefore, the first word of every sentence is the cause of the second word.
MIDGE: Even if what you said was true, constant conjunction wouldn't prove that the connection was a causal one.

13. Concept development

In applying a concept to a specific set of cases, children should be able to identify those cases that fall clearly within the boundaries of the concept and those that clearly fall outside the boundaries. Children should be encouraged to cite counter-instances if they think the boundaries of the concept have been incorrectly drawn. Exercises and discussion plans should deal with both clearcut and borderline cases.

SETH: If you betray a friend, can you still be friends afterward?

LOU: Afterwards, maybe, but not while it happens, it seems to me.

Note: Seth is trying to discover the contours of the concept of friendship by confronting a highly problematic instance. Lou's response seems to evoke experience (friends might later be reconciled, if a breach in the friendship were to develop) and logic (the definition of friendship might be logically incompatible with that of betrayal). If one's concepts are very fuzzy, one's value judgments can hardly be very clear. Seth and Lou are trying to be clear.

14. Generalization

Students working with data should be able to note such regularities or uniformities as do exist and to construct generalizations that would apply to these and similar instances. Students should also be aware of the hazards involved in such generalizations.

a. NORA: Everyone in the class has said that the doctors they have gone to have been careful. On the basis of that, what can we say?

ROGER: As far as we know, doctors are generally careful.

b. TRICIA: Each state we've visited has had a border with some other state, and we've visited practically all of them.

PAT: I guess it's safe to say that all states have common borders with other states.

Note: Obviously, Roger is appropriately circumspect, and Pat is not. In matters of value, generalizations are not impossible, but they can be hazardous. (As an example, consider value generalizations in art history.)

15. Drawing inferences from hypo-thetical syllogisms

Students should be able to distin-guish between valid and invalid inferences when working with hypothetical ("if-then") syllogisms. In hypothetical deduction, it is valid to affirm the antecedent or deny the consequent. It is invalid to deny the antecedent or affirm the consequent. For example, it is valid to say, assuming, of course, the truth of the premises, "If I push this button, the world will blow up. It didn't blow up. So I must not have pushed the button" (denial of consequent).

a. BURT: If the gas in the *Hindenburg* dirigible had been helium, it wouldn't have burned.

HARRY: But it did burn. So the gas in the *Hindenburg* couldn't have been helium.

b. DAISY: Is it true that if Hank had a chance, he'd sell his own mother?

TINA: Yes, but he hasn't sold her yet, so I guess he hasn't yet had a chance.

Note: This is one of the most powerful of all the reasoning skills. Understanding of the valid patterns comes with acquisition of the language and does not need to be specially acquired; the same is true with most aspects of formal logic.

16. Ability to recognize and avoid —or knowingly utilize—vagueness

Vague words lack clear cut-off points to their applicability. Students should be able to distinguish contexts in which vague words are accepted from those in which they are unsuitable.

ROSE: Can two countries fight each other without declaring war?

DOUG: Sure.

ROSE: Can two countries declare war on each other without fighting?

DOUG: Sure.

ROSE: So "war" and "peace" are really very vague terms!

DOUG: Of course they are, but so are "hot" and "cold" and "dry" and "wet" and lots of other terms that are extremely useful in spite of being vague.

17. Taking all considerations into account

In value questions, as in inquiry generally, it is important to see comprehensiveness. When we neglect to take all relevant considerations into account, we can be accused of jumping to conclusions. Students can develop skill in asking one another—and themselves—if they have overlooked anything in the course of their inquiry.

CONTRACTOR: Have you checked out the safety factor for this new design of the school roof? I'm worried about its ability to withstand a really heavy snow.

ARCHITECT: We checked the records back for some years, and we found it doesn't often snow heavily in these parts. I wouldn't worry.

Note: Often it is only by hindsight that we discover we have failed to take some critical factor into account. Not every consideration turns out to be critical (those that do become established as *criteria*). But in terms of ethical education, children must be alerted to the importance of *considerateness,* not just of one another but of all the relevant features of a situation.

18. **Recognizing interdependence of ends and means**

When a goal or objective is cited or recommended, there is an obligation to spell out the means by which it is to be achieved. (Things are means only relative to specific ends; thus what is a means in one situation need not be one in a different situation.) Students should be able to suggest ends for proposed means and means for proposed ends.

a. TEACHER: In addition to using it as a coat hanger, what uses could you put this thing to?

MEREDITH: It's what I open the car door with when my father's locked his keys inside.

b. TEACHER: The railway system is a means of transportation. What is its end or purpose?

FRANCIS: It helps people get to their destinations, and every person has a different goal. So I guess one means can serve many ends.

Note: In a, the teacher asks that a new purpose be thought of for a given object; the student recalls how an unusual end (getting into the locked car) dictated recourse to an unusual means (the coat hanger). In b, the student suggests that there is no contradiction between means being public and shared in common, while ends are individual.

19. Knowing how to deal with "informal fallacies"

Many informal reasoning fallacies are due to our reliance on irrelevant considerations or our omission of relevant ones—hence they hinge on judgments of relevance. They may occur in written form and as violations of dialogical procedure as well. Students can be alerted to their presence and to ways of treating them. Skills for coping with some of these fallacies have already been identified for ambiguity (see #6); for vagueness (see #16); for composition (see #8); for division (see #8); and for post hoc (see #12). There are still a great many others to which students can be introduced; the "fallacy of illegitimate authority" may be taken as representative.

HANK: I wonder who could tell us about the effects of dumping toxic chemicals in rivers.
DAISY: My uncle Pete.
HANK: Is he an authority on chemicals or on the environment?
DAISY: Neither one, but he sure is good in Scrabble.
Note: Authority may be understood as based on *credentials* or on *status*. Within a given institution, say, the family, appeal is generally to status authority. Where there is not common institution, appeal is authorities with expert experience or to the process of inquiry itself.

20. Operationalizing concepts

Students should be able to cite observable effects for the concepts they employ and to express those in the form of conditionals. Thus if a thing is not readily scratched by other things, it is called "hard." If it falls, it is said to have "weight." (The specific behavior is the antecedent of the conditional and is the criterion of the concept itself, which is the consequent of the conditional.)

a. JOE: Why do you say he's a bigot?
   KEN: If for no good reason you hate some ethnic group, it's what I call bigotry.

b. TESS: What are the marks of a good teacher?
   BEN: Liking ideas and liking kids.

   Note: Obviously there is a close connection between this skill and that of defining terms.

21. Defining terms

There are some very general rules about definitions, such as they should not be too inclusive or restrictive, they should not be negative, and they should not be circular. One of the most traditional procedures for defining nouns is to ask questions: what sort of thing is it, and how does it differ from other things of that sort?

a. BETTY: What's a gem?
   MELISSA: A *stone.*
   BETTY: What sort of stone?
   MELISSA: Why, a *precious* stone.

b. WILMA: What's liberty?
   GRACE: Freedom.
   WILMA: What's freedom?
   GRACE: Liberty.
   WILMA: We seem to be going around in circles.

22. Identifying and using criteria

Whenever we make judgments of value (such as in ethical or aesthetic matters) or of practice (in estimating quantities or qualities) or even of fact (as in governing the admissibility of evidence), we employ standards or criteria. It is important that students know the criteria they employ in making such judgments and that they utilize the criteria that are most appropriate to the situations in which the judgments are to be made. Criteria are, of course, especially important in the construction of definitions and in the operationalization of concepts. When confronting a problem, we try to take all considerations into account, but those considerations that are decisive are criteria.

a. WILBUR: Using the criterion of *per capita income,* India is a poor country.

FLO: Yes, but using the criterion of *natural resources,* India is a rich country.

b. YOLANDA: Using the criterion of *population,* Japan is a large country.

ZEKE: Okay, but using the criterion of *geographical size,* Japan is a small country.

c. GAIL: I think *The Merchant of Venice* is a good play, but what are the criteria by which I judge it to be good?

SANDRA: Judging it as a tragedy, it isn't very good.

LEON: And judging it as a comedy, it isn't very good.

GAIL: Well, if those aren't the criteria, there must be others that we haven't thought of. I guess I'll just have to keep trying to figure them out.

23. Instantiation

Many children who have difficulty generalizing and developing abstract concepts nevertheless have facility in offering instances and examples—just the reverse of what is true of many adults. But ability to instantiate is essential to the capacity to apply ideas to concrete situations. Likewise essential is the ability to offer counterexamples as a means of refutation.

a. RUTH: Can you give me some examples of colors?
JACK: Sure—green, lavender, scarlet, and purple. I'm sure glad you didn't ask me what *color* is.

b. GENE: What goes up must come down.
JOY: Like a space rocket, right?

Note: Joy's counterinstance effectively refutes Gene's claim.

24. Constructing hypotheses

Hypotheses are ideas that represent possible ways of resolving problematic situations. When we encounter surprising or disturbing facts, we invent hypotheses to account for them. Skill in constructing hypotheses both entails and encompasses skill in making predictions, by means of which the hypotheses in question are either confirmed or disconfirmed.

a. MAX: I think this stuff here is an acid. Look at it fume!
LUCY: Let's see if it turns litmus red. If it does, you're right.

b. TIM: I'm puzzled by that guy over there who keeps watching us play these machines.
JEFF: Well, if he should turn out to be a truant officer, that will explain everything.

Note: In b, if the man turns out *not* to be a truant officer, then Jeff's hypothesis is irrelevant, and a new hypothesis is needed. If he turns out to be a truant officer, but not looking for Tim and Jeff, then the hypothesis is disconfirmed, for it does not explain why he is watching them.

25. Contextualizing

Students should be able to recognize how assertions change their meaning—and possibly their truth values—when applied to a variety of contexts. Thus in asserting that something is true, one should be prepared to say *under what circumstances* it might be false, and vice versa. Also, one should be able to provide, from prior experience, contexts that would make elliptical statements meaningful.

TONY: Listen to what Othello says: "Put out the light and put out the light." That's redundant!

LOUISE: No it's not. You have to supply a different context for each "Put out the light," and when you do, each has a different meaning.

26. Anticipating, predicting, and estimating consequences

To a considerable extent, rationality involves foreseeing the future impact of what happens in the present, whether or not the present activity is of our own doing. It is difficult to hold people responsible for what they did when it is evident they were unable to anticipate what would happen as a result of what they did. All the more reason to develop skills in anticipating, predicting, and estimating consequences.

CLARE: Bill, I wouldn't do that if I were you. There's a stiff punishment for turning in false fire alarms.

BILL: Aw, I won't get caught. Nobody's looking.

CLARE: But while the firemen are chasing after false alarms, they're unable to put out the real fires.

BILL: That's tough.

CLARE: Sure it is—especially if it's in your own house!

Note: Clare is trying to reason with Bill. She's trying to think of reasons that might dissuade him. In this instance, these reasons involve citing disadvantageous consequences. Clare could, of course, simply cite the law rather than the penalties. But she probably suspects that the formation of Bill's character into that of a law-abiding person should have been achieved long ago and that this is not the time to complete his unfulfilled moral education.

27. Classification and categorization

There are two kinds of classifying: sorting and grading. Sorting does not specifically involve distinguishing the better from the worse; grading does. In selecting a set of classes into which a number of individuals are to be grouped, one should seek classes that are mutually exclusive and jointly exhaustive of the totality of individuals.

BIFF: Countries can be classified as either democratic or non-democratic.

PAM: But non-democratic countries can be classified as either totalitarian or authoritarian.

BIFF: I disagree with you, and on two counts: first, totalitarian countries are also authoritarian; and second, there are countries that are non-democratic but not authoritarian.

Note: Biff's right. Pam's classification was neither mutually exclusive nor jointly exhaustive of non-democratic countries.

Notes,
Bibliography,
and Index

Notes

Chapter 2

1. Jacques Derrida, *Qui a peur de la philosophie?*
2. Plato, *Republic,* Book 7, trans. Francis Cornford. New York: Oxford University Press, 1945, p. 261.
3. Gilbert Ryle, "Plato," in *The Encyclopedia of Philosophy,* ed. Paul Edwards. New York: Macmillan, 1967.
4. Plato, *Gorgias* (p. 485), in *The Collected Dialogues of Plato,* ed. Edith Hamilton and Huntington Cairns. Princeton, N.J.: Princeton University Press, 1961.
5. George Santayana, "Ultimate Religion," in *Obiter Scripta,* ed. Justus Buchler and Benjamin Schwartz. New York: Scribner's, 1936.

Chapter 3

1. Robin G. Collingwood, *Essay on Philosophical Method.* Oxford: Clarendon Press, 1933, pp. 26–52.
2. Eduard Hanslick, *On the Musically Beautiful,* Ed. and trans., Geoffrey Payzant. Indianapolis, IN: Hackett Publishing Co., 1986.

Chapter 4

1. David Hume, *An Inquiry Concerning Human Understanding.* New York: Liberal Arts Press, 1955, p. 173.
2. See, for example, Robert Bellah et al., *Habits of the Heart,* Berkeley: University of California Press, 1985, as well as recent comments by E. D. Hirsch, Jr., in which he claims to be able to identify "what every American needs to know" (*Education Week,* April 15, 1987, p. 9).

Here is Hirsch explaining that what students need in order to be "culturally literate" is not simply thinking skills but facts:

We should incorporate the elements of cultural literacy into the structure of textbooks, courses, and school requirements. We should teach more surveys that cover large movements of human thought and experience. Yet even now the goal of teaching shared information is under attack by the latest version of educational formalism, the "critical thinking" movement. This well-meaning educational program aims to take children beyond the minimal basic skills mandated by state guidelines and to encourage the teaching of "higher order" skills. Admirable as these goals are, the denigration of "mere facts" by the movement's proponents is a dangerous repetition of the mistakes of 1918.

Any educational movement that avoids coming to terms with the specific contents of literate education or evades the responsibility of conveying them to all citizens is committing a fundamental error. However noble its aims, any movement that deprecates facts as antiquated or irrelevant injures the cause of higher national literacy. The old prejudice that facts deaden the minds of children has a long history in the nineteenth and twentieth centuries and includes not just the disciples of Rousseau and Dewey but also Charles Dickens who, in the figure of Mr. Gradgrind in *Hard Times,* satirized the teaching of mere facts. But it isn't facts that deaden the minds of young children, who are storing facts in their minds every day with astonishing voracity. It is incoherence—our failure to ensure that a pattern of shared, vividly taught, and socially enabling knowledge will emerge from our instruction.

The notion that thinking skills can be entrusted with the task of giving coherence to masses of inert, atomistic facts is difficult to take seriously. Without concepts or ideas, such facts are simply residues of alienated information. There are difficulties galore with any notion of a "common culture," but none is more problematic than Hirsch's, with his primitive view that such a culture is an aggregate of facts. (See E. D. Hirsch, Jr., *Cultural Literacy.* Boston: Houghton Mifflin, 1987, pp. 132–33.)

3. Cf. R. M. Hutchins, *The Conflict in Education in a Democratic Society.* New York: Harpers, 1953.

4. Benjamin Bloom et al., eds., *Taxonomy of Educational Objectives.* Vol. 1. New York: David McKay, 1956–64.

Chapter 5

1. Aristotle, *Nicomachean Ethics,* in *The Basic Works of Aristotle,* ed. Richard McKeon. New York: Random House, 1941, pp. 935–43.

2. Immanuel Kant, *Fundamental Principles of the Metaphysic of Morals.* New York: Liberal Arts Press, 1949.

3. John Stuart Mill, *On Liberty* and *Utilitarianism,* in *The Six Great Humanistic Essays of John Stuart Mill,* ed. Albert Wm. Levi. New York: Washington Square Press, 1963.

4. John Dewey, "Moral Judgment and Knowledge," in *Theory of the Moral Life,* ed. Arnold Isenberg. New York: Holt, Rinehart and Winston, 1908, 1960, pp. 120–46.

5. For a comparable examination of a similar list of cognitive skills as applied to matters more factual than valuational, see Matthew Lipman, "Thinking Skills

Fostered by Philosophy for Children," in *Thinking and Learning Skills, Vol. 1: Relating Instruction to Research,* ed. Judith W. Segal, Susan F. Chipman, and Robert Glaser. Hillsdale, N.J.: Lawrence Erlbaum Associates, 1985, pp. 83–108.

6. The numbers stand for the skills as presented sequentially in the Appendix.

Chapter 6

1. Quoted in Justus Buchler, *The Concept of Method.* New York: Columbia University Press, 1961, p. 13.

2. Stuart Hampshire, "Logic and Appreciation," *World Review,* 1952.

3. Something may be called unique because it is "one of a kind," that is, the only instance of a given type. But the fact that something is unique does not prevent it from belonging to an order or, for that matter, to countless orders.

4. See Buchler, *Concept of Method.*

5. For a discussion of those extraordinary and highly individualized acts that far exceed what is morally expected of a person, see J. O. Urmson, "Saints and Heroes," in *Essays in Moral Philosophy,* ed. A. I. Melden. Seattle: University of Washington Press, 1958, pp. 198–216.

6. Robin G. Collingwood, *The Principles of Art.* Oxford: Oxford University Press, 1937, pp. 15–16.

7. Cf. Gilbert Ryle, "Thinking and Self-Teaching," *Rice University Studies* 58, no. 2 (Summer, 1972).

8. This has been argued for by Gilbert Harman, *The Nature of Morality.* New York: Oxford University Press, 1977, p. 127.

Chapter 9

1. Charles Glock et al., *Adolescent Prejudice.* New York: Harper & Row, 1975.

2. Matthew Lipman, *Mark.* Upper Montclair, N.J.: IAPC, 1980, Chap. 1.

Chapter 10

1. Ronald Berman, Op Ed column, *The New York Times,* Jan. 29, 1978, p. 4.

2. Kenneth Koch, *Rose, Where Did You Get That Red?* New York: Random House, 1973; and *Wishes, Lies, and Dreams.* New York: Chelsea House, 1970.

3. John Dewey, *Art as Experience.* New York: Minton, Balch, 1934, pp. 35–57.

Chapter 14

1. Cf. W. E. Kennick, "Creative Acts," in *Art and Philosophy.* 2nd ed., ed. W. E. Kennick. New York: St. Martin's Press, 1979, p. 166.

2. The notion of treating all human activities as games is often associated with Wittgenstein, but one should see also Johan Huizinga, *Homo Ludens: A Study of the Play-Element in Culture.* London: Routledge and Kegan Paul, 1949, pp. 199–213.

3. See, for example, his discussion of "technique" in *The Principles of Art.* Oxford: Clarendon Press, 1938, pp. 26–28.

4. Kennick, "Creative Acts," p. 181.

5. Carl R. Hausman, "Creativity Studies: Where Can They Go?" *The Journal of Aesthetics and Art Criticism* 45, no. 1 (Fall, 1986): 87–88.

6. Charles Peirce, "The Probability of Induction," in *Philosophical Writings of Peirce,* ed. Justus Buchler. New York, Dover Publications, 1955, p. 180.

7. Cf. Michael A. Wallach, "Creativity and the Expression of Possibilities," in *Creativity and Learning,* ed. Jerome Kagan. Boston: Houghton Mifflin, 1967, pp. 36–57.

Chapter 15

1. C. I. Lewis, *An Analysis of Knowledge and Valuation.* La Salle, Ill.: Open Court, 1946, pp. 469–78.

Bibliography

Baier, Kurt. "Response to Matthew Lipman's 'Philosophical Practice and Educational Reform,'" *Journal of Thought* 20, no. 4 (Winter, 1985): 37-44.

Baier, Kurt, and Nicholas Rescher, eds. *Values and the Future.* New York: Free Press, 1969.

Bandman, Bertram. "The Child's Right to Inquire," *Thinking: The Journal of Philosophy for Children* 2, no. 2, pp. 4-11.

Baron, Jonathan. *Rationality and Intelligence.* New York: Cambridge University Press, 1985.

Bellah, Robert, et al. *Habits of the Heart.* Berkeley: University of California Press, 1985.

Benderson, Albert. "Critical Thinking," *Focus* 15 (1984): 7-9.

Berman, Ronald. Op Ed column, *The New York Times,* Jan. 29, 1978, p. 4.

Bloom, Benjamin, et al., eds. *Taxonomy of Educational Objectives.* Vol. 1. New York: David McKay, 1956-64.

Brandt, Anthony. "Teaching Kids to Think," *Ladies Home Journal* (Sept., 1982): 104-6.

Brumbaugh, Robert S. *The Philosophers of Greece.* Albany, N.Y.: State University of New York Press, 1981.

Bruner, Jerome. *The Process of Education.* Cambridge, Mass.: Harvard University Press, 1977.

Buber, Martin. *Between Man and Man.* New York: Macmillan, 1965.

Buchler, Justus. *The Concept of Method.* New York: Columbia University Press, 1961.

Chance, Paul. *Thinking in the Classroom.* New York: Teachers College Press, 1986.

Collingwood, Robin G. *The Principles of Art.* Oxford: Oxford University Press, 1937.

Descartes, René. *The Philosophical Writings of Descartes.* Cambridge: Cambridge University Press, 1984-85.

Dewey, John. *The Child and the Curriculum.* Chicago: The University of Chicago Press, 1902.

———. *How We Think.* rev. ed. New York: D. C. Heath, 1933.

———. *Human Nature and Conduct.* New York: Henry Holt and Co., 1922.

———. *Theory of the Moral Life.* New York: Holt, Rinehart and Winston, 1908.

———. *Theory of Valuation,* in *International Encyclopedia of Unified Science,* Vol. II, no. 4. Chicago: University of Chicago Press, 1939, pp. 40–50.

Durkheim, Emile. *The Division of Labor in Society,* trans. George Simpson. New York: Macmillan, 1933.

———. *Suicide,* trans. John A. Spaulding and George Simpson. Glencoe, Ill.: Free Press, 1951.

Edgeworth, Maria, and Richard L. Edgeworth. *Practical Education.* 2nd ed., 3 vols. London: J. Crowder, 1801.

Edgeworth, Richard L. *Essays on Professional Education.* London: J. Johnson, 1809.

Ende, Michael. "Literature for Children," *Thinking: The Journal of Philosophy for Children* 5, no. 2, pp. 2–5.

Epictetus. *Enchiridion,* trans. George Long. Chicago: Henry Regnery, 1956.

Glock, Charles, et al., eds. *Adolescent Prejudice.* New York: Harper & Row, 1975.

Golding, William. *Lord of the Flies.* New York: Capricorn Books, 1955.

Goodman, Nelson. *Languages of Art.* Indianapolis: Bobbs-Merrill, 1968.

Gutek, Gerald. "Philosophy for Children," *Phi Delta Kappan,* April, 1976.

Hampshire, Stuart. "Logic and Appreciation," *World Review,* 1952.

Harman, Gilbert. *The Nature of Morality.* New York: Oxford University Press, 1977.

Hausman, Carl R. "Creativity Studies: Where Can They Go?" *The Journal of Aesthetics and Art Criticism* 45, no. 1 (Fall, 1986): 87–88.

Hirsch, E. D., Jr. *Cultural Literacy.* Boston: Houghton Mifflin, 1987.

Hobbes, Thomas. *Leviathan.* New York: Liberal Arts Press, 1958.

Huizinga, Johan. *Homo Ludens: A Study of the Play-Element in Culture.* London: Routledge and Kegan Paul, 1949.

Hume, David. *An Inquiry Concerning Human Understanding.* New York: Liberal Arts Press, 1955.

Hutchins, R. M. *The Conflict in Education in a Democratic Society.* New York: Harper's, 1953.

Johnson, Tony W. "Philosophy for Children and Its Critics—Going beyond the Information Given," *Educational Theory* 37, no. 1 (Winter, 1987): 61–68.

Kant, Immanuel. *Fundamental Principles of the Metaphysic of Morals.* New York: Liberal Arts Press, 1949.

Kennick, W. E., ed. *Art and Philosophy.* 2nd ed. New York: St. Martin's Press, 1979.

Koch, Kenneth. *Rose, Where Did You Get That Red?* New York: Random House, 1973.

———. *Wishes, Lies, and Dreams.* New York: Chelsea House, 1970.

Last, Jane. "I Think, Therefore I Add," *The Times Educational Supplement,* June 15, 1984.

Lewis, C. I. *An Analysis of Knowledge and Valuation.* La Salle, Ill.: Open Court, 1946.

Lipman, Matthew. *Harry Stottlemeier's Discovery.* Upper Montclair, N.J.: IAPC, 1974.

——— . *Kio and Gus.* Upper Montclair, N.J.: IAPC, 1982.

——— . *Lisa.* 2nd ed. Upper Montclair, N.J.: IAPC, 1983.

——— . *Mark.* Upper Montclair, N.J.: IAPC, 1980.

——— . *Pixie.* Upper Montclair, N.J.: IAPC, 1981.

——— . *Suki.* Upper Montclair, N.J.: IAPC, 1978.

Lipman, Matthew, and Ann Margaret Sharp. *Ethical Inquiry.* Lanham, Md.: University Press of America, 1985.

——— . *Growing up with Philosophy.* Philadelphia: Temple University Press, 1978.

——— . *Looking for Meaning.* Lanham, Md.: University Press of America, 1984.

——— . *Social Inquiry.* Upper Montclair, N.J.: IAPC, 1980.

——— . *Wondering at the World.* Lanham, Md.: University Press of America, 1984.

——— . *Writing: How and Why.* Upper Montclair, N.J.: IAPC, 1980.

Lipman, Matthew, Ann Margaret Sharp, and Frederick S. Oscanyan. *Philosophy in the Classroom.* 2nd ed. Philadelphia: Temple University Press, 1980.

——— . *Philosophical Inquiry.* Lanham, Md.: University Press of America, 1984.

Locke, John. *John Locke on Education,* ed. Peter Gay. New York: Teachers College Press, 1964.

——— . *Two Treatises on Government.* 2nd. ed., ed. Peter Laslett. London: Cambridge University Press, 1967.

Matthews, Gareth B. *Philosophy and the Young Child.* Cambridge, Mass.: Harvard University Press, 1980.

——— . *Dialogues with Children.* Cambridge, Mass.: Harvard University Press, 1984.

McManus, Michael. "Using Classroom as a Community of Inquiry," *Chicago Sun-Times,* Nov. 28, 1984.

Mead, George Herbert. "The Psychology of Social Consciousness Implied in Instruction," *Science* 31, (1910): 688–93.

Montaigne, Michel E. de. *The Essays of Michel de Montaigne.* New York: Heritage Press, 1946.

Munchausen, Baron. *Gulliver Revived: Or the Vice of Lying Properly Exposed.* London: Smith, 1785.

Nelson, Leonard. *Socratic Method and Critical Philosophy.* New Haven, Conn.: Yale University Press, 1949.

Nickerson, Raymond, and David Perkins. *The Teaching of Thinking.* Hillsdale, N.J.: Lawrence Erlbaum, 1985.

Oakeshott, Michael. "The Voice of Poetry in the Conversation of Mankind," in *Rationalism in Politics.* New York: Basic Books, 1962.

Peirce, Charles. "The Fixation of Belief," in *Philosophical Writings of Peirce,* ed. Justus Buchler. New York: Dover Publications, 1955.

——— . "The Probability of Induction," in *Philosophical Writings of Peirce,* ed. Justus Buchler. New York: Dover Publications, 1955.

Piaget, Jean. *Judgment and Reasoning in the Child.* London: Routledge and Kegan Paul, 1928.

——— . *Language and Thought of the Child.* London: Routledge and Kegan Paul, 1932.

Plato. *Republic* and *Gorgias,* in *The Collected Dialogues of Plato,* ed. Edith Hamilton and Huntington Cairns. Princeton, N.J.: Princeton University Press, 1961.

Pritchard, Michael S. *Philosophical Adventures with Children.* Lanham, Md.: University Press of America, 1985.

Reed, Ronald F. *Talking with Children.* Denver: Arden Press, Inc., 1983.

Richards, I. A. *Interpretation in Teaching.* New York: Harcourt Brace, 1938.

Rousseau, Jean-Jacques. *The Social Contract,* trans. G. D. H. Cole. New York: Everyman's Library, E. P. Dutton, 1913.

Ryle, Gilbert. *Collected Papers.* New York: Barnes & Noble, 1971.

——— . "Plato," in *Encyclopedia of Philosophy,* ed. Paul Edwards. New York: Macmillan, 1967.

——— . "Thinking and Self-Teaching," in *Rice University Studies* 58, no. 2 (Summer, 1972).

Santayana, George. "Ultimate Religion," in *Obiter Scripta,* ed. Justus Buchler and Benjamin Schwartz. New York: Scribner's, 1936.

Segal, Judith W., Susan F. Chipman, and Robert Glaser, eds. *Thinking and Learning Skills, Vol. 1: Relating Instruction to Research.* Hillsdale, N.J.: Lawrence Erlbaum Associates, 1985.

Sheils, Merrill, and Frederick V. Boyd. "Philosophy for Kids," *Newsweek,* Sept. 20, 1976.

Sternberg, Robert J. "Critical Thinking: Its Nature, Measurement and Improvement," in *Essays on the Intellect,* ed. Frances R. Link. Alexandria, Va.: Association for Supervision and Curriculum Development, 1985.

Urmson, J. O. "Saints and Heroes," in *Essays in Moral Philosophy,* ed. A. I. Melden. Seattle: University of Washington Press, 1958.

——— . "On Grading," *Mind,* 1950, pp. 398–401.

Vico, Giovanni Battista. *The New Science of Giovanni Vico.* Ithaca, N.Y.: Cornell University Press, 1968.

Vygotsky, L. S. *Thought and Language,* ed. and trans. E. Hanfmann and F. Vakar. Cambridge, Mass.: MIT Press, 1962.

Wallach, Michael A. "Creativity and the Expression of Possibilities," in *Creativity and Learning,* ed. Jerome Kagan. Boston: Houghton Mifflin, 1967.

Weber, Max. *"The Protestant Essay and the Spirit of Capitalism,"* in *Man in Contemporary Society.* Vol. 2, trans. Peter Gay. New York: Columbia University Press, 1956.

Index